FLOW TO LEARN

A 52-WEEK PARENT'S GUIDE TO RECOGNIZE & SUPPORT YOUR CHILD'S FLOW STATE

—the optimal condition for learning—

Carmen Viktoria Gamper

New Learning Culture
PUBLISHING

Flow To Learn: A 52-Week Parent's Guide To Recognize and Support Your Child's Flow State–The Optimal Condition for Learning
Copyright © 2020 by Carmen Viktoria Gamper
NewLearningCulture Publishing. All rights reserved.

Cover Art and Illustrations: Sybille Kramer
Back Cover Photo: Robert Hickling
Editors: Dana Villamagna and Susanne Stover

Quotes with kind permissions from Mihaly Csikszentmihalyi, Rebeca Wild, Dr. Tsabary Shefali, Janet Lansbury, O.Fred Donaldson, Katherine Thornalley, Teacher Tom, Joy Gallina.

Library of Congress 2020905972
ISBN 978-1-7347970-0-8 (Ingrams paperback)
ISBN 978-1-7347970-2-2 (Amazon paperback)
ISBN 978-1-7347970-3-9 (Barnes & Noble paperback)
ISBN 978-1-7347970-4-6 (eBook)

Gamper, Carmen Viktoria, 1976-, author
Flow to learn : a 52 week parent's guide to recognize and support your child's flow state / Carmen Viktoria Gamper.
San Francisco, CA : New Learning Culture, 2020. | Includes bibliographical references.
LCCN 2020905972 (print)
LCSH: Education--Parent participation. | Child psychology. | Child development. | Child rearing. | Educational change. | BISAC: EDUCATION / Parent Participation. | FAMILY & RELATIONSHIPS / Education. | PSYCHOLOGY / Developmental / Child. | FAMILY & RELATIONSHIPS / Parenting / General.
Classification: LCC LC226 .G36 2020 (print) | LCC LC226 (ebook) | DDC 371.19/2--dc23.

NEW LEARNING CULTURE PUBLISHING · SAN FRANCISCO, CALIFORNIA
www.NewLearningCulture.com

Dedicated to all children
and the child in all of us

CONTENT

PART TWO | YOUR CHILD
A YOUNG MASTER OF FLOW

PART THREE | THE ZONE
CREATING FLOW ACTIVITY STATIONS

PART FOUR | YOU
A FLOW COMPANION

PARENTING INSIGHTS

PREFACE

YOU'RE INVITED to come on the transformative FLOW TO LEARN journey and discover your child through the lens of a flow companion and a mentor. I'm an innovative teacher, and early in my life, I realized that children are highly capable young masters who know how to learn. While playing, they naturally drop into the deep, focused state called "flow," which is increasingly recognized by science as the ideal state for learning.

The insights on children and learning presented in this book are the result of more than 15 years of work and research in the field of child-centered education. After becoming disillusioned with being a teacher in standardized school, I joined the worldwide grassroots movement of visionary educators, researchers, and parents who decided to trust children as competent learners and to create environments where children can thrive on their own terms.

My interest in childhood education started many years ago in a summer camp for the European SOS Children's Villages in Northern Italy. SOS Children's Villages is an international organization for orphans, founded by the Austrian philanthropist Hermann Gmeiner after WWII when many children were orphaned, and many women were left widowed. These orphanages, now present in over 130 countries worldwide, are much more than institutions. They are organized around the genuine needs of children and their caregivers. In essence, children are grouped into families consisting of a primary caregiver who serves as their mother and commits to staying with the children long-term. In addition, each family is supported by psychologists and social workers who assume roles as uncles and aunts and accompany the whole family in a relaxed and loving way. All these families together form a village.

For four summers during my time off from university studies, I worked as a translator and storyteller at one of these SOS summer camps in Northern Italy. There, for the first time, I had the opportunity to witness hundreds of children playing and learning as their hearts desired, and as they naturally dropped in and out of flow states. I observed that even though children were allowed to swim and run around all day, they also chose to sit at tables, drawing, writing, and solving puzzles, just like in schools but without an adult directing them. I discovered that an inspired Montessori teacher had prepared the many play and learning opportunities for self-directed access, so children could choose how to spend their time.

Even though these children were free to choose any pastime, from circus games to ball play, they often chose school-like activities over sports and games. In their own playful flow, they voluntarily practiced academic skills. Moreover, when I saw these children play, I realized that play and rest, socializing and individual work were naturally chosen in perfect balance by each child, leaving them feeling happy and fulfilled. I began to see the inherent intelligence in children's spontaneous activities, and I was fascinated.

After my university graduation, I enrolled in an independent Montessori teacher training at Claus Dieter Kaul's Institut für Ganzheitliches Lernen (Institute for Holistic Learning) in Munich. I also began studies with the Ecuadorian educators Rebeca and Mauricio Wild, whose school in Quito, Ecuador, had inspired a new movement of innovative, child-centered schools throughout Europe and the world. Beyond Montessori education, these Rebeca Wild based schools (RWB schools) are radically based on supporting children in their self-chosen efforts to learn in a state of flow.

NOTE: "RWB schools" is short for "Rebeca Wild based schools," an umbrella term that I coined for my work to refer to schools that incorporate Rebeca and Mauricio Wild's education approach (to find out more, read the Afterword).

Deeply inspired by RWB schools, I went on to become a teacher, director, co-creator, and consultant for them in Italy and Austria. I co-created and served as educational director at two of these schools. I recreated the school learning environment at Kinderhaus Miteinander (literally translated as "Children's House All-Together") in Wörgl, Austria, and I wrote their new mission statement, which assisted this private school with its accreditation to be a public school option. Working with a group of parents in my hometown of Merano, Italy in 2004, I helped create Die Pfütze — La Pozzanghera, Aktive Montessorischule mit Nicht-Direktiver Begleitung (Literally, "The Puddle, Child-Led Montessori School With Non-Directive Learning Companions"), an RWB school for grades 1-12 that thrives to this day.

Working at these child-based schools, I found my earlier insights confirmed over and over again: children know how to learn! They are brilliant young masters in their own right when they get the support and nourishment they need. I felt a powerful motivation to continue researching in this field. My passion for spreading these exciting findings and improving the quality of life for children, teachers, and parents everywhere brought me to California, where I live today.

I combined what I had learned with best practices in child-centered education and created the New Learning Culture (NLC) approach and school model. I started training teachers and parents in this modality and became a consultant for innovative, child-centered education. Finally, I realized the need for literature in this field, and I started writing books. I wrote the book you are reading now, along with several other forthcoming books about the NLC school model, a customizable template for learning environments that support play, flow, and academic skills.

Back in the early 2000s, when I was a teacher and "flow companion" (another term I created for my work to refer to an adult who supports flow states in children), I noticed my creativity increase as I relaxed with the children. Every day I discovered new ways of connecting, inspiring, teaching, and learning. As I observed the children's spontaneous activities, I started to perceive long-term learning processes that I had not recognized before. I increasingly trusted in children's natural willingness and capacity to learn over time as they kept surprising me with their creativity, honesty, and love for learning. As I earned the children's trust, I, in turn, became a trustworthy authority figure. I became empowered to kindly and firmly stand up for my wishes and boundaries in the school environments, and was able to remain bonded and authentically communicate even during conflicts and disagreements. Daily, I proved to the youngsters that no matter what difficulties arose, I could be counted on not to abandon our bond. Over time, boundaries were increasingly accepted as part of this school and I enjoyed my role as one of the three benevolent guardians of our classroom environments. Together, we created an extremely fertile ground for learning. All these rich experiences, insights, and discoveries have come together in this offering to you, the reader, as a practical guide and inspiration.

My hope for parents and caregivers is that to whatever degree is possible in your lives, FLOW TO LEARN will help you to create magical play and learning moments for your children, which also enrich your own soul! Even though that may seem out of reach in this day and age, please give it a try—keep inviting flow into your home. Throughout this guide, you'll find small adjustments that can make a big difference. Every moment spent in flow nurtures your child's and your own creativity, love for learning, emotional well-being, and perhaps even, your superpowers!

Carmen Gamper

March 2020

INTRODUCTION

PARALLEL TO THE ADULT WORLD we know as "normal," there is a secret world unfurling, alive, and vibrant. Embedded in our busy lives of work, school, appointments, and daily chores exists the world of the child who marches to the beat of a different drum; in fact, the child doesn't march—the child *flows* and meanders happily from one adventure to the next.

If allowed to be in its natural form, a child's world is slower; it's full of wondrous things and magical places. Children become deeply connected with their environments as they explore nooks and crannies and play with what they find. Using their rich imagination, they change the corner of a hedge into their fort and castle; sticks become their swords and wands. The smells, tastes, and sounds of our childhoods shape us forever.

For a child, playing and learning are the same, and that feels perfectly natural to them. During play, children effortlessly drop in and out of the deep, energized focus called "flow," which psychology describes as "optimal experience," and in education is increasingly used to describe the optimal state for learning. Professor of psychology at Claremont Graduate University, Mihaly Csikszentmihalyi, coined the concept of flow in his seminal book *Flow: The Psychology of Optimal Experience.*

Children are masters of flow: that state of deep focus and absorption that occurs naturally during self-chosen play, where each step flows seamlessly into the next. Time is forgotten, and small and big decisions are continuously made in a state of knowingness, willingness to risk, to be creative, and to experiment.

Flow is innate in all children, no matter into which culture they are born; no matter their gender or economic status. The more children can play freely and spontaneously, the more they learn. In fact, as children, we are young masters of learning. If nurtured, learning in flow will continue into adulthood.

During their focused, self-chosen play, children take charge of their experience and set their own meaningful goals. They stretch their comfort zone on their own terms while experimenting with their skills. This kind of state is very similar to what adults experience in their most fulfilled moments and their highest achievements in fields such as dance, sports, music, and chess. Inevitably, flow is also a state of optimal performance.

When we allow children to be in flow, they get a taste of that fulfilling state and develop the basic flow skills that can later on lead to mastery in a chosen field. Mastery is an expression of flow and is developed during flow. An advanced skill level takes more than thinking, reading, hearing about, or just wanting something. Proficiency takes practice, and the most powerful, effective practice is done in self-chosen flow. It takes deep, focused engagement—flow—to become fluent in any skill. Flow cannot be forced or directly instructed by a teacher or parent; instead, it must be allowed to expand. It needs a place to be. This book will help you invite, cultivate, and celebrate moments of child-led flow.

Most mainstream educational settings today are not conducive to flow; they actually obstruct and prevent flow. This reality is one we must examine: the one-size-fits-all classrooms, the strictly guided lessons, the frequent subject changes, the pressure to succeed on someone else's terms, and the underlying atmosphere of obedience instead of collaboration and mentorship. All these elements and many more combine to suffocate a child's natural love for learning. What children need most is not direct instruction, even though that may be part of the learning process. Given the right conditions, children have a natural curiosity, and they experience internal waves of intense willingness and openness to learning.

We are living in a time of great crisis, and in a time of great opportunity. Old paradigms are crumbling before our eyes and new solutions are emerging. Individualizing education, being in flow as adults, and allowing children to be in flow offer great solutions for the future – in the education system and also on the job market. As New York Times bestselling author Daniel H.

Pink explains in his book *A Whole New Mind: Why Right-Brainers Will Rule the Future*, today's coveted jobs in higher management, sales, health care, and law, to name just a few sectors, require impeccable social skills and empathy, and especially the ability to see the big picture and find creative solutions. These skills are systematically neglected in standardized education, yet naturally acquired during flow. What will be needed for an abundant, thriving society are professionals who cannot be replaced by machines. These will include entrepreneurs, inventors, innovators, designers, marketing specialists, programmers, artists, nurses, and teachers. In that near-future world, researchers see technology replacing routine work. "Old-school" skills such as obedience, perfectionism, and memorization will become obsolete. Already, employers ask themselves: Can a computer or robot do it faster and more accurately? Can someone overseas do it more cheaply? The innately human skills of intuitive creativity and social dexterity cannot be automated. Yet, there is little to no space for allowing these skills to flourish in flow within standardized education.

FLOW TO LEARN will help you to create conducive conditions for flow outside of school, and support teachers in bringing it into schools as much as possible. Whether you are a parent, educator, nanny, grandparent, guardian, or another special person in a child's life – you can be a nurturer of flow for them, a "flow companion." This book also helps you learn how to see children as guides to accessing your own flow states. Your willingness to play and your creativity deeply matter in this world. Flow is how you experience yourself most authentically as a living, breathing creature. Supporting the emergence of flow in children and in yourself is an act of pure love.

HOW TO USE THIS BOOK

FLOW TO LEARN is a rich tapestry of inspiration and information that steadily accompanies you through the 52 weeks of the year. Each Week offers two parts: first, you will find reflections and information about flow, then an array of practical suggestions, "TRY THIS," on how to facilitate flow in your life with children.

1. *Read the book Week by Week to regularly increase flow in your life. This is a great way for couples and co-parents to shift paradigms together.*

2. *Randomly open the book and see what finds you.*

3. *Use the Table of Contents and the Index to look for particular items, and use the list below to quickly find ideas for activities.*

QUICKLY FIND IDEAS FOR ACTIVITIES & FLOW STATIONS

ABOUT THIS BOOK

THE FLOW TO LEARN PHILOSOPHY OF EDUCATION includes elements from methods that promote flow, such as Montessori, Reggio Emilia, Fröbel, and, especially, the RWB (Rebeca Wild based) schools, which have been my primary field of research. As you read, you will find many examples from these child-centered schools, where I used to be a teacher and regularly observed children learning in a state of flow. In this book, you will discover how to..

☆ Support the flow state in children to help them grow and thrive.

☆ Create a home, a sanctuary, where you and your child love to spend time, find fulfilling activities, and can replenish from school and work.

☆ Identify qualities in your child's educational setting that promote flow and optimal learning and qualities that block them.

☆ Create spaces and choose toys and learning materials that help children drop into flow states.

☆ Debunk current myths in education, including the overuse of rewards and the misguided expectations of academic rigor in early grades.

☆ Help your child process their time at school and other potentially stressful experiences with tension-release supports.

☆ Nurture mutual respect between you and your child.

☆ Reinvigorate your own life with flow experiences.

FLOW TO LEARN suggests many actionable items, some of which you may already do, and some may not fit your situation. Enjoy what works for you, and leave the rest. Nothing in this book is meant to be a cookie-cutter solution; you are unique, and your child is unique. You can't go wrong when you base your decisions on your child's and your genuine individual needs, which this book helps you discover. Our genuine needs always guide us in a helpful direction. By the end of this book, you will see why children, as well as your inner child, are young masters of flow. You will discover many ways to bring more of your mojo back! Because flow is where the fun is, where we find purpose and meaning. In flow, we belong to ourselves, we own our experience, and we fully participate in life! Flow truly makes life worth living!

FLOW-FRIENDLY PARENTING

SINCE THE RELATIONSHIPS between teachers and learners in RWB schools differ from those in families, and since I don't have children of my own, I consulted with several parenting experts (see Resources) and worked with many parents who have been using the suggestions in this book. Eventually, I was fortunate enough to find Susanne Stover, who, together with her husband, practices FLOW TO LEARN's recommendations with their two wonderful children.

Susanne became the primary parenting advisor for this book and you will find her insights in between the Week chapters. She has practiced FLOW TO LEARN's approach with her children for over six years, and developed an intimate understanding of the benefits and challenges of supporting the flow state in her children. She shares about her family's journey:

I met Carmen in 2009 through mutual friends. Hearing her stories about the RWB schools she worked with fascinated me. I was astonished and inspired by the existence of schools where children explored freely in a hands-on learning paradise, supported by adults who trusted their choices. Excited to learn more, I enrolled in her New Learning Culture (NLC) online course. My husband Joe and I found Resources for Infant Educarers (RIE) through that course, in which Carmen introduced Magda Gerber and Emmi Pikler as among the earliest influencers of respectful parenting and learning approaches based on the core tenet that infants, toddlers, and children can be trusted to initiate, explore, and self-learn as whole people with whom adults can have deep and meaningful relationships.

It was a paradigm shift for us and we read everything we could get our hands on in the time before our first child was born. Initially, it felt one-sided and awkward to speak to our infant son as if he were already a whole person. We both remember his unmistakable responses to our cue, "I'm going to pick you up now," at only three weeks old: sustained eye contact, limbs all a-wriggling, and his adorable little grunts that were used exclusively to tell us, "I am ready!" Many of our doubts dissolved and the communication with both our children has grown immeasurably in scope and sophistication through the years. It is still awkward and difficult at times, as is any authentic intimate relationship. Even in our stumbling efforts at respectful and flow-based parenting, we have seen the research confirmed time and again.

The wonderful truth behind children learning in a state of flow is that from their earliest moments on throughout childhood, the intricately woven, multidimensional cognitive map of everything they learn doesn't suddenly switch off or need to be captained by an adult once the child reaches a certain age. Instead, we adults can encourage children as they discover what brings them joy, allows them to learn deeply and permanently, and nurtures their thirst for knowledge. This is backed by decades of evidence. As Dr. Seuss and I always say, "A person's a person, no matter how small," and learning in flow is the best place of all! The role of a parent does not feel easy or simple most days. As babies grow into children, so does the parenting learning curve grow steeper. Confronted by children's intensive limit-testing and other age-typical behaviors, the adult brain tends to respond to this stress according to its own conditioning. In our case, the responses included behavior management tools like rewards, punishment, admonishments, yelling, threats, guilt, or manipulation. Even though my husband and I were committed to being respectful with our kids, it got increasingly more difficult to bridge the gap between how we wanted to parent and how our own brains were wired to react. As life has a way of doing, a number of external stressors converged at once when our daughter was six months old, and the basic structure of our lives fell apart. In a very real way, this was a gift, because we were unable to continue trying to muscle through our own conditioning to create the nurturing home we knew was possible. We had to find out why we couldn't respond the way we wanted to during conflict with our kids. We were obligated to deal with the most difficult child of all: our inner child. Despite many years of personal growth, I still haven't completely let go of the pervasive animosity commonly held toward the idea of the "inner child." It sounds weak and vulnerable, because it is. These are natural characteristics of children. On the other hand, our adult armor is tough: we push through; we make it work; we survive. But that armor didn't let me connect with my kids in the way they needed me to. It wasn't until I fully engaged with Carmen's flow-based parenting approach that I had the breakthrough I'd been searching for: I could not offer a loving response to my children when they were upset or did something wrong until I could offer the same loving kindness to my adult self, even after a day full of my own mistakes.

Through myriad influences, today's society often confuses tenderness with weakness, kindness with deficiency. We mistake emotions for flaws. We've forgotten that children must express the full breadth and depth of their experiences to grow properly. The evidence-based tools in FLOW TO LEARN remind us that when children develop in environments of tenderness and kindness, they will be much more likely to become adults whose emotions do not commandeer their actions. Eventually, the same child who feels truly heard and accepted as he wails angrily at his mother because he's convinced that she "made the air cold" will grow up to become a successful, kind human being, in healthy balance between recognizing and meeting his own needs and doing the same for those around him.

Digging into this process of rewiring our own brains as parents has been an ongoing process for my husband and me. It will be a lifelong practice, but when we make progress, our kids relax more, and spend more time in flow. What that often means for us as parents is that we are not responsible for our children's happiness from one moment to the next, while at the same time feeling the deep assurance that they are in the best possible space for learning and growing: their own creative flow. If this sounds incredibly freeing for a parent, I can assure you, it is! In order to help this happen as often as possible, we set up five spaces inside and outside our home that encourage flow:

— The living room: Toys, fabrics, and musical instruments in baskets on a shelf; a cupboard with board games and puzzles; two small crates filled with children's books; music and storytelling on CDs that kids can access on their own, or from the internet with the help of an adult.

— The *"Calming Corner:"* Generation Mindful feelings charts and calming activities, cushions, pillows, blankets, and books.
— A kitchen table that can hold snacks, drinking water, as well as arts, crafts, clay and cooking projects.
— Their bedrooms, which have one or two toys and books for them to "zone out" with when they need quiet time.
— Outdoor space with trees, pet animals, plants, soil, hoses, sand, and all manner of natural components for play.

The deep, focused silence of our son's flow-state is very different from the playful, colorful narration of our daughter's. What they have in common is a palpable joy, evident during and after their flow experiences. They might play alone for extended periods and spend their next play session together. They might role-play, and they might argue, and they typically need support many times, although there are blissfully quiet stretches as well. We know that caring for children will always have its messy, loud, and exasperating moments, or days, as the case may be. FLOW TO LEARN does not attempt to "fix" the challenges inherent to parenting, but it does address many of the difficult issues we face as modern parents and caregivers.

What we strive for in our home is that every solution we try on allows both parents and children to maintain our dignity and our connection with one another. Day in and day out, through the grind of showing up for each other, that connection is a reserve we draw on during the tough moments, and build on during times of playfulness, silliness, and joy. We are grateful for the FLOW TO LEARN blueprint as it integrates respectful parenting, child-led learning, and flow-based education to support us in nurturing our children's best selves throughout the enormous amount of time we spend influencing their lives, while healing ourselves in the process. May we all learn to grow with the flow!

PART ONE

FLOW

THE OPTIMAL STATE FOR LEARNING

The great Tao flows everywhere.
All things are born from it,
yet it doesn't create them.
It pours itself into its work,
yet it makes no claim.
It nourishes infinite worlds,
yet it doesn't hold on to them.
Since it is merged with all things
and hidden in their hearts,
it can be called humble.
Since all things vanish into it
and it alone endures,
it can be called great.
It isn't aware of its greatness;
Thus it is truly great.

—Verse 34 of the *Tao Te Ching*

With everything I do, I just try to be myself.

—Kevin Durant

WEEK 1

WHAT IS FLOW?

Children in flow—Adults in flow

"FLOW" EMERGED AS A TERM for "optimal experience" out of the ongoing research on happiness. Under the lead of professor Mihaly Csikszentmihalyi (ME-high CHEEK-sent-me-high), some central questions have been asked anew in modern psychology and human science: *Why aren't more people happy? When exactly are people happy?*

Studies with over a hundred thousand individuals around the world from many different walks of life have revealed that happiness is not something that just happens, but neither can you go looking for it. Even though family, friends, success, money, and other circumstances contribute to happiness, research indicates that lasting happiness is an individual state of consciousness that must be cultivated internally.

Happiness is determined by how much delight we can derive from mundane or extraordinary experiences. It is our ability to enjoy our own activity so much that nothing else seems to matter. It is being fully involved with our present moment, thereby letting go of worries and self-consciousness. It is what many adults crave in their lives and what children naturally experience during self-chosen play.

In Csikszentmihalyi's words: "It is what a painter feels when the colors on the canvas begin to set up a magnetic tension with each other, and a new *thing*, a living form, takes shape in front of the astonished creator. Or it is the feeling a father has when his child for the first time responds to his smile." In these moments, we feel alive and in charge of our fate. Indeed, flow is directly connected with a feeling of being in command of our own experience, as opposed to feeling pushed in one direction or another. When we decide what, when, and how we do something, when we are motivated from within, even strenuous activities can give us happiness. As Csikszentmihalyi describes: "Optimal experience is thus something that we *make* happen. For a child, it could be placing with trembling fingers the last block on a tower she has built, higher than any she has built so far; for a swimmer it could be trying to beat his own record; for a violinist, mastering an intricate musical passage. For each person there are thousands of opportunities, challenges to expand ourselves."

Flow is the energized focus that naturally arises when someone is fully satisfied with their activity. It is the optimal state for learning, because during flow activities people stretch their limits at their own personal pace. In this self-chosen state, life force can flow freely. It is simultaneously instructive and healing because it speaks to our innermost need for discovering the world from an authentic place within.

Flow contains all that makes life worth living: deep, satisfying focus; personal goals that give meaning; a lifelong joy of learning; and a rich inner world that feels purposeful. Flow contains awe and magic. It elevates us. Maybe it takes us beyond what's human; maybe it makes us *more human*.

THE ELEMENTS OF FLOW

Below are 14 basic elements of flow, and how they relate to a child's natural way of learning. Note: Not all elements need to be present for an activity to become a flow experience.

The self-chosen challenge: Choosing a personal challenge that feels worthwhile achieving is crucial to flow experiences. Life force is fueled when we feel genuinely interested in our activity and empowered to pursue it.

Focus and concentration: Flow requires the ability to concentrate. Children and adults naturally focus on activities they genuinely enjoy even when they are strenuous.

Absorption: This term relates to a completely open mental state when one is ready to learn from an activity. The educator Maria Montessori (1870-1952) started using the phrase "the absorbent mind" at the beginning of the 20th century to describe children's ability to deeply engage while learning.

Lack of self-consciousness: During flow, one is naturally free of self-doubt and self-criticism, and therefore it is possible to relax into one's activity. Young children are naturally self-confident and unworried and hence have easier access to the flow state.

Clear goals: A self-chosen goal is the guiding light during a flow activity; it gives each moment direction and purpose. Children may change their goals while playing or working on something.

Balance between skills and challenge: Flow experiences emerge from an ideal balance between what one can do and what one wants to achieve or learn. Children naturally choose activities that correspond to their inner world, meaning that flow activities allow them to practice what they already know, and learn new things at just the right pace.

Feeling of timelessness: During flow children and adults experience timelessness; an hour can feel like a few minutes. Children still have easy access to timelessness, so they need help with knowing how long something may last or when a timespan is over.

Embodied experience: In flow, our minds are in tune with our bodies— we *become* an experience; we are fully in it. Children naturally learn best when they can move as they wish. Activities learned in flow become body memories and are rarely forgotten.

Intrinsic rewards: One of the most important markers for flow is a feeling of deep fulfillment during and after a flow experience. There is no need for prizes, gold stars, or other external rewards.

A lack of awareness of bodily needs: As adults we have enough life experience to know what our body needs, when it is time to drink water, eat, or rest. When children are in a state of flow, they need our help with this.

ADDITIONAL FLOW ELEMENTS FOR CHILDREN

Emotional safety: For children to deeply engage in their play they need to feel emotionally safe. Children aren't able to give themselves emotional safety yet; they need adults to provide them with truly safe and respectful environments. Learning cannot be separated from feeling.

Physical safety: Young children often don't yet know when they are in actual physical danger. When we provide them with supervised freedom, they can remain safe and focused while learning to handle "risky" objects such as needles, glassware, or scissors or when they develop important vestibular skills such as balancing, climbing, and jumping.

Imagination: If an activity is invented and planned by a child, there is usually an element of bright imagination. A child doesn't merely climb a playground ladder; in their imagination they climb the ladder to a sailboat, a ladder to their home, or a ladder into a magical land.

Playfulness: Children love to play. When they are emotionally safe, they are lighthearted. The outcome of an activity is often not as important as the mere joy of the process (especially for young children). *How* children learn is as equally important as *what* they learn.

TRY THIS

Notice your own moments of flow

Remember times and activities in your life when you experienced flow. What stands out for you? Over the next week, notice when..

☆ You choose your own activity because you love it.

☆ You feel intrinsically rewarded by an activity.

☆ The activity allows you to lose all self-consciousness.

THE SCIENCE OF PLAY AND FLOW
Research on child development

FLOW STATES NATURALLY ARISE repeatedly during children's play, because as children our brains are wired for playing and learning in flow. Scientists have found that the benefits of play are not only visible in a child's psychological well-being and cognitive development, but also traceable in a child's biochemistry.

An extensive body of research confirms that unstructured, free, spontaneous play is extremely beneficial for children and crucial to their healthy brain development. Research on flow and play has emerged primarily from the fields of developmental and cognitive psychology, as well as neuroscience, using CAT scans (Computerized Axial Tomography) and MRIs (Magnetic Resonance Imaging) to measure anatomy and brain chemistry under different circumstances.

A NOTE OF CLARIFICATION: This book uses "flow" as a term initially coined by Mihaly Csikszentmihaly, who describes flow as the psychology of optimal experience. For Csikszentmihaly, flow refers to profound happiness, focus, and fulfillment in the present moment experienced in many different ways, including but not restricted to outstanding performance. Flow can be the happiness of smelling a flower, the fulfillment of feeling the wind on your skin, the joy of a well-cooked meal, and, especially for children, it is the joyful focus during their self-guided play.

Csikszentmihaly's research, starting in the 1970s, sparked great interest and has since been applied and adapted to many different fields, including business, virtual reality, and sports. Especially in sports, flow has become popular referring to the science of peak performance, measuring and describing the focus and physical endurance needed to reach outstanding goals under extreme pressure such as free-climbing a steep rock wall. For adults, extreme pressure to succeed can lead to acute present moment awareness and optimal "brain plasticity" (the brain's ability to change and adapt instantly according to circumstances). This kind of flow differs from the relaxed flow states we naturally experience in childhood because as children we experience flow that originates from trust, curiosity, and a more gentle internal pressure and drive for play and exploration. The childhood brain is wired for flow and extraordinary, intense experiences aren't needed to activate it. As Sir Ken Robinson puts it in his book *The Element: How Finding Your Passion Changes Everything*: "[Flow is] a way of feeling deeply connected with our own sense of identity and curiously comes about through a sense of relaxing, of feeling perfectly natural to be doing what you're doing." In addition to Csikszentmihaly's work on flow, many other researchers, including Dr. Joseph Chilton Pearce, Dr. Stuart Brown, Dr. Joe L. Frost, and Dr. Dan Siegel have studied childhood play and learning as it relates to psychology and neuroscience. Below are some of the most important scientific insights about flow and play.

NEUROSCIENCE IN A NUTSHELL

The brain consists of several billion brain cells that communicate over a network of trillions of connections called synapses. Neurons are the specialized type of brain cells that send messages across the synaptic connections via electrochemical and neurochemical signals such as dopamine, serotonin, and endorphins. Each of these neurochemicals carries specific information that changes emotions, moods, thoughts, reactions, and responses to events. During children's spontaneous play, especially during the state of flow that frequently occurs during play, many feel-good neurochemicals are transmitted that make learning in flow a highly rewarding experience. While more research needs to be done, the following neurotransmitters are known to be released during flow:

Dopamine: Is released when receiving positive feedback from an activity, when "it works," and when completing tasks; it increases attention, regulates body movements, motivates healthy risk-taking, and contributes to feelings of pleasure, excitement, and satisfaction.

Anandamide: Known as the "bliss molecule," relieves pain, increases experiences of reward and pleasure, and reduces anxiety.

Serotonin: Regulates moods and anxiety, helps with emotional stability, and promotes a positive outlook on life.

Oxytocin: Motivates social connections and increases trust in others.

PREFRONTAL CORTEX ACTIVITY

The prefrontal cortex (PFC) is the part of the brain that's active when we use our higher brain functions or executive functioning skills such as decision-making, regulating emotions, impulse control, and self-observation. The PFC develops at a slower pace alongside all other parts of the brain and is said to be fully developed only at around age 25. Yet, the quality of infancy and early childhood environments significantly influences a person's healthy PFC development in later years. Extensive human and animal studies confirm that early affection, safe environments, and healthy nutrition play a major role in relation to executive functioning skills. A challenged PFC leads to a distorted sense of self, excessive self-doubt, and self-consciousness.

During the flow state, the PFC is quiet, and as a result, we are far less critical of ourselves and far more courageous. With a quiet PFC, we can melt with our body instead of observing it, and thus we can lose ourselves in an activity. Since the PFC is generally far less active in children, and they naturally monitor themselves less, they are often less self-conscious and can access the flow state more readily. There is a great need for further studies and data regarding children's flow states and brain development.

BRAINWAVES DURING FLOW

Simply put, we distinguish five brain waves, listed here from slowest to fastest waves: namely Delta (deep sleep), Theta (daydreaming or meditation), Alpha (relaxed thinking), Beta (alert thinking), and Gamma waves (Aha! moments). In their normal waking state, most adults show Beta waves. During the flow state, adults register a wave pattern between Alpha and Theta waves.

For adults, Theta brainwaves are usually only measured in meditative states or during the conscious period between being awake and falling asleep. For children until the age of approximately 13, Theta waves are part of their normal waking state. This may be one of the reasons why –in conducive conditions, such as safe, inspiring environments– children can readily drop into a flow state. Further research needs to be done.

LEARNING AND FEELING CANNOT BE SEPARATED

When children play, neurons communicate (called firing), connections are made, and the self-organizing network of intelligence grows; but when they don't fire frequently enough, the neural network shrinks and communication possibilities are lost. Each moment in flow and play is meaningful and helps to both reinforce existing synapses and to establish new ones in the brain. In Joe L. Frost's words: "The casual observer does not grasp the profound relationships between achievement and the endless games that the very young play—the patty-cake, peek-a-boo, and sing-song rhythms that are in reality storehouses or machines for programming the brain for language, art, music, math, science, kinesthetic, and interpersonal abilities and intelligence." By the age of three, children have trillions of synapses in the brain, estimated at twice that of an adult's brain. Some synapses are reinforced through a child's environment; others are pruned due to lack of use. There is scientific evidence that suggests there can be too much or too little stimulation in a child's environment. Merely filling a child with information is of no use; the information has to be absorbed in a warm, emotionally safe context, and in alignment with the child's will and readiness. Every child has different needs in this regard. Environmental input, combined with genetics, is what can either support or hinder a child's growth and development.

In addition to stimuli in the environment, children are informed by and react to the internal, emotional states of other people, especially of their significant adults. A special type of neuron, the so-called mirror neurons, pick up, for instance, if another person feels safe or anxious, present or distracted, benevolent or judgmental. In this way, an adult's emotional state often co-determines that of a child, including whether the child feels safe and relaxed enough to learn and thrive.

Healthy children continue to play throughout their childhood, into adolescence, and even into adulthood, yet the ways children play change as they grow. Spontaneous play meets children's current genuine needs and equips them for skills they need later in life; in so doing, children learn and refine basic life skills such as communication, flexibility, inventiveness, and versatility, as well as motor, language, and negotiation skills. Spontaneous play helps build and maintain a stable identity and inner resources that support the individual in times of crisis.

PLAY IS CRUCIAL FOR MENTAL HEALTH

Research and anecdotal evidence suggest that much of the violence committed by adults is directly related to a lack of play and nourishing attachment with a caring adult in childhood. If children aren't allowed to play of their own volition, then they don't develop the neuroplasticity (flexibility and imagination) needed to imagine alternative solutions to life's setbacks. The constant carrying out of orders against one's own will limits thinking to a narrow box of fear, isolation, anxiety, pessimism, sarcasm, and even sadism.

One of the first and most revealing studies on this topic was conducted under the lead of psychiatrist, play researcher, and founder of The National Institute for Play, Stuart Brown. He investigated a dramatic incident that occurred in 1966 known as the Texas Tower Massacre, where Charles Witman barricaded himself inside the top of a university tower and shot 44 people. Brown found that Whitman had a brutal father who did not allow him to play; hence, he never developed typical child play patterns. Following this insight, Brown's research continued with 26 convicted Texas murderers, and revealed that 90% lacked typical childhood play, and participated in inhumane acts such as bullying or cruelty to animals.

Many more studies have been conducted that confirm the utter importance of spontaneous childhood play. In their 2019 recommendations on children's health, the World Health Organization (WHO) states that children need to sit less, sleep more, and play more. In the Declaration of the Rights of the Child (1959) and again in the Convention of the Rights of the Child (1989) the United Nations Organization (UNO) recognized that it is "the right of the child to rest and leisure, to engage in play and recreational activities." There are countless organizations of pediatricians, teachers, and parents who advocate for childhood play. There are grassroots movements that create play-based, child-centered schools, and political efforts to create policies that bring playgrounds, nature parks, and gardens back to urban communities. Everyone who cares for children can participate in these efforts and help "wire" children's brains with positive experiences, emotions, and healthy social interactions to keep those healthy connections "firing" in the brain.

CHILDHOOD TRAUMA CAN BE HEALED

If you had unstable or abusive childhood experiences, or for other reasons, did not get enough play during childhood, please know that with conscious intent our brains can and will keep changing, growing, and learning. Childhood trauma and conditioning can be healed, but consistent effort must be made to help the brain rewire.

There are many ways to heal and even transform the pain of negative childhood experiences into wisdom and compassion. Respect yourself as a survivor and learner and allow yourself to rest and recuperate. Give yourself kudos for your extraordinary efforts. Eat a healthy diet. Re-learn to play, which can be done side by side with children. Feel your emotions and let yourself mourn.

For additional help, I suggest the "Emotional Freedom Technique" (EFT), a powerful healing technique that has helped many war veterans heal from trauma and can be applied to all forms of anxiety. As introductory reading, I suggest *Wired for Joy* by Laurel Mellin, an associate clinical professor of family medicine and pediatrics. *Wired for Joy* is a simple, practical guide to rewiring your brain toward joy and a positive outlook on life.

TRY THIS

Tinker and create without expecting results

Playing without pressure is healing for the inner child. Choose play activities for yourself that lack a specific goal and let the process of playing be more important than the result. When we experience how much can be learned during free play, we will feel comfortable and excited watching children play. If we don't understand the value of free play, it might be difficult for us to watch children "only playing" instead of sitting at the desk studying or being guided in their activities by a grown-up. In many professions where creativity is required, adults let themselves play freely with the subject before results are expected. Since we are mostly conditioned to show accurate or attractive results, activities like the ones proposed below will free your creative spirit. This part of the process is needed for us to understand both children and ourselves. Even if an exercise feels awkward in the beginning, keep on playing until something lights you up. That light is your inner, very personal creativity, a precious aspect of human consciousness that is all too often buried. Every activity is more delightful when you remove pressure and add an element of play. Here are some ideas for your free play with or without children:

☆ Take apart an old camera or other gadget you don't need anymore just to see what's inside.

☆ Experiment with a musical instrument, with sound-makers, or simply your voice, in your own way, just for yourself.

☆ Make noises and sounds—melodic, gibberish, whatever comes out.

☆ Dance or move in a way that feels good.

☆ Take leaves, pebbles, and branches you find outside and create patterns that the wind will blow away.

☆ Draw anything on paper knowing you will throw it out.

☆ Create something ugly on purpose.

☆ Play dress-up, or "put on" a silly character or voice.

☆ Pretend to be an animal or a tree.

☆ Talk with yourself and state affirmations, perhaps even in a joking manner, "Great job, buddy!"

☆ Show yourself some love. It takes self-love to make something fun for yourself when you are alone. Entertain yourself; make yourself giggle because you are doing something weird or funny.

WEEK 3

FLOW AND MENTAL HEALTH
From deep focus to life purpose

DURING FLOW, CHILDREN ESTABLISH emotional, mental, and behavioral patterns that support their mental health throughout life. For instance, let's look at simple, flow-friendly activities such as building a block tower or knitting a scarf. While creating something tangible, children develop skills that are crucial to mental health. They experience themselves as genuine learners; they learn how to learn. The activity gives constant feedback on what is working and what is not, so they learn to quickly adapt to changes and the requirements of a situation; they learn flexibility. They learn what it takes to reach a goal; they learn self-discipline. They learn to do something meaningful for themselves and they learn what it means to be autonomous. They learn that mistakes are part of every process. Self-chosen activities call them back to try again; they learn patience and perseverance.

Hands-on and whole-body experiences help children create a healthy identity, and over time, find meaning and purpose in their lives. In flow, they get closer to finding out who they naturally are and who they want to be. Flow provides opportunities to discover what motivates them to be active and what fuels their life energy. On the go, children discover their innate talents and preferences; they experience what nourishes their spirit, and, eventually, what kind of contribution to society might come naturally to them. As you bring more flow experiences into a child's life, you will witness how the child becomes increasingly intelligent, not just intellectually, but as a well-rounded personality. There is something about a fulfilling activity that calms our nervous systems at any age; it is a feeling that we are in the right place at the right time. In flow, we are doing something meaningful that renders us more capable, more confident, and more energized.

Young children have a natural inner emptiness; they are free from the thought-clutter that most adults experience. For the average adult, it is an achievement to get one's mind to calm down enough to enjoy the innocence of an activity. But once you get the taste of learning in flow, nothing compares. It's the ultimate comfort for being a separate individual, for being alone. It's how you can have fun with yourself. It's self-comforting and self-uplifting. It's the capacity to find joy by yourself.

In your flow, "in your zone," you don't need anyone. You are completely happy with just being you, alone in your comfort zone that you stretch at your own command, whenever you are ready, with no pressure whatsoever from outside. Just you and your own willingness to grow and learn; to achieve what seems worth achieving to you. For a young child this is their normal way of life. Until it is not. Sadly, in most schools, especially in standardized education, this individual state of learning goes undervalued or unrecognized. Instead of being encouraged to learn in flow, children learn to suppress their inner impulses. They learn to sit still and focus on something they did not choose, which is often something completely disconnected from their experience. They learn to study using only a fraction of their potential—the intellectual mind. The whole rest of their learning capacity is disengaged.

This disengagement impacts not only intelligence but also mental and emotional health. It creates anxiety and tension that come out in many ways, such as mistrust of adults, disease, and aggression. Not only do children find themselves disconnected from their natural interests, but also from the adults they would love to trust. In most schools, a child's world is greatly reduced from the first-hand experiences of active learning to a second-hand, abstract world where they memorize information out of books. The joy of flow is gradually forgotten and buried under a load of homework, exam preparations, behavior control, and worries.

Most children, at school and elsewhere, are continuously exposed to a harshness inherent in our current society, whether from well-meaning adults or peers dealing with a deep loss of agency over their own lives. These children experience pressure, criticism, data-overload, and unrealistic beauty and performance standards. They are trained to be consumers instead of creators. Moreover, the human mind has a natural negativity bias developed out of a primal need for survival. Positivity and a life-affirming mindset need to be actively cultivated in order to limit anxiety and depression, and avoid addictions.

In today's culture, it takes effort to create time and space for children to learn in flow, but so many parents and innovative schools show that it is possible. And it's worth the effort. Flow has to be invited; it has to be practiced and cultivated to keep shaping a child's inner landscape toward meaning and purpose. Flow needs what children should ideally have as long as possible: time for timelessness, no (or very little) worry, inner quiet, self-esteem, time for play without pressure, curiosity, and a basic love for life itself.

Mental health and well-being are ongoing practices. A young mind must be supported to anchor itself in flow experiences, in the tangible world, and in nature, so the mind can become an ally in navigating this world, instead of one's own worst enemy.

CHILDREN'S MENTAL HEALTH MARKERS

We often talk about mental health only when a child already shows heavy signs of mental illness such as depression, anxiety, aggression, and other behavioral challenges that create an inability to fit into school. Often children's mental health challenges can be remedied before medicating them by changing their environment. Look for the below simple, yet powerful mental health markers to make sure your child is doing well now.

☆ Likes to play.

☆ Laughs with you.

☆ Moves and is curious.

☆ Has a vivid imagination.

☆ Is eager to explore nature.

☆ Tests your boundaries and their own limits.

☆ Enjoys loving touch and rough and tumble play.

☆ Recovers relatively quickly from sadness and upset.

☆ Feels safe to share with you when they are sad or upset.

☆ Experiences moments of flow during a self-chosen activity.

NOTE: Limited ability to be flexible and empathic are age-typical (as explained in Week 21), and will naturally mature in a loving environment with healthy boundaries. Rebellion and frustration are normal responses when children don't like the one-size-fits-all strategies in schools. Not being able to fit into standardized education is often a sign of great mental health because it reveals the willingness of the individual to defend their self-motivation and authenticity. Support your child with loving conversations, regular opportunities to play, and a plan of action to mitigate any long-term negative impact the situation may have.

TRY THIS
Three mental health anchors for your child

A child needs various points of stability in their life in order to be anchored in good mental health and find comfort during challenges.

Anchored in healthy relationships: Even one significant adult who genuinely cares for the child can make a huge difference in a child's well-being.

Anchored in nature: Regular access to outside time, running, and exploring freely in a nature place such as an urban park, the forest, or the beach. Playing with pebbles and sticks, listening to the sounds around them, discovering plants, animals, and insects—all of this nurtures a child's mental health.

Anchored in flow experiences: Flow offers an invitation to claim one's life and to own one's experiences. Flow in art, music, and movement helps us to express and consciously feel what goes on within and thus transform and heal it. This can have a positive ripple effect that helps to heal other parts of our lives and establish a strong and healthy core rooted in sanity and self-love.

WEEK 4

THE SELF-CHOSEN CHALLENGE
The ultimate game-changer

CHOOSING A CHALLENGE fueled by inner necessity and intense self-motivation is where a child's life force resides. A self-chosen challenge is the ultimate game changer because it goes hand-in-hand with a drive for learning self-discipline, patience, and resilience. We can and should offer children many different invitations for learning, but even though it may be tempting or it may seem like the responsible thing to do, we should never push an activity. Invite, inspire, make enticing, but don't force a child. When *we decide for a child*, we deprive them of many crucial learning opportunities.

The self-chosen challenge is the beginning of true self-discipline that does not need external pressure to be sustained; it is the sweet spot where a child is fully engaged and will not only learn but also mature. In the Rebeca Wild based (RWB) schools, I supported many children who set their own goals. Often, these goals were hard to reach—such as crafting a complete chess set in the woodshop or sewing long poems on a pillow.

It's fascinating to see how children develop patience when striving for something they really want. There is a struggle between frustration and the desire to achieve; a tug of war between giving up and continuing. These inner dynamics lead to important maturation processes and inform children for the rest of their lives. They learn that positive and negative feelings are a natural part of almost any creation process; they become familiar with comfortable and uncomfortable feelings and they learn to persist during challenges. They discover what it feels like to be frustrated, to give up, to hang in there, to continue even though it's hard. And what it feels like to achieve a goal, to celebrate that moment of success. It is empowering to be able to follow a self-chosen challenge (no matter what it is) and it provides a child with a feeling of command over their experience that is deeply fulfilling.

Children choose their challenges for various reasons. First, as long as they are able, they learn because they are curious about life, and they are willing to expand, explore, grow, and discover. They have a spontaneous joy of life and act from a place of inner contentment and self-confidence. Second, a challenge is often chosen to fulfill a personal genuine need and improve one's own quality of life:

"I must know what these letters mean!"

"I want to write a message for my friend."

"I would like to make a dollhouse out of this shoebox."

"I made a gift for you!"

Finally, there is learning to prove to oneself and others that one can do it and thereby experience the excitement of a self-chosen competition. Living up to a challenge through self-discipline feels exquisite: "You weren't sure if I could do it . . . there, I counted all the rice kernels in the bag!" or "I knew I could jump higher than you today; maybe you will jump higher than me tomorrow."

Finishing self-chosen tasks, completing a project, or keeping a commitment or promise becomes increasingly important as children get older, when they naturally develop increasing genuine interest in the results of their activities and a deeper understanding of linear time. Young children need not be forced to develop self-discipline prematurely. As young children, we are not interested in the result of our activities as much as we take delight in learning profoundly from each activity and experience *just as it is*. If the idea that the value of an activity is based on its tangible results is introduced too early, children often develop anxiety, which keeps them from enjoying their learning processes in the moment. Children have an inner compass that guides them to appropriate activities in alignment with their current learning edge. "Come on, try a little harder!" can be equally distracting as our fearful comments, "I'm worried about you. Be careful!" Within boundaries that feel safe to you, lean back, admire and trust your child's self-chosen challenges, and you will be surprised at their ingenuity and competence.

TRY THIS

Help your child with an ongoing practice

When children have the opportunity to experiment with a variety of activities, they may find a practice they would like to deepen. Children don't know yet that mastering anything involves time and commitment, so be patient with them and receptive to their feedback. Adults can lovingly help children reach their goals, but not at the cost of their joy and never without their consent. An ongoing practice could be anything that needs a long-term commitment such as growing plants, playing an instrument, crafting a wooden toy, tending to a pet, or learning to ski. Here are some ways in which you can help your child reach a self-chosen challenge:

☆ Provide everything the child needs for practicing, such as equipment, a quiet place, and uninterrupted time.

☆ Leave the instrument or materials needed out, visible, and within reach, so your child can practice anytime they want.

☆ Watch the child practice, if that helps them, otherwise create a place where they can practice on their own.

☆ If needed, in agreement with your child, find the right amount of practice time; maybe 30 minutes a week is enough, maybe 15 minutes a day feels right. Adjust the practice schedule to your child's needs over time.

☆ Create rituals around practice time. For instance, children love helping set timers, lighting a practice-time candle, or reciting a poem connected to their challenge.

☆ Be a role model and participate in your own way.

☆ Offer ongoing help and support.

☆ If a child wants to give up, inquire what is happening: Is it too hard? Is the teacher intimidating? Do they just need a break? Feel free to ask open-ended questions as well.

☆ If the commitment creates too much tension, let them take a break, come back to it later, or find a more suitable practice.

The Self-Chosen Challenge at Home

Giving children agency over their learning process is not to be mistaken for a "laissez-faire" or a "free-for-all" approach, which assumes a lack of boundaries that can be frightening for children and adults. At the RWB schools, we use very clear boundaries and prepared environments within which the learner's self-chosen challenges can happen. Similar conditions are needed at home. Susanne, FLOW TO LEARN's parenting advisor shares her experiences:

There is a common misconception that allowing a child to make independent choices results in an overly permissive environment or even in giving up our role as parents. Children need to feel safe within the healthy boundaries we set as their grown up, trustworthy leaders. As their parents, we maintain the responsibility to help them meet their needs when we recognize they cannot do so themselves.

It's an ongoing practice for me to discern what can be my child's choice in a given moment (learning decisions, play decisions, creative process decisions, self-care decisions, and so on), and when I should choose for them. For example, I might observe that my three-year-old is quite tired, and that she needs to take a nap before she can return to her innate flow state. I have seen that her ability to be in safe command of her environment drops significantly when fatigue sets in. However, if asked, "Would you like to go rest?" she might insist she isn't tired and doesn't need to rest. Perhaps she'd rather keep playing, or she might not yet understand what 'feeling tired' is, so her choice at that moment would not be in her best interest. In this example, it's clear to me that she needs my guidance to go rest, so asking if she would like to do so is offering her a false choice, since <u>her</u> choice would necessarily be overridden by <u>my</u> responsibility to keep her safe and well.

From the RIE (Resources for Infant Educarers) approach, I have learned that giving my children a controlled choice will increase the level of trust they have that I always mean what I say when offering them options. A controlled choice in this instance could be: "You seem really tired, so I am going to help you go rest in your bed. Would you like to walk or be carried?" In this way, I calmly set the caring, respectful boundary and provide a clear, controlled choice designed to keep my child safe while allowing her to feel autonomous.

I let her know what is happening before engaging in any physical touch so she can prepare for being carried or led to her napping place (or she may very well choose to go on her own!). Of course, there are times when an adult must scoop up a child who is in danger or is so fatigued that they can no longer manage verbal comprehension. When this happens, I might lovingly say things like: "I hear you are upset. You wanted to keep playing. I picked you up to keep you safe and I'll take you to nap now. I'm so sorry I startled you. It's okay to cry. Would you like me to lie down with you for a while?"

If a child feels emotionally safe throughout a challenging transition such as the one I just described, they become increasingly able to trust the benefit of their caregiver's decision, for example, understanding that the adult they trust helped them to rest, and now they feel much better. All caregivers know that requiring a child (or an adult!) to stop before they're ready to do so will usually result in opposition, and understandably so. Naturally, disagreements between us and our children about what is best for them happen often, which is all the more reason we try to ensure that they feel validated in their experience. This is one of the greatest balancing acts of respectful caregiving: encouraging children's self-led choices and independent thought while we simultaneously maintain our responsibility to keep them protected and healthy.

In our case, meeting these moments with honesty, firm boundaries, and respect for our children's emotions and desires has deepened the bonds we have with them. They know we still love and respect them as individuals, even as we set limits on their self-chosen challenges.

WEEK 5

RECOGNIZING FLOW
Train your eyes to see children differently

LEARN TO SEE CHILDREN as *young masters of flow* so you can support their emotional well-being, creativity, and superpowers. Children's superpowers include skills such as crystal clear focus, open-minded presence, boundless self-motivation, and deeply devoted, genuine interest in their own activity (refer to Week 14 for more details).

When children feel emotionally safe and can spend time in prepared environments, they spontaneously create flow-experiences for themselves. During flow, children are enthusiastic, open, and focused; they experience their mind at its best, as an ally and supporter. *If there is one thing we can learn from children, it is how to be playfully focused in flow.*

However, no one has ever told us this is so. "The kids are just playing," is what we commonly hear. But numerous studies from learning psychologists, educators, and pediatricians confirm what many of us intuitively know: children's play is their natural way of learning about their world. During spontaneous play, such as pretend play, playing with blocks, or tinkering away at something, children drop in and out of flow continuously and effortlessly when given the freedom to do so.

During the moments, minutes, or hours in flow, when children are fully focused on their activity and their body and emotions are on board with their mind's focus, that's when whole-body learning happens. The child learns something that they never forget, such as using scissors, riding a bicycle, or reading. Once you can read, you never go back to not being able to read. It is in these moments when a child's whole being is most receptive to absorbing all they can learn from an activity.

Let's say you see a child tinkering at the table with paper, scissors, and glue. You find out that their goal is to craft a paper airplane, not any paper plane, but an exciting, perfect paper plane that will fly from the window all the way to the squirrel on the tree in the backyard and deliver a walnut. How are you going to react?

Most people are not aware that such a complex child-chosen activity allows for countless new pathways to be formed between creative and logical thinking. It provides an enticing, steep learning curve from having an idea to realizing it, as well as the chance to hone practical skills like learning how to fold, cut, and tape paper. For the child, these are all just means to an end, and for the trained eye, these are effective exercises for creativity, coherence, and fine motor skills.

The child willingly chooses these exercises, without any pressuring or caregiver orchestration. Children love to learn in a child-friendly, playful context where they can follow their own process. The child doesn't consciously plan to learn. Rather, lasting learning happens as a result of intense interest in their self-chosen challenge.

Of course, we adults play a crucial role in the basic psychological imprint upon this child. Will the child find a supportive voice and the space and time for experimenting and discovery? Or, will the child be interrupted, ignored, or swooped up to do something else? Will the child get doubtful, patronizing looks, admonishments to be careful, or unsolicited help and advice? Will the child get too much praise, diverting them from flow to external rewards? Will they find our support to fully experience their own joy or disappointment when their plane finally flies? That's up to us.

TRY THIS
Watch a child play

Now that you know more details about flow, observe your child during the day or watch the learners in your classroom and notice if there is any span of time, even minutes, when a child is in flow. Become a quiet, friendly observer; when they look at you, return a friendly smile to signal you are not going to interrupt them and what they are doing is fine. Some children may be in the habit of expecting encouragement or approval in order to continue with their project. If this appears to be the case, it may take a while for a child to realize they are free to drop into flow without interruption. As they begin relaxing into their own process, limit your verbal feedback (if any is needed) to warm, short narration of their choices, simply reflecting their actions. Often, a few exchanges of this nature will give children reassurance that they are indeed safe to drop into a deep state of flow. Look for the elements of flow:

☆ When is your child fully concentrated on their activity?

☆ When can you tell the activity is intrinsically rewarding?

☆ What are the conditions that helped this child get into flow?

☆ How can you bring in more of the beneficial elements that helped this child to be in flow?

☆ What abilities might the child have improved?

☆ Which kind of intelligence might your child practice? According to the developmental psychologist Howard Gardner, there are nine types of intelligence and I added three more that are important when we observe children. This makes twelve kinds of intelligences in total, and they are found in infinite combinations, specifically in over 6 billion combinations – each person has their own unique flavor of intelligence.

12 KINDS OF INTELLIGENCE

Practical intelligence: The ability to find a solution to a problem and achieve a desired result.

Visionary intelligence: The ability to imagine, visualize, and dream of something that does not exist in the world.

Linguistic intelligence: Enables children to understand and use spoken and written words in useful, fun ways.

Mathematical intelligence: Enables children to use numbers and other measurements to better understand and work with their surroundings.

Spatial intelligence: The ability to picture something in the imagination exactly as it was seen it before.

Bodily-kinesthetic intelligence: The ability to move the body gracefully and efficiently, and to handle objects skillfully.

Musical intelligence: The ability to create, practice, and enjoy music, sounds, and rhythms.

Empathic intelligence: The ability to understand, imagine, and feel what another person or an animal is experiencing.

Introspective intelligence: The ability to know yourself.

Naturalist intelligence: A keen interest in the natural world, plants, animals, and their diverse habitats.

Existential intelligence: Existential intelligence is the desire to ask questions about humanity: Why are we here? Where are we going? Is there a God?

Intuitive intelligence – the flow state: Intuitive intelligence is the ability to do a task really well without having to think about it. Intuitive intelligence often comes in the form of a flow state.

THE CHILD MASTER IN YOU

Constantly return to your beginner's mind

WE ARE BORN WITH what Zen Buddhism calls a beginner's mind—an open mind, full of curiosity and wonder. As children, when we feel safe, we eagerly explore our surroundings. In our minds, everything is possible. Over the course of a day, when we find something interesting, as children we naturally and masterfully drop into the state of flow.

It's our beginner's mind that gives us easy access to flow and allows us to become fully absorbed in an activity we love. And it's our beginner's mind that leads us to reap the ultimate benefit of flow in childhood—learning deeply and permanently about our world. We don't forget what we learn in flow. It becomes our body memory.

Dropping into flow requires the childlike quality of looking at an activity with an open mind. It is a mind free of preconceived notions, doubts, and judgments, that sees clearly and directly instead of being filled with thoughts such as "I will never be able to do this" or "I already know I won't enjoy this." Young children have no doubts that they are capable. They trust their personal process of learning. A beginner's mind is receptive and allowing. It opens a doorway to flow states for yourself, and it enables you to understand the mindset of a child. Have you ever experienced a young child asserting, "Let me do it myself"? How outraged they get when you do it for them! That is why Maria Montessori, one of the first educators to value the state of flow, translates for children by stating, "Help me do it myself!"

Children are telling us to "be my companion on the learning path, but don't do it for me." Often, simply narrating their actions can be enough assistance to reinforce their intrinsic desire for hands-on, autonomous learning. Motivated by a genuine need for growing independence as well as belonging, children naturally return to the beginner's mind to ever so eagerly start new explorations. Think of a toddler's first attempts to open a door. The child sees other people using the handle. As soon as she is tall enough to reach it, she begins experimenting. If allowed, she will play with it until she is able to open the door or decides on her own it is time to ask for help. After some practice in deep focus and flow, opening a door handle becomes easier, and eventually it becomes a body memory—there is no need to practice this anymore. Onward to the next learning experience!

As we see in the RWB schools, this kind of learning, if allowed, happily continues as children grow. This is how humans naturally learn how to read, write, or play an instrument. As long as we are supported in doing so, we naturally keep returning to our beginner's mind—and we return with more skills each time. We integrate what we learn and start a new learning cycle from a more skilled perspective. Each new mastery becomes woven into the interconnected, complex web of knowledge that lays the groundwork for more difficult learning experiences. The deeper the learning, the more solid the foundation for next learning steps.

Let's use drumming as an example. While at first a child may randomly beat a drum following no special rhythm, over time they may discover various ways to play it. They initiate and develop new rhythms. When the child is fascinated by it, they naturally continue to practice drumming in flow. You might ask to join the party and through your own play provide suggestions for new rhythms or techniques and see how the child responds. They may not be ready to play with others or receive feedback and suggestions, if they are still deeply engaged with their own flow process.

As a flow companion, you will learn when to respect those healthy boundaries set by a child, and how to recognize a genuine invitation into their sacred space of learning in flow. In this way, the child's motivation for learning the task at hand is preserved, and the practice is likely to avoid the pitfalls of obligation or lack of ownership that can lead to abandonment of the process.

If we are supported to learn in flow, our beginner's mind is constantly being refined with layered and more important information about the world. In fact, as adults we can return to our beginner's mind with many additional treasures that we (ideally) have learned growing up: as adults we are more aware of dangers, we know how to take care of our physical and emotional needs, and we have the social skills needed to integrate our flow states into social environments.

BALANCE YOUR BRAIN'S NEGATIVITY BIAS

As infants and young children our heads are often free of busy thoughts. At this young age, a serene mind tuned in to a healing stillness feels natural to us. Young children's thoughts are almost always in direct connection with a present moment event. Though they might stretch to include a longer story, not much worry or anticipation is present yet (both are thinking activities disconnected from the present moment.)

As we gather more life experience through interaction with people, places, and items, we start to think more. Thoughts pop up in our inner reality that nudge us to evaluate events, assess risks, judge, like, and dislike things based on how they make us feel. Our brain begins to serve as a kind of protective device trying to help us avoid discomfort, stay safe, and feel more pleasure. As we grow up, we become increasingly used to scanning for problems, and expecting the other shoe to drop. For instance, as children it's easier to have a completely positive experience and to feel fully uplifted by its memory. As adults, our brain's learned negativity bias filters the memory, all too often getting hung up on the one upsetting detail that happened that day. While your child remembers the fun and connection of your day together on the beach, you might be stuck focused on the moment when you snapped at them for getting sand in your bag.

If an event feels scary enough, a child's negativity bias may very well kick in. For example, if they fall into cold water and experience great shock or fear, combined with their parents' reactions, that event may stand out as the most salient memory of their day at the beach. Consequently, a child's whole being will focus on this traumatic experience to process, transform, and release it in many ways, and mostly by "playing it out" (as explained in Week 17). As adults, this function can become an impairment—instead of processing to release, our brains tend to overthink and make things more complex and disturbing to our inner world than they are in reality. Most of us need to put effort into rebuilding positive thinking habits— otherwise our brain's negativity bias can tarnish even the most innocent, sweet experiences we have with children, with others, or for that matter, even with ourselves.

This negativity bias most likely developed as a survival mechanism and served a good purpose throughout human evolution. Those who survived then passed on the brain training genetics to detect danger soon enough to avoid it, which reinforced it over millennia. In this day and age, there are large swaths of humanity that do not need to reckon with regular, life-threatening danger. Yet, the negativity bias remains a strong part of all our wiring.

Constant thought feels normal to most adults, and if we are unaware of it, this constant thinking tends to be negative; many of us have forgotten what it feels like to have a peaceful mind, to think less, worry less, and simply trust an experience. And often it is exactly this overactive mind that keeps us from finding more pleasure and flow in the present moment.

With a little effort, it is possible to retrain our brain and relearn to enjoy, trust, and relax into life experiences. For instance, at night, when you lie in bed, before dozing off, create a new habit of listing at least three positive things that happened that day. You might find your body relaxes and you fall asleep more easily. You can also start a gratitude journal, by yourself or together with your child, where you take daily notes of things you are grateful for. Simple habits such as these make a big difference for your brain circuitry, and gradually, perhaps without noticing at first, your ability to think positively and fully enjoy sweet moments with your child will increase, and so will your ability to drop into flow.

Find out more on balancing the brain's negativity bias in Loretta Graziano Breuning's book *Habits of a Happy Brain: Retrain Your Brain to Boost Your Serotonin, Dopamine, Oxytocin, and Endorphin Levels.*

TRY THIS
How to encourage the beginner's mind

Experiment with reawakening and using your beginner's mind, especially when you find yourself in new circumstances, but also in daily life. Support children in trusting their own initial impressions of an item or an activity and you will observe how the joy of discovery increases.

FOR ADULTS
USE YOUR NON-DOMINANT HAND TO DO FAMILIAR TASKS

Try to experience your beginner's mind by letting the hand you always use rest, and by using your other hand to do mundane tasks you need to do anyway. This may slow you down, and perhaps bring up some impatience, but if you keep going, you will reap the benefits of re-wiring your brain and expanding your habitual view of how you do things.

This week try this:

☆ Brush your teeth with your other hand.

☆ Write your name with your other hand.

☆ Use the computer mouse with your other hand.

FOR CHILDREN
USE NON-INVASIVE LANGUAGE

One way to keep the beginner's mind alive in children is to use non-invasive language. Instead of answering children's questions with words and labels right away—"This is thyme," "That's Da Vinci's Mona Lisa"—we can allow a child to have their own first impressions of novelties with questions like "What do you see?" or "Tell me more about that." Instead of pointing out elements in the environment, we can allow a child to make their own discoveries, for instance, instead of saying "Look at the beautiful butterfly!" we can say, "I can see something special right now, can you?"

THE POWER OF HANDS-ON ACTIVITY

Bring joy back to learning

CHILDREN NATURALLY USE THEIR HANDS and their whole bodies in flow. This is what makes learning attractive, lasting, and joyful for them. It is awkward and painful for a child to use only their thinking mind and disregard their emotional and physical impulses during the learning process. They need to see, touch, hear, feel, smell, and play with something in order to learn about it.

It is during hands-on activities that children are most likely to experience flow, the deepest, most suitable inner state for learning. Natural, relaxed focus allows the brain and heart to absorb new information and integrate it seamlessly into the child's being. Whatever is learned in flow remains in a child's long-term memory. It becomes a reference point in their internal world that helps with all abstract thinking and theoretical contemplations, as well as allowing for the development of increasingly complex hands-on skills and coordination.

Everything children learn in preschool and elementary school can be taught with hands-on learning materials in playful ways. The most impressive example of this is math. Many children have extremely negative feelings toward math in its traditionally taught forms. Many adults cringe when they think back to math lessons and have concluded that they're just not smart enough to understand it. But how can something so magical, perfect, and splendid as math, a sacred language for the multi-dimensional world around us, become so abhorred? It is because it was reduced to rote memorization, pen and paper, and a complete lack of meaningful, creative connections with our world; the life was literally taken out of it. It was diminished to an isolated, abstract subject that seemed to have nothing to do with our vibrant and colorful reality.

In my mid-twenties, I relearned math during my Montessori teacher training with hands-on learning materials and had a stunning revelation: I wasn't too dumb for math! It was the theoretical way that it was explained to me that didn't work. For the first time, I saw math as a descriptive language, a tool I can use to better understand the world and myself. There is a huge difference between scribbling fractions in a book, and their practical counterparts: slicing a pizza or an apple into halves, quarters, and eighths; sharing game tokens equally among friends; or creating a budget for a school trip. The latter hands-on experiences are needed many, many times in childhood so the concept of "fractions" can be incorporated into our whole-body knowingness. Then, when we calculate fractions on paper, math merely becomes what it is meant to be: a language for what we know firsthand; a language that helps us perceive the reality we know in more complex and evolved ways, even allowing us to imagine things far beyond the everyday tangible experience.

Rebeca and Mauricio Wild were especially fond of Montessori and other hands-on math materials. A few years before Rebeca passed away in 2015, I asked her what she would most want to communicate to parents in the U.S. She responded with the following message, translated from German:

"Since in our culture, most people are guided by external information, many of our internal networks are blocked. But if we dare to go new ways with our children, they can begin to perceive the difference between what they heard from others and assumed to be true, and what they have learned through their very own experiences and have gradually understood. One way to reactivate internal authentic understanding is to interact with hands-on math materials. But only if we give up our agenda to teach children 'better' and 'faster,' and instead let them make new discoveries to share with others who are curious about what they learned. For us [Mauricio and Rebeca], it has become increasingly clear that hands-on math is not simply a different way of 'doing math,' but that there is much more to it. Through interactions with the various counting boards, beads, and cubes, a learner's internal understanding builds structures that connect their reticular system with the limbic system as well as with the various other areas of their brain – it truly is a visceral experience. Often adults or adolescents would share with us that during their work with these materials, they suddenly understood why, for example, they have difficulties with their partner or their parents. This is definitely more than mathematics!"

TRY THIS
An example of child-directed learning

Joy, a public school teacher from California who visited the RWB school I helped create in the Italian Alps, remembers the following experience she made in the school:

Every morning yoga was offered in the theatre. It was a lovely way to start the day. Sometimes it would be just Anna, me, and Renate, and other times there were quite a few of us. But, every day, without fail, two young boys waited rambunctiously outside the theater door, eager for us to finish. Once our mats were packed up, and we opened the doors, the boys rushed in and began building forts. I quietly observed their process, one special morning, doing my best not to intrude on their learning space. They went to the corner where large geometrically-shaped stuffed objects were stored and began flinging them into the center of the room. They then dragged out a couple of ladders and pulled different colored cloths from the shelves. I observed as they went on to systematically and with great fervor build the most intricate and well-balanced 'buildings.' I was fascinated by the way they worked together to adjust certain pieces, learning what did and did not work, what would stay up and what didn't have enough support, how each edge could fit into certain nooks, and so on. The creations they made were forts suited for royalty. They then climbed in and began to enjoy the fruits of their labor...so determined, and in flow, learning in pure joy and concentration.

This day of witnessing such a scene made a huge impact on me. Just three weeks before, I had taught my 3rd grade students back in public school in Oakland about 3-D shapes. It was a struggle for them. We were using small wooden pieces of each shape and worksheets that required students to count the sides, vertices, faces, and so on of each piece. The kids were compliant and 'did their best,' but the lessons felt flat and without real meaning.

And then fast forward, here I was sitting in this schoolroom in Merano, with no 'teacher' to guide, only two six-year-old boys and an inspired environment, and these boys were learning on such a deep level the intricacies of 3-D shapes. They were not only 'learning about' them ... they were experiencing them, holding them, touching them, turning them, building with them, revising their plans, creating, and enjoying their 'work.' In this moment, I really got how play and work are one and the same, and why it is a huge disservice to our children to teach that they are separate.

LEARNING HOW TO THINK

Flow skills prepare for academic skills

THERE IS AN ALARMING TREND in education to push academic skills on children even before preschool, at a time when they are unable to comprehend what is asked of them, or even physiologically capable of the task. A child-centered approach assures children the right to learn at their own pace, on their own terms, when they are ready. Reading, writing, foreign languages, and basic math might be exciting for some children at an early age, but should never be forced at the cost of spontaneous play.

During playful discovery and thought experiments that include natural learning curves based on trial and error, children form the mental and intellectual abilities needed to develop academic skills within an optimistic growth mindset: "I can learn this! I couldn't do it last week but today I can do it!" Many hands-on experiences ensure that fundamental thinking capacities are being practiced and reinforced for permanence. These foundational experiences are best acquired in flow.

Teaching children primarily through spoken and written words separates them from the direct experience of their environment. Children learn that they need another person in order to interpret and interact with the environment, so this approach can be quite disempowering. Furthermore, verbal teaching leaves much room for misunderstanding. For example, when children learn division using only numbers on paper, they usually do not realize that the result of a division equals what "one person" receives. When division is experienced by a group of children evenly dividing a basket of apples, children understand division with their whole bodies and minds. They see that the result of division is "what one gets." Such holistic experiences are the most natural, efficient, effortless, and fun ways to learn.

In flow, children learn how and when it is best to think and when it is better not to think. Being in flow shows children that there is a higher intelligence in us than our thoughts; an intelligence anchored in our bodies; an inner, organizing, and integrated intelligence that can be trusted. They learn that practicing and trusting oneself are the avenues that repeatedly lead to success. Below is a list of intellectual skills that most children learn with ease during their spontaneous play (by themselves and with others) in prepared environments; these skills are needed *before* academics can make sense to them:

— Focusing on a chosen topic
— Problem-solving and planning next steps
— Estimating and anticipating results
— Spatial thinking, developing the capacity to know what something that is not present looks like
— Developing a strategy
— Envisioning and dreaming of what is not yet materialized
— Calculating a risk
— Discerning between real and imagined
— Perceiving the environment with all senses
— Recognizing patterns and varieties in nature, such as the growth of plants and movement of insects or clouds and patterns in human and animal behavior
— Allowing the mind to rest from thought in order to open up to the "lightbulb" or "sudden knowing"

— Cultivating positive thinking versus negative thinking habits
— Being encouraged and encouraging oneself with positive thought
— Contemplating the present moment
— Contemplating what happened in the past
— Using the mind as a tool to relax the body and nervous system

The following are core academic skills most children can learn once their intellect is ready:

— Critical thinking
— Listening and learning through discussion
— Reevaluating assumptions
— Speaking without fear
— Researching data and information
— Memorizing
— Taking notes, summarizing and extracting information from texts
— Writing essays and articles
— Preparing and presenting about a subject
— Math and science
— Basic technology and engineering
— Civics, government, and economics
— History, geography, computer science
— Taking an exam
— Time management
— Digital skills

In well-prepared, flow-friendly, educational environments, such as RWB schools, children can learn the following skills, playfully, and at their own pace:

— Sorting, adding, subtracting, dividing, and multiplying with real-life objects
— Communicating thoughts and emotions clearly

— Expressing oneself with clarity and ease

— Simplifying complex content

— Prioritizing tasks and information

— Deducing important information from random facts

— Remembering chosen content

— Memorizing chosen songs, poems, texts

— Associating personal, relevant content with our instructive, collective stories and myths

EXPANDING OUR UNDERSTANDING OF INTELLIGENCE

Conventionally, we think of intelligence in the context of an IQ score. Yet, neither academic nor intellectual skills completely determine a child's intelligence. Harvard psychologist Howard Gardner helped us expand our traditional notion of intelligence with his theory of multiple intelligences (Week 5). Yet, in order to deepen our understanding about a child's (and our own) intelligence, we need to go even further: A child's intelligence is determined also by their ability to connect and to feel connected. In fact, children develop high intelligence through feeling connected. Intelligence is generated with the heart as well, and considers all sides of an issue in the context of genuine interest for what one is learning, while caring for all people, nature, and oneself.

In his books and interviews, Joseph Chilton Pearce, (1926-2016), professor of humanities and visionary author, summarized and interpreted the research on the intelligence of the heart, which has influenced many educators and parents around the world from the 1970s onward. In simple terms, he explained what had already been proven scientifically: Our heart is not only a physical pump, but also highly intelligent. Our heart's reactions, feelings, and emotions are an important part of our brain and nervous system. The degree to which we listen to our heart's reactions determines our capacity for joyful, self-directed learning, flow, relaxation, and clear, balanced thought.

SILLINESS, PLAYFULNESS, AND LEARNING

As a ground rule, children learn anything more easily in a playful, warm, and even silly context. Playfulness, silliness, and lightheartedness allow a child's nervous system to feel safe and at ease. This doesn't necessarily mean adults should come up with ways to be silly with children (even though that may be wonderfully fun at times); instead, allow children to be silly with you when it naturally arises for them. Don't force them to focus when they need to chuckle and giggle. Whenever you can, let children tell you their jokes and stories and receive them with a smile that says, "I see you and your brilliant mind!" I feel it's an honor if a child trusts an adult with insights into their world. Once this dialogue, this back and forth, is allowed, children will also be more likely to and listen to what a parent, teacher, or tutor has to say.

Learning (that goes beyond memorization) and feeling cannot be separated. Feeling respected, loved, and supported while learning is a catalyst for more advanced learning processes. Being silly with children or benevolently allowing them to make funny faces or to tell you a knock-knock joke creates a relaxed atmosphere and signals to a child that they are safe and accepted in your presence. The established trust allows a child to authentically receive from you the teaching you would like to offer to them.

TRY THIS

How to create intellectual safety

Intellectual safety is a nurturing foundation for creativity and flow. Creativity starts hiding when it feels judged harshly. So many people have lost the joy of painting, singing, creating, or experimenting because they encountered one or more adults who inhibited their joy in childhood and beyond.

Some examples of how adults do this, often with good intentions, is by judging a child's creative process negatively *or positively*; overtaking the creative process by regulating how it should proceed; superimposing the "ideal" method before a person is interested in learning it or telling them their way of creating is the "wrong" way; or reducing the creative process to an end-product goal, and often then judging it by supposedly objective metrics, which are by nature generated by someone other than the original creator.

Contests and performance can be a wonderful celebration of creativity, but not at the expense of the inner motivation and joy of the process itself, which is the most meaningful part for anyone who creates from a place of flow. Here are some suggestions for creating intellectual safety for children:

☆ Foster an environment where everyone's perspective is welcome.

☆ Talk to children with respect and appreciation for their own knowing.

☆ Show children it is okay to have different opinions; it's okay to disagree. You can "agree to disagree," still respect each other, and get along.

☆ Reframe mistakes as valuable, essential steps for learning.

☆ Never laugh at a child's question or answer that was given in a sincere manner.

☆ Avoid comparing learners with each other.

☆ Avoid judging children's expressions in art, language and other disciplines; instead, ask if your constructive feedback is welcome or simply express neutral observations (You used a lot of purple!).
☆ Celebrate a child's achievement together with them.

EMOTIONAL SAFETY

The quality of relationship is up to you

IN RELATIONSHIP WITH CHILDREN we become archetypal mothers, fathers, teachers, and companions. Our presence, our voice, and our advice become a child's inner voice in adolescence and beyond, when children become increasingly aware of themselves. The quality of our bonding with a child will become a model for their bonding with significant others and their own children throughout life. It is well worth taking the time for deep, authentic bonding with a child, as this genuine need, when fulfilled, can change the course of a child's life.

For a young child, it doesn't really matter who *you* think you are, as long as you are kind and patient. A young child looks at you with the eyes of innocence, and since you are tall and grown up, they trust you know your way around, and hope you will genuinely listen to them and give them what they need. Children live in their own world, and we are the ones who have the capacity to understand *them*—they cannot yet understand our adult ways. So, please, always remember: Whatever a child does, you never need to take that personally—never, ever. Children never act *against you*; children instinctively always act *for themselves*. Much of the time, they cannot control their reactions and emotional expression, until the appropriate parts of their brains related to impulse regulation literally are formed. Remain kind, remain patient, and provide stability as much as you can. A child must be able to rely on at least one significant adult in order to feel emotionally safe. On a primal level, this is a child's urgent need to constantly know that they will not be abandoned, no matter what. This primary need is to be bonded with adults, not with peers. Children are not yet ready to provide emotional safety for each other, because they are in an egocentric stage of life in which they must learn to take care of their own needs first.

Take responsibility for an emotionally safe environment through remaining kind and connected with children including during challenging situations. For children, feeling safe with you means knowing *they are always okay,* and they don't ever need to be "perfect," or "up to grade level" for us to respect them, always. They need to know we regard them as learners on a path. They need to know from you that *it is okay* to feel their feelings, cry, laugh, be upset, have a conflict, ask questions, or play alone. When we allow children to be upset, release tension, and process emotions, while gently holding firm boundaries to ensure everyone stays safe during these times, they relax on a deep level, and learn social skills over time, by our example. In psychology, this is known as "secure attachment." A parent's message to their child and a flow companion's message to a learner is always:

It's okay to be you. You are okay the way you are. There is nothing wrong with you. It's okay not to know yet. It's okay to ask. It's okay to make mistakes. You will learn everything you need to know in your own time.

It's okay to feel what you are feeling. It's okay to be sad. It's okay to be upset. It's okay not to like something. It's completely normal, and I will stay with you until you're feeling better.

It's natural to have conflicts sometimes and I will help you to solve them. It's human to hurt someone sometimes, and I will show you how to say "I'm sorry" and make amends.

For children, feeling emotionally safe means knowing they will always be cared for, fed, and sheltered. It means feeling protected and knowing that no other child can hit them, scare them, or take their things away. It means knowing they won't be left alone to solve conflicts with peers. When children feel genuinely safe, they will surprise adults with their intelligence, empathy, and willingness to cooperate.

Always, as best you can, remain bonded with a child who is entrusted to you. Be one team with that child. Don't withdraw your loving attention when you or the child gets frustrated or when there is conflict. Believe in the child's good intentions. Even when the child displays egocentric behavior and is hard to deal with, remember that this behavior is a stage of childhood development that naturally softens if it is not suppressed (as explained in Week 21).

TRY THIS
What do You need to feel safe?

In order to help children feel safe and to take responsibility for your relationships with children, it's important that *you* feel safe first. Feeling safe is largely determined by your nervous system, which is directly connected to your breath. If you breathe at a fast pace even though you didn't run, or if you breathe very lightly as opposed to breathing deeply, your nervous system might be in the "I feel threatened" mode, which is known as the sympathetic state that regulates our fight-or-flight responses (as explained in Week 15).

You can calm yourself, intentionally switching your nervous system over to the "I feel safe" mode, the parasympathetic state of rest, by consciously breathing slower and more deeply. This gives a signal to your nervous system that you notice your body, that you are caring for your own well-being, and that you are safe. Notice how you feel in different environments, with different people, or after different foods. Within the same environment, some may feel safe while others feel vulnerable. Become aware of tension in your body, and situations where you feel uncomfortable. Try to find out why without pointing fingers or blaming anyone or anything. Just notice and inquire what could be changed in the tangible environment or within yourself to calm your nervous system, feel safe, and thus improve your quality of life.

As you continue practicing this self-observation, you may find there are issues from your own childhood relationships with adults that come up. The better we understand ourselves and consciously make loving efforts to heal wounds we may carry from our experiences, the more patient, kind, open, and aware we can be as we care for the children in our lives. Make notes about your own feelings as they arise and ask yourself these questions..

- What makes me feel safe?
- What gives me inner peace?
- What thoughts create tension in me?
- Which thoughts give me happiness?
- When am I naturally grateful and relaxed?
- What brings about a sense of vulnerability for me?
- What makes me feel uncomfortable?
- What can be changed in my home or classroom environment to make me feel more comfortable?

Helping Your Child Through Big Emotions

Strong emotions are age-typical for young children. When young children see they will not upset or drive away their adult leaders with big emotions they can't yet control and that often feel scary to experience, it builds in them a fundamental sense of safety. Challenging interactions can become important moments for developing trust between children and their caregivers. This allows them to fully integrate strong emotions in healthy ways, building more confidence that they can undertake the kinds of self-chosen challenges presented in this book. Susanne, dedicated mother of two young masters of flow and FLOW TO LEARN's parenting advisor, shares how her family strives to make it through emotional exchanges in their home:

Like most parents, it can be challenging for me to experience my children's big emotions, the rapid shifts of mood and demands, and eruptive crying commonly known as the terrible twos (and threes, and fours, and fives!). Yet, early on in my parenting, I realized intuitively, and found confirmed by other parents and researchers, that a child having a 'meltdown' is not trying to manipulate; in fact, they've lost control of their response to the situation, and they need help.

All children have a genuine need to be met with acceptance, so the adult should never take a child's emotions or reactions personally. Practicing the act of self-expression when emotions run high strengthens children's self-knowledge and trust that they can become fully capable of making the right decisions in their best interest. Like any skill developed over time, it takes repeated practice and learning by example. When I committed to providing a safe "container" for my children's authentic expressions and release of emotion, it became easier for me to handle these moments from a place of acceptance. I keep reminding myself that as children grow, knowing they are okay to express themselves and learning how to be with their big emotions will certainly help them develop self-regulation more easily.

Here is an example from our lives, based on the RIE model for handling emotionally charged interactions with young children. As a three-year-old, my son is playing with his food and throwing spoonfuls of his dinner onto the floor. I say: "Oh, I want you to stop throwing soup on the floor, please. (He continues.) Remember, the place for your food is in your bowl. (He continues.) We need to clean up the soup before leaving the table. Here are two washcloths. I'm going to clean it up now. You may help me if you like." (He throws the bowl on the floor, yelling in anger.) Staying as unruffled as I possibly can, I continue narrating his actions: "You threw the bowl on the floor again, and you seem upset. You're showing me that you're done eating, and we can try again at breakfast. I am going to help you go upstairs for bath time. Would you like to walk by yourself or may I help you? You aren't answering so I am going to help you go upstairs. I see you are angry!"

Rather than becoming annoyed by my son's actions, taking them personally, or allowing a power struggle to develop, I am training myself (it's always a work in progress) to remember that their brains are not yet capable of impulse control. In moments of overload for their system, my children are physiologically and psychologically unable to sit down, handle their food according to house rules, express themselves with words, or whatever the case may be. To verbally repeat the boundary until I do get frustrated at their apparent disregard, or to ignore their call for help (as outbursts usually are) would be unkind to both of us. When I can stay calm and embrace my supportive, loving role while also holding firm to a boundary right away before I become irritated, my terribly upset child feels comfort in my guidance.

This practice is certainly not perfect, but the goal is that my children know on a deep level that they're safe with us even though it's scary for them when they lose control of their emotions and actions. In this way, they know I've got them, I love them, and it's going to be okay.

REALITY CHECK

What does my child naturally do?

TAKE A FEW MINUTES and assess what your child naturally does at home. If they already have many hands-on activities they enjoy, you can enrich their natural interests with additional materials. Ask yourself, what are the activities my child currently does in our home? Use this checklist:

— Block and toy play

— Drawing, painting, crafting, tinkering

— Reading

— Outdoor activities: sandplay, ball play, movement games

— Homework

— My child likes to do what I do

— Screen time (which specific games or videos)

— Other activities: _____

Ask yourself, where does my child currently spend most time at home? Number the places with 1 for most time, 2 for second most time, etc.

_____ In the kitchen

_____ In the living room

_____ In their playroom or bedroom

_____ In the backyard

_____ Other places in our home: _____

_____ Wherever I am

Ask yourself: Why does my child spend a lot of time there? Underline what applies.

— Because I am usually in this area
— Because my child is undisturbed in this place
— Because it's sunny/shady/cool/warm
— Because there are specific toys and places for activities
— Because it's comfy, beautiful, clean, chaotic (a wonderful mess), orderly, exciting, safe
— Other reasons: _____

Finally, ask yourself: Where would I like my child to spend a lot of time? Look around your home and decide where you could create places for flow experiences.

TRY THIS
Schedule a day of rest and play

If your family lives a busy life, try to schedule at least one day of rest per week for you and your children. On that day, turn off the screens, including your phones when at all possible. Resting does not necessarily mean doing nothing. It simply involves taking a break from the often hectic routines of daily life. This can be a day where you nurture yourself, cultivate being a family, and do things that make your inner child and your children happy.

If your child spends most of their time at a screen, you can consider (with the help of this book) slowly weaning them off screen time, and gradually introducing more time for hands-on activities, movement, and nature. Letting go of screens, can feel intimidating at first. Meet resistance with kind but firm positions that this will be the "new normal" for your family. Getting a pet for your child can be very helpful in this process. Animals are immune to the addictive effects of screen time and have a pure and dependable grounding effect in children. A bridge to the natural world that is fluffy, funny, or cuddly, pets can be quite healing to children and adults.

Your day of rest can include time when everyone individually does what they most love and time when you all come together to share a meal or other activities. When you come together, share what you each have done individually. Here are some suggestions for your day of rest and play:

☆ Do a crafting project, such as creating a decoration for the house.
☆ Go for a nature walk.
☆ Play a family board game.
☆ Cook something special together.
☆ Paint a big picture together.
☆ Write postcards or letters to extended family and friends.
☆ Various self-care activities, for instance, meditating, stretching, and taking a long, relaxed bath.
☆ Create a photo album.
☆ Decorate a shelf or window.
☆ Create additional comfortable spots in the house.
☆ Create a fun spot in the yard.

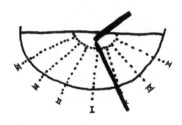

Permission to Play

Taking the time to play with children can be challenging for modern households with overfull schedules. Parenting advisor to FLOW TO LEARN, Susanne, shares what happens in her home when she, her husband, and children come together in play:

One Saturday morning at home with our children, I was at my desk after breakfast, trying to fit in some work to meet a deadline. The kids were independently in flow and I was glad to be dropping into my own. They began to touch base with me often, and each interruption felt more jarring. I suggested games, promised I'd play later, and even gave them the firm confirmation that I was unavailable. However, it was clear that their genuine need was to connect with me. I decided to be present with them for a few minutes, knowing that shortly I'd return to my work.

Our three-year-old daughter wasted no time once she felt me engage, effortlessly diving into a role-play game: It was time for me to go to bed in the "Calming Corner," a space where we have our Generation Mindful posters, along with books, blankets, pillows, cushions, and a colorful rug on the floor. "You have to lie down and go to sleep, Mama. Tomorrow we are all going to the playground. Okay, please lay your head on the pillow." I complied willingly, amused by her enthusiasm. Her eyes sparkled with delight. "But first you need to drink some water." I sat up. "Okay, good, now it's time to sleep, go ahead, I'm right here." I lay back down. Suddenly, we weren't alone. "Oh no! Do you hear that?! It's a monster! Quick, hide under the covers!" I quickly hid, a little startled by the sudden turn of events. Our five-year-old son happily joined in, now a monster, now bringing a delivery, now a dad, now a silly dog. I reveled in their creativity and their gentleness. We danced, hid, slept, made music, and pretended. It was so much fun that I easily chose to embrace this chance to simply play with my kids, uninterrupted.

When lunchtime came, there were no arguments. We were content and filled with a sense of satisfaction. It was a wake-up call for me: this was so easy, compared with how it goes when the to-do list comes first at all costs. I often find myself slipping into a "logistics" mindset around our routines—using our time together to check off the list as efficiently as possible. It's completely understandable, and at times it's necessary. Still, I was grateful to be reminded that a small investment of quality time with the children is well worth our while. Even 15 minutes of being fully present with each other calms everyone's nervous systems. It helps us remember how to slow down and just be together.

Another way we use play in our home is to break up tension. If I notice I'm feeling tense, I might start talking silly talk or singing a funny song, literally releasing tension out of my body through movement and song. One of our favorites is sung in a gravelly voice and minor key: "Mama's in a baaaaad mood/ Who spilled this milk on the floor?! / Mama's in a baaaaad mood/ Get yourselves right outta that door!" We know it well and raucously take turns making up rhyming verses. This turns the moment into a fun bonding experience while acknowledging that I was, in fact, in a terrible mood.

Our children readily share their own playful approaches to life's routines whenever they can. Asking their Dada to toss bottlecaps into the intricate traps they create is one of their favorite pastimes. Another favorite is "opposite day," in which a parent must sternly instruct them they'd better not do a task on their own, like put on their clothes or brush their teeth, or they'll become extremely disobedient children! They laugh in response and say defiantly, "Oh yes, I will!! Look at what I'm doing!" It's incredibly efficient—they get everything done, flip authority on its head, practice doing lots on their own, and have a blast in the meantime.

If I'm just too worn out to play, I try to remember that's okay, too. I know it's good for our children to see us set authentic, healthy boundaries for ourselves. Each parent or caregiver must determine where the balance lies for ensuring that their needs are sufficiently met, giving themselves permission to fill their own cups by scheduling activities that replenish their reserves. I notice how much more willing I am to play with our children when I'm reasonably rested and taken care of.

Playing together is healing, for children and adults alike. Through play, we connect with our kids from a non-hierarchical place—where they can call the shots and make decisions. The precious gift of permission to play is a safety net we can fall back on when life gets scary or overwhelming. It reinforces children's natural lightheartedness, engages their "I feel safe" mode, and it exercises our abilities to create and enjoy our own play, without needing to be entertained by external sources. I feel that being invited into a child's flow space is one of the holiest ways to spend my time as a parent. Play is one of the best ways to say, "I love you."

WEEK 11

HEALING NEGATIVE SCHOOL EXPERIENCES
Tension release is healing

TENSION RELEASE IS A SIGNIFICANT part of self-healing in children and adults, and it is unavoidable when we become more present with ourselves in flow experiences. Children who go to a less than ideal school are in a daily reality that doesn't respect their most pressing genuine developmental needs for movement, exploration, spontaneous play, and connection. Of course, this creates inner tension. During the many school mornings of sitting, listening, and trying to focus, children increasingly lose touch with their genuine needs and curiosity. Their parents or significant caregivers are often the only ones they can turn to when they need support.

Most of all, children need adults who are true allies, whom they can trust to love them exactly as they are. If they have this deep bond with at least one significant adult, parent, teacher, grandparent, or friend, children will develop a strong inner core and the skills to face all challenges. Younger children naturally release tension during spontaneous play, self-talk, and time in nature. If your child still plays and talks during play—no matter how old they are—that's a very good sign that their tension release mechanisms still work well.

Older children often stop playing and need different forms of tension release to express their frustration. Allow them to vent and complain, while you listen with patience and understanding. (Computer games and other screen time aren't ideal forms of tension release. Due to the screen's addictive potential, and the passivity of the body during screen time, it may create more tension). Stay with a child until they feel better. You can offer ways of tension release as described below.

NINE WAYS TO HELP YOUR CHILD
RELEASE TENSION

<u>1) Allow children to cry.</u>

Crying as part of feeling sad, disappointed, excluded, or treated unjustly is the most direct way to process uncomfortable experiences. Shedding tears is one of the most powerful ways of healing. Tears release emotional stress and physical toxins from the body. Usually children feel completely renewed after a good cry, especially in the safe presence of an understanding adult. Sometimes children cry even when there is no apparent reason, or for seemingly unrelated reasons to be able to feel the relief of crying.

<u>2) Allow children to laugh and laugh with children.</u>

Children love to laugh. Uninhibited laughter is a joyful, effective way of tension release. When children laugh together with peers or adults, it is a powerful bonding experience, as long as all involved understand the reason for the laughter, and don't feel insulted or hurt by it. You may have noticed children have a different sense of humor than adults; nevertheless there are plenty of opportunities for children and adults to laugh together as long as the adult's heart is open to the world of a child. For instance, adults may not find the repetition of the same knock-knock joke as funny as a seven-year-old, or they may not giggle as much about the poo-poo joke of a three-year-old. However, as adults, we can still open our hearts to a child's light-hearted happiness and perceive it as what it is: an attempt to connect, release tension, and restore inner balance. Children's laughter can be healing for both children and the adults around them.

3) Support children in resting.

Resting is a natural way of replenishing energies and releasing muscle tension after a period of intense physical movement or intellectually strenuous tasks. Let a child cuddle up in pillows or stretch and move on the floor as long as they want to without any pressure to do anything. Children find their own perfect balance between activity and rest and naturally restore their energy when needed.

4) Offer places for pretend play.

Pretend and role-play are natural avenues for children to release tension. (Read more about healing play in Week 17).

5) Provide places for movement.

Most children are in constant movement. When they play a game on the floor, they stretch and frequently change position. When they sit at a table, they sway back and forth and move their legs. They are what adults sometimes call "fidgety." All these movements release inner tension. Allow children to move as much as they wish. Wherever possible, provide areas and safe opportunities for movement with hanging ropes, swings, climbing walls, boxing bags, jumping ropes, hula-hoops, and the like.

6) Help your child physically feel their emotion and let it go.

We can heal mind, body and heart by becoming deeply aware of our feelings and how they manifest in our bodies. When a child is upset, sad, or scared, you can try to lead them through a simple process.

Ask: "Where are you feeling this in your body? Is it in your throat, belly, or jaw? Point to where you are feeling this. Now, gently lay your hand on that place and let's breathe deeply and feel this." Then, see what happens. Often acknowledging a feeling is enough for a child to let it go.

7) Offer art supplies to draw, paint or craft.

Arts and crafts aren't only for play and learning, but also for healing. Children release tension through creating something and tearing it up, drawing out scenes from their imagination, dreams, or memories, or painting on large surfaces with big brushes with the fulfilling attitude that it doesn't matter if the painting can be displayed in the end. You can lead your child to a tension release art project with questions such as "What would your feeling look like if it came through the door?" and "You could paint how you are feeling now, and then how you would like to feel."

8) Let the child talk and simply listen.

As children get older (sometimes young children, too), they have increased verbal skills to reduce tension. Just like adults, children speak about challenges they face and just like adults, they are mostly not seeking answers or someone who solves their problem for them. Instead, they need someone to listen, someone who simply accepts and witnesses what they are going through. Listen with your heart when a child speaks and detect their genuine needs behind their words. Empathize honestly, "I'm sorry you have to go through this, and I'm here for you through all of it."

9) Allow screaming where it's appropriate.

Screaming is another effective way of tension release. Think of places where it would be okay for your child to scream. Perhaps at the beach or in nature with not many people around. They might scream into pillows to dampen the sound. A friend allows her child to yell all the four-letter-words she isn't supposed to say into the pillows, so they don't "get stuck inside."

TRY THIS

Temper your child's negative school experiences

Here are a few ways you can stand up for your child's rights in standardized school:

— Opt your child out of state testing.

— Help teachers understand your child.

— Kindly ask teachers to reduce or stop your child's homework.

— Request that your child may go to the restroom according to their needs.

— Request that your child be able to drink water anytime they are thirsty.

More ways to support your child's school experience:

☆ On the evenings together and on days off, give your child a voice in decisions that affect them: let them choose their clothes, food (from only healthy choices), and room arrangements.

☆ Reduce or eliminate unnecessary appointments.

☆ To avoid rushing, ensure the whole family gets up early enough to allow ample time for getting ready for school.

RECLAIMING GENUINE ACTIVITY
From dull routines to a mindful life

OUR LIVES ARE FILLED WITH repetition. We are used to our daily routines and can do most of them on automatic pilot. Every day we need to get dressed, eat, drink, walk, wash our hands, and so on, and we are used to our own ways of doing all that. However, as soon as a young child is in the mix, especially for parents, it may become hard to keep doing daily routines as usual. Being with a young child feels almost as if a Zen master were to slow down our every move, forcing us to pay attention to things we haven't deemed important in a long time, and then throw in a healthy dose of chaos for good measure.

If we allow it, a young child helps us notice the subtle differences and changes, the textures, flavors, and smells of daily life that have the power to comfort and delight us. Everything we do offers a new opportunity to become present, to respond with interest, to learn on deeper levels, and to become aware of the miracle and mystery of being alive.

Suddenly, when there is a young child, you can't just get out of the door quickly to rush somewhere. Young children couldn't rush or multi-task if they tried. They focus on one thing at a time, and it takes as long as it takes. We can fight that fact and struggle every day with that young child, creating tension and upset, or we can surrender our agenda, allow ourselves to relax into the slower pace as much as possible, and adapt to what life is asking us to do: *slow down and become present.*

As young children we still instinctively know that it does not only matter what we do—what matters most is *how* we do it. There are many different ways one can do the same thing. All our daily activities can be done either with care or haste. Think of drinking tea: one can do it inattentively, risking burning one's tongue or being surprised when the cup is suddenly empty, or one can enjoy a cup of tea by mindfully relaxing with each sip after a long day. Or, one can elevate serving and drinking tea to a ceremony and make it the center of attention, as has been a longheld cultural tradition in Japan. For many young children it is a pleasure to serve pretend tea and cake, perhaps even with a slice of mudpie. The same activity can be a dull routine or an act of celebration.

This insight is also reflected in the Buddhist teachings on mindfulness that are being used increasingly in psychotherapy, business environments, and schools. Experiencing something consciously is an act of self-comfort and self-love that over time can heal our inner world. Although it may feel stressful at first, one key to being present along with children is to let go of getting to the "next task" as quickly as possible. This is a cultural habit that can be changed as we practice reframing what a successful day, or afternoon, or weekend looks and feels like. We might still accomplish many tasks, and the likelihood of having enjoyed those tasks is exponentially increased through the practice of mindfulness. Children do this naturally, as real-life masters of staying present.

Focusing on our own activity, even on the most mundane task, is a skill that can be practiced and we can learn it from young children. Yet, it takes our own initiative, courage, and willingness to cut out unnecessary appointments and slow down enough to create time for mindful activities. Even though young children are prone to the state of mindfulness, this skill must be nurtured by their environment in order to mature. When children never see role models of mindfulness, they forget and start treating things carelessly. This is why Maria Montessori, at the beginning of the

20th century, provided classrooms filled with precious, beautiful items that were freely accessible to her young students. Learning materials were made of smooth wood, delicate glass, and fine china—items that break if mishandled, which is an important learning experience on how to treat delicate items. Montessori patiently, repeatedly showed children how to treat things mindfully, with care and respect. She never rushed children. She confidently trusted her students to mature their natural tendency for mindfulness at their own pace.

We can't avoid that children also will do things automatically or less mindfully over time as they grow up, yet we can help them not to wander too far off from the body memory of mindfulness by nurturing ourselves and them with our gentle presence.

The moments in which we are mindful differ from absent-minded moments; they are the moments when inner harmony can be restored. The initial gentle self-discipline it takes to be present with one's hands and aware of one's feelings reactivates our body intelligence and is a powerful gateway to drop into flow. During mindfulness practice, one connects with oneself. That connection then, the more it is practiced, may transform into a deeper state of focus and, eventually, into flow.

TRY THIS
Step by step to mindful activity

Choose a daily life activity you are going to do more mindfully with children this week, such as eating breakfast with your child, washing your hands and your child's hands, or reading a book. Accompany your activity with simple, clear, friendly, and descriptive language. Narrating keeps you present and provides a clear structure for a young child during an adult-led activity.

MINDFULLY GUIDING AN ACTIVITY
WITH A TODDLER OR YOUNG CHILD

☆ Together, choose any activity you would like to do with a child, and ask if they would like to participate, such as "Would you like to read a book with me?"

☆ Once your child is on board, accompany each single step of your activity with simple, descriptive words: "Now we are choosing a book. Now, we are looking for a comfortable place where we both can sit. Now I am reading the book title. Now I am turning the page carefully. Would you like to turn the page carefully?"

☆ If there are learning moments for the child, show each learning step with patience, as often as needed, and then allow the child to imitate you. For instance, "Let's be gentle with the book. This is how one turns a page carefully."

☆ When you feel the activity is over, you can say, "We just read the book and now we are done, and I am going to put the book back on the shelf, or would you like to do that?"

☆ Accompanying your own activity with words, or internally with your thoughts, is also a powerful way to keep yourself present and take command of your thinking mind. You can use this technique anytime you do something to stop your mind from wandering.

FLOW IS THE REWARD
No additional rewards needed

HOW DO YOU KNOW A CHILD was just in flow? They are happy and they look at you, smiling and fulfilled. They are not expecting any rewards from you for doing what they love to do. Even praise isn't really needed. Acknowledgement, yes. Celebrating what just happened, yes, but as a companion, not as an authority who judges.

We have all been trained out of simply loving what we do. Early on we learn, you do something to get something. We do chores to get an allowance, we play sports to compete and win, we study to succeed in a test, we do homework to get good grades, and we get a job to make money. This makes total sense until we turn our attention inward and realize it doesn't feel as good as it should if this system of reward were true.

There are endless accounts of people who succeeded in having everything, managing to get *all* the rewards, and yet they feel empty inside. Tom Shadyak, the incredibly successful director of many Jim Carrey movies, reveals this impressively in his documentary film *I Am*. The day he moved into his new multi-million-dollar mansion, he felt desperate and decided to change his life. He turned his back on external rewards and started creating a life where he felt positively connected to his inner landscape of genuine needs.

In this world, doing something just for the fun of it, just because you love it, because you love to learn and discover, is a revolutionary act.

It says, "I'm not only here to survive, I am here to thrive!" Allowing a child to do something just because they enjoy it, without competition, comparison, or reward, is a powerful act of love. And it can deeply and positively influence that child in the long run.

Rewards such as gold stars, good grades, or behavior charts, are, as Maria Montessori put it (already over a hundred years ago), "beneath the dignity of the child." Only when children enjoy an activity because they love the activity itself, not the adult-created reward, does true authentic, sustainable learning occur, that contributes to a healthy identity.

Self-chosen activities with intrinsic rewards add to a child's self-esteem, enforce their connection to inner authority, and promote critical thinking. Activities undertaken for disconnected rewards are all too often done lovelessly and hastily. They condition children to look outside for motivation and worthiness instead of following their inner compass and confidence.

Every year there are more multidisciplinary studies demonstrating that intrinsic motivation is absolutely necessary for long-term learning and continued high performance. What we achieve for the sake of an extrinsic reward is easily forgotten once the reward is received, whereas when we learn for ourselves, reaching for mastery, we retain it for much longer, even forever. We value it much more. It becomes part of who we are. As Alfie Kohn's memorable book title states, children are *Punished by Rewards*. Rewards are counterproductive and indeed train us out of flow.

WHY CANDY REWARDS ARE HARMFUL

Candy as a reward is especially harmful because of the addictive potential of sugar. Food should never be a reward. Healthy food is a basic genuine need that should always be freely accessible for children and everyone—even if it is not like that in the rest of the world, let it be so in your own home to establish an island of sanity. Refined sugar is unhealthy, so reduce it as much as possible. Take it out of sight and remove it from your home, so it's forgotten. When children experience cravings, give them healthy options to choose from, and allow their feelings to be expressed at the change. Firm and loving boundaries are again required.

WHY MONEY REWARDS FOR CHORES ARE UNSUITABLE

A money reward should not be the reason a child contributes to the family household. A child is not an employee; they are a beloved family member. Money rewards disconnect the child from the intrinsic value of their contribution to the household. Instead of feeling like a valuable member of the household, the emphasis is on the reward. Instead of learning that their actions have a positive or negative effect on the family, they learn to put too much focus on a monetary reward.

Teach your child that a household has genuine needs that must be met. Explain what each family member contributes and then ask them what they think they may be able to contribute. Help them find age-appropriate chores for which they have enthusiasm. Young children often love to help with chores, but they want to do them their way, maybe slower, maybe not as perfectly as you would do them. Find the patience and help your child grow into doing chores in the spirit of "this is how our family works." Experiencing togetherness and fun during what is often seen as drudgery allows a child to deeply connect to the family in ways that support their emotional and mental health.

A WORD ABOUT PUNISHMENTS

There is no need to ever punish a child. Children make mistakes because they are learners. They don't have access to the worldly knowledge, empathy, and wisdom needed to avoid trespassing and hurting others, but they *can* get there with our help and patient guidance. Punishments have lasting detrimental effects on a child's psyche, and often lead to self-punishment, shame, and aggression down the road. When children experience forgiveness, they learn to forgive themselves. Understanding what can be done better next time, making amendments, realizing the impact of personal actions and feeling sad about it, apologizing and being given chances to learn, and receiving that comforting reassurance that we are worthy of forgiveness, all of these lead to humble self-esteem and wiser decisions in the future.

SO WHAT CAN WE DO INSTEAD OF PUNISHING?

If a child made a mistake, broke something, stole something, hurt someone, talked back, or was inappropriate while upset, first help them calm down and see what happened. Try to understand why they were acting out and consider how the cause can be remedied without punishment.

Explain what needs to be said and set the boundaries that need to be set. But most of all, believe in a child's benevolence and good will. Help them make amends and repairs, and support them with integrating the negative experience to transform it into a learning experience. Withdraw if you need space to keep your calm, or allow your child to withdraw for a while, if necessary. Don't withhold beloved toys or wholesome activities that help the child heal. It might be tempting to interpret a young child's behavior as intentionally hurtful—remember that young children are not developmentally capable of sophisticated manipulation. Such an interpretation stems from our adult life experience and fears.

Never withdraw your love and respect. *A child is never against you, they are always simply for themselves*, learning to meet their own needs. If children receive benevolence, patience, and understanding in a difficult situation, they will learn to be that way for themselves and others when they are older. If you need to keep them safe or keep their siblings safe while they calm down, ensure you connect with the child before leaving them, or it may feel like you are leaving them in the lurch of their own extreme discomfort as a punishment.

And if you punish a child or hurt a child because you were stressed out, don't then punish yourself. You are the trailblazer; you are the one stopping generational abuse by forgiving yourself and your child as quickly as you can. Own your mistakes aloud with your children. Ensure that you make amends with your children to model taking responsibility for your mistakes in a loving, authentic way. Keep returning to your confidence in each other's benevolence. Cultivate goodness. If a child hears and feels that you believe in their inherent goodness, they are much more likely to be able to return to this inner core, to forgive themselves and develop an identity that is good and reliable for others. It is our self-punishment and harsh self-judgments that keep us from believing we are decent, good people.

TRY THIS

When, why, and how do you reward your child?

A reward can be a fun addition when playing a game, such as a treasure hunt, but it shouldn't be used as an educational tool, or to manipulate behavior toward an adult's desired outcome. Ask yourself the following questions..

— When does a child expect a reward from me?
— Why do they expect a reward?
— What is the reward I use?
— What could I do to make an activity rewarding in and of itself?
— What are the instances in which I think a reward is needed? (If there are any such instances, that is okay. Overall, try to move into the direction of intrinsic rewards.)

PART TWO

YOUR CHILD

A YOUNG MASTER
OF FLOW

There is in the soul of a child
an impenetrable secret
that is gradually revealed as it develops.
It is hidden like the pattern
followed by the germ cell in its development
which is only seen in the process of development.

—Maria Montessori

It is when we act freely, for the sake of the action itself
rather than for ulterior motives,
that we learn to become more than what we were.
When we choose a goal and invest ourselves in it to the limits of
concentration, whatever we do will be enjoyable.
And once we have tasted this joy,
we will redouble our efforts to taste it again.
This is the way the self grows.

—Mihaly Csikszentmihalyi

WEEK 14

CHILDREN HAVE SUPERPOWERS

We underestimate children

WE USUALLY TALK OF SUPERPOWERS only in fiction, describing highly unusual or impossible skills such as telepathy and flying. However, children do have superpowers—you had them too, and might still have some you don't know about.

Children are highly underestimated in our culture. Since they are dependent on adults for so many years, we might think they are completely helpless and clueless. While it is true they need many things they cannot provide for themselves (as every caregiver knows and may grow weary of at times), as their needs are met, they are extremely capable.

There is a fable recorded in many different versions about an eagle, the king of the sky, who grew up in a chicken coop. He learned to behave like a chicken, pecking on the ground and never flying. In some books the eagle finds out who he is and raises up to the sky; in other books he never finds out and lives his life as a chicken on the ground. Are you and your child finding out about your superpowers?

Sadly, we don't always think of children's natural abilities as superpowers, but nevertheless, they are. If as adults, we are able to use our inner child's wisdom, we tap into a vast resource. Our connection to our inner child fuels our superpowers!

For instance, adults in high level leadership positions need childlike qualities such as an open mind, fearless creativity, and a willingness to take risks. Many spiritual teachings suggest adults become like children again because it is in our childlike innocence that we can look at others and ourselves without conditioning or negative judgments. It is our inner child who helps us to be happier, to gain true self-esteem, and to authentically live life at moments in flow. With intention and effort, we can reawaken some or all our superpowers in adulthood.

Some children have superpowers that cannot be overlooked, such as a two-year-old fluently reading, a three-year-old mastering the piano, a four-year-old beating adults in chess, and a five-year-old solving advanced math problems. At the age of three, my cousin played the accordion like an adult and everyone who heard him was in awe. Children under the age of ten who realize outstanding accomplishments are commonly called prodigies. Even though they have remarkable skills, they still have age-typical needs for play, rest, and connection.

Superpowers, like the people who command them, come in all kinds and combinations. Many children communicate, process information, learn, and play in different ways from most others in their age group. These children may struggle in standardized schools because they don't fit in. They often don't function well in environments with fixed, conventional expectations for what is considered "normal" communication, movement (or lack thereof), performance, learning types, or social interaction. In order to better understand and meet the genuine needs of these exceptional children, we must adjust our assumptions of how children should conduct themselves within the constructs of our society.

A wonderful example of how expectations are shifting to embrace the superpowers of atypical, exceptional children is seen in how they are being welcomed into the corporate world. A growing number of companies have changed the structure of their interview process in order to ensure the success of qualified and talented candidates who are not comfortable maintaining eye contact for extended periods of time, or at all. By creating an environment that welcomes neurodiverse individuals, these companies have increased their access to a pool of highly skilled workers. This trend is increasing, especially in the technology sector, where candidates who are on the autism spectrum often offer uniquely advanced skillsets.

Although diagnostic tools are helpful to connect with and better serve children with special, atypical abilities, for example by talking about children being "on the spectrum" (of autism / autism spectrum disorder or ASD), we are mostly referring to their higher or lower ability to function in a social environment. As such, we must take great care to ensure we use these labels to benefit the children, rather than limit their potential or take away opportunities for them to shine in their unique superpowers. As another example, when some children aren't able to learn languages or math in the same ways as their peers, they might be diagnosed with dyslexia or dyscalculia (a different brain organization where the right brain is more active than the left brain). Altogether too many children, especially the ones who cannot sit still on command, are diagnosed with ADHD (attention deficit/hyperactivity disorder).

Please be aware that while these diagnoses may be valid and useful within standardized schooling and in a treatment context, they may also be a hindrance to a child's holistic development that includes their specific and valuable superpowers. In fact, being in the focus of flow is one of the superpowers that can be found in the majority of children diagnosed with ASD, dyslexia, and ADHD. There are tens of thousands (probably more) of anecdotes about children who were diagnosed within the standardized school system and went on to thrive in different environments such as experimental schools or homeschooling.

Whether a diagnosis is true and helpful, partly accurate and helpful in understanding a child's needs, or not accurate at all, the crucial message we are finally beginning to understand is that all children have genuine needs that we as adults must attune ourselves to. We may need to train ourselves to listen differently, speak differently, and connect differently in order to meet their genuine needs. Rather than viewing those who stand out from the crowd as beings to be worked with toward the goal of "normalizing" them to fit into our society, we must question whether it is we who need to attune to the communication and superpowers they already possess, and help them find ways to help them share their gifts with the world. What leads these children to develop their unique skills is being exposed to environments, caregivers, and activities that spark their interest and meet their needs. Given the opportunity, their superpowers may include developing countless outstanding accomplishments in a chosen field, or—simply and powerfully—to live a happy and fulfilled life.

THE MANY SUPERPOWERS OF CHILDREN
AND YOUR OWN INNER CHILD

There is a wide spectrum of human superpowers, and collectively, we are increasingly value our superpowers. The lists below are far from complete, yet they can help shift our perspective of all children—and especially of children with different abilities. We hear enough of children's shortcomings and weaknesses—let's celebrate the superpowers of the human offspring! Some superpowers we almost all had as children; some superpowers only a few children seem to have; some are witnessed only in children with special conditions and abilities.

SUPERPOWERS WITNESSED IN MOST CHILDREN

Here is a list of superpowers witnessed in most neurotypical children, as well as atypical children.

☆ Accessing flow states

☆ Keen present-moment awareness

☆ Boundless imagination

☆ High levels of creativity

☆ Capacity for invention and fantasy

☆ An innocent, open, and playful mind

☆ Fearless curiosity

☆ Intense self-motivation

☆ Keen interest in their self-chosen activity

☆ Courage, self-esteem, and confidence

☆ Self-healing powers

☆ Self-educating powers

☆ Highly refined observation skills

☆ High sensitivity to sound, touch, light, tastes, and scents

ADDITIONAL SUPERPOWERS OF CHILDREN
WITH DIFFERENT ABILITIES

In addition to the superpowers almost all children have (listed above), children with special conditions often have additional superpowers. ASD, ADHD, dyslexia, Down syndrome, and other exceptional states of being must not be reduced to mental health diseases or genetic disorders; the children who show these traits have unique gifts that can shift our unquestioned thinking patterns.

Our challenge as parents and educators is to drastically expand our habitual ways of perceiving, tending to, and communicating with these children. We must develop new methods of education that include thoroughly prepared, child-directed, hands-on learning environments where these children can learn at their own pace, developing their own gifts. Included below are four lists of some of the superpowers children with different abilities possess, just to mention a few.

Superpowers of children on the autism spectrum

☆ Honesty

☆ Intense, prolonged focus on a self-chosen subject

☆ Vivid internal world

☆ Super-memory for data and numbers

☆ Photographic memory and spatial thinking (memorizing data, maps and complex drawings)

☆ Highly refined mathematical thinking

☆ Musical abilities

☆ Artistic skills such as exceptional drawing

NOTE: Temple Grandin, professor of animal science and Greta Thunberg, the young woman who recently became a world leader for climate activism, are two of many impressive role models of how an ASD diagnosis can be transformed into a superpower.

Superpowers of children with ADHD

☆ Creative thinking and thinking out of the box

☆ Innovating

☆ Hyperfocus when the activity is self-chosen

☆ Productivity when self-motivated

☆ Keen sense of freedom and autonomy

☆ Keen inner guidance

☆ Spontaneity and high energy

☆ Passion, emotion, excitement

☆ Low tolerance of boredom

NOTE: According to Additude Magazine, the following people with outstanding accomplishments learned to live with and/or turned ADHD into their superpower: Simone Biles (gymnast), Justin Timberlake (singer and actor), Adam Levine (singer), Solange Knowels (singer), Emma Watson (actress), Michael Phelps (swimmer), Scott Kelly (astronaut), Shane Victorino (Baseball player), Zooey Deschanel (actress), and many others.

Superpowers of children with dyslexia

☆ Right-brain thinkers

☆ Seeing the bigger picture

☆ Identifying patterns and understanding complex images

☆ Spatial thinking

☆ Thinking in pictures

☆ Facility for invention and creativity

☆ Keen intuition

☆ Highly sensitive

☆ Deep feeling

☆ Consideration of many alternatives

☆ Spatial, visual, big picture thinking

NOTE: According to the Helen Arkell Dyslexia Charity, the following people with outstanding accomplishments were diagnosed with dyslexia: Maggie Aderin-Pocock (astronomer and space scientist), Orlando Bloom (actor), Richard Branson (founder of Virgin Records), Walt Disney (American icon who built the Disney empire), Jim Carrey (actor and comedian), Albert Einstein (one of the most influential physicists), Sally Gardner (children's book writer), Whoopi Goldberg (actress, comedian, and author), John F. Kennedy (35th U.S. president), John Lennon (singer, songwriter of the Beatles), Jamie Oliver (chef), Steven Spielberg (director), and many others.

Superpowers of children with Down syndrome
☆ Love and kindness
☆ Connection
☆ Empathy
☆ Creativity
☆ Appreciation for the moment
☆ Appreciation for small things
☆ An uplifting effect on others

NOTE: Here is a list of people with Down syndrome who have made outstanding contributions to their communities and industries: Zack Gottsagen (actor), Isabella Springmühl (fashion designer), Jamie Brewer (actress), Lauren Potter (actress and activist), Pablo Pineda (educator and actor), Ángela Bachiller (public office), and many others.

Superpowers witnessed in many children
☆ Super-memory
☆ Advanced math skills
☆ Mental calculation
☆ Composing music and mastering an instrument

☆ Perfect pitch and singing voice

☆ Fluency in multiple languages

☆ Advanced vocabulary and other intellectual abilities

☆ Writing poetry, plays, and novels

☆ Dancing

☆ Painting, sculpting and other visual arts

☆ Advanced chess playing

☆ Seeing sound as colors

☆ Seeing energy around people and plants

☆ Healing powers

☆ A keen sense of empathy

☆ Excellence in the fields their parents are passionate about

TRY THIS

Superpowers in you and your child

Think of yourself and your child as having superpowers. Focus on all the strengths and talents you can detect. Make a list of your superpowers and update it over time. What we focus on gets stronger!

Superpowers witnessed in parents, teachers, and caregivers

☆ Unconditional love and unending patience

☆ Putting their child's needs first

☆ Boundless effort to improve their family's lives

☆ Deep empathy and connection

☆ Kindness even when it's hard

WEEK 15

TWO WAYS OF EXPERIENCING THE WORLD
Feeling safe or feeling threatened

THERE ARE TWO NOTICEABLE WAYS of experiencing the world that affect how open or how guarded we are, for children and adults alike. Our whole being changes whether we feel *safe* ("I feel safe" mode) or whether we feel *threatened* ("I-feel-threatened" mode.) This in turn defines whether we thrive in our environments or merely survive. Safe and threatened, in this context, are very primal, foundational *states of being*. They influence our physical well-being, and our thoughts and emotions.

When children are in the "I feel safe" mode, a calm relaxed state, referred to as the parasympathetic state, and a rest and digest state, they trust their environment and are therefore open to connecting, exploring, learning, and expanding their horizons. In medical literature this is called the parasympathetic state. Emotional and physical safety permits children to drop into flow frequently.

On the other hand, when children are in the "I feel threatened" mode, (also called the sympathetic state), their capacity for connecting and learning drastically diminishes. This mode includes a *fight, flight,* or *freeze* response, as well as the lesser known *fawn* response, which refers to an unhealthy state of people-pleasing at the cost of one's own needs. The "I feel threatened" mode is an involuntary response based on circumstance and personality; it is highly instinctive and cannot be controlled by the child. Even adults cannot simply think or will their way out of this alerted state; instead, it takes patient effort and ongoing relaxation practices to keep the nervous system in the "I feel safe" mode. Therefore, suggesting to a child or to your inner child to "relax," to "calm down," to "get used to it," or to "get over it" is rarely effective. Shifting the nervous system to a relaxed state on a regular basis is an ongoing, holistic process that may involve environmental and lifestyle changes for children as well as adults.

For children, feeling safe or threatened is highly individual, and not necessarily rational to the adult mind. It is the result of many components such as innate personal sensitivities, social pressures, trauma, environment, and conditioning; where some children feel safe, others don't. Here is one of many possible scenarios: in a traditional classroom, background noise and bright lights may not bother some children while others may feel overwhelmed and therefore unsafe. Their environment puts their nervous system into constant alertness at best and defensiveness or shutdown at worst, rather than relaxed focus. Even more unfortunate is that since the majority of young children are not aware of physical subtleties like their pulse or breathing rates, they likely will not understand that their nervous system is on alert, and therefore not know why they are acting in a defensive or disruptive manner.Children who feel continuously threatened reveal their inner turmoil in many different ways. They may be excessively introverted, disinterested in their environment, avoid eye contact, use coping methods more often, such as twirling hair or sucking their thumbs, or they may withdraw, hidden behind books or in older children, cell phones. Conversely, they may act out, "make trouble," or become excessive risk-takers, diving head over heels into dangerous situations. In this "I feel threatened" mode, children feel disconnected, alone, and they suffer. They are usually much more easily upset or annoyed, and less likely to collaborate.

Some adults might argue the "I feel threatened" mode prepares children for our rough world, and that it's beneficial for them to be constantly aware of the dangers that will inevitably arise in order to survive. Our excessively competitive school systems teach children early on to live primarily from a strategic, defensive place, trying to avoid setbacks, humiliation, or punishment, and getting ahead to win, even if it is at the cost of others.

However, success based on survival thinking is often merely that: survival. The constant competition keeps children as well as adults in separation and lonesome struggle, and thus their empathy and communication skills partially shut down. On the other hand, when we allow children to remain in a state of "I feel safe," and steadily teach them how to collaborate, they aren't helpless at all. On the contrary, instead of being defensive, they become much more resourceful and react to challenges with creativity and inner strength. They will find likeminded people to create teams and help others reduce their competitive patterns. The more practice they have with building this resource of collaboration, the stronger they become, and the greater success they will have meeting difficulties head-on. Over the course of history, those who can think calmly and creatively on their feet not only better recognize true danger and survive it, but also thrive within the broader contexts of their lives.

Most present-day perceived threats are not physical, but verbal, mental, or emotional. When an emotionally safe person is attacked, they will have the expanded mind needed to ask *why* the other person is attacking. Instead of merely defending or attacking back, they have developed the inner spaciousness to discuss a problem and find solutions. An emotionally safe child will be wary when they are in an abusive situation and simply leave, instead of playing along as a victim or an enabler. They have learned that thriving comes from respecting and being respected. Instead of wasting vast amounts of energy in conflicts, emotionally safe children use their energy to find solutions and create what they wish, once they have matured to an age when they are cognitively able to do so.

In the rare situations where true danger arises, adults who were provided with safe environments in which to develop their body awareness will be able to immediately recognize it as such. They will be in touch with their bodies and its responses, and highly practiced at responding to their state of being. They can sense when they are in true danger or unsafe conditions that require quick action. This keen emotional resilience is available to children and adults alike, as we more fully inhabit our bodies (as opposed to relying on and being subject to our limited thinking capacities). This has been practiced in martial arts traditions for millennia. Deep body awareness has a time-honored effectiveness much greater than the limited fight, flight, or freeze responses. We have the golden opportunity with children to encourage mastery of this higher skillset.

TRY THIS

Emotional safety through practicing consent

One very important way of creating emotional and physical safety is by practicing consent with children. Through involving children in decisions, especially decisions that directly concern their body and whole being, we show our sincere respect. We show that we truly care, which in turn creates the foundation for children to truly care about themselves and others, recognizing mutual respect as a cornerstone of safety.

The most direct way of practicing consent is by asking children before touching their bodies, by allowing them to say "yes" or "no" to being touched, and by fully respecting their answer. The repeated overriding of such an intimate, personal boundary can be incredibly confusing for a child and damaging in the long-term. Children need to experience regular human touch as comforting, calming, and pacifying, never as invasive. Invasive touch puts the nervous system into the "I feel threatened" mode.

Each child has individual preferences of how often and how to be touched. Respectful, gentle touch by an adult stimulates the skin, relaxes muscles, and opens the child's mind up to the world. Patiently find out how your child likes to be touched by asking directly or by keenly observing their reactions and possibly voicing what you observe, for example: "It seems like you don't want me to hug you right now, is that how you're feeling? It's okay to need your own space."

Sometimes children love to be stroked on their backs or their heads, which could be one reason why they love to pretend to be puppies. Sometimes they love to be picked up or rocked gently in our arms. Often children love to be carried or put on one's lap to be rocked and cuddled. They enjoy warm, soft covers with lots of pillows, and love to build cozy shelters where they playfully hide and maybe even re-experience the safe, dark warmth of the womb. This week, and in general, be aware of the below guidelines for interactions based on consent.

Avoid pressuring children to talk, shake hands, sit on laps, or even hug and kiss you or other people when you can see they are not interested. Simply respect their decision, speak for them when appropriate and excuse them by saying they are feeling shy today, which is okay.

Never tickle or roughhouse with children against their will, and immediately stop if a child says "no" or you notice that they are uncomfortable. Ask them if, where, and how they would like to be tossed or tickled. Often making the mere gesture of tickling in the air is enough for a child to laugh. Tell them where they may tickle you and see how delighted they are to be able to make you laugh. Tell them when you've had enough and model setting calm boundaries. Some families use the phrase "not fun" when someone has reached their limit and needs physical touch to stop.

Unless it is an emergency, don't pick a child up before asking. For infants and toddlers, announce that you are planning to pick them up and see how they react. Whenever possible, allow a little time for them to connect with you, and feel safe about being picked up or guided. For example: "I am going to help you move your body soon, because it is time to leave. If you want to move your own body, you can choose to do that instead." Or, "Would you like to walk, be carried, or hold my hand while we go out the door?"

Let Children Rely on Your Firm Boundaries

Giving in repeatedly to a child's demands that involve a "breaking of the rules" in your home may seem like an easy way out of conflict, but it will likely create more challenges down the road. Susanne, FLOW TO LEARN's parenting advisor, offers her experience with managing limit-testing in their home.

I have learned that my children don't feel safe when they're given too much power to shift the way our home functions. They count on our fair and logical "house rules" to help them build their understanding of how the world works. I now know that what lies beneath my child passionately trying to change a rule is often their need for me to see them, support them, and lovingly show them the rule still stands. How do I know this is true? Because if the limit in question is not held, our children will continue to test until they find the firm, reassuring new limit. Like all children, it's their job to vigorously test a limit until they're sure it's rock-solid.

When enforcing limits with my son (five years old) or daughter (three years old), I first make eye contact with them, gently and clearly stating what I want them to do or stop doing and ensuring they have understood. If they again test the same limit, my response is a calm but firm course of action (as opposed to another verbal warning, followed by another, and so on). This way, I have a much better chance of staying unfazed and able to accept all their feelings without shaming or blaming them.

Of course, there are times we bend the rules or make exceptions. Sometimes, we even plan out and celebrate these "special occasions" with fanfare. Our children revel in creating elaborate descriptions of the next special occasion, when we will stay up all night, eat chocolate-vanilla ice cream and cake, and jump on the bed until the sun rises. They joyfully break all the rules from the safety of their imaginations, while the foundation of their reality, our ground rules, remain solidly in place.

Imagine a world in which every time we yawned, the rules of gravity would change and the things around us would float to the ceiling. We'd never know which ones it would be—the chairs, the plates, or the kitchen appliances! We would quickly associate yawning with this disturbing instability of our surroundings and would surely look for a pattern within these new laws of physics. Similarly, if we don't calmly enforce a rule every time a child is incapable of following it, we pull the rug out from under the child's understanding of their world. They are then biologically obligated to "act out" until they're sure of the new rules.

For example, if my son shakes buttery quinoa off his hands at the table instead of using a napkin, my first (ideal) response would be to make encouraging eye contact with him and nonchalantly say, "Oh, love, please don't shake your hands, it throws quinoa everywhere." Feeling rested and secure, he might reply, "Oh, right! I forgot, sorry." I would then thank him, we'd clean it up together, and that would be the end of it.

However, let's say he is needing extra connection or rest in that moment and does it again. If I take this personally and respond with a rebuke, his already-tired primal brain goes into high alert. I imagine it saying something like this: "Alert! Mama didn't see I need help. And she's mad now. What will get her attention so she will see me and what I need? Maybe catapulting my fork into the living room will do the trick? Okay, try it!" As parenting expert Janet Lansbury often reminds us, this is a scary place to be as a child, because it's an involuntary response made even scarier because the child knows it's unwelcome. If I'm paying attention, I will recognize the fork flying into the living room as a call for help and take action by going to him, gently acknowledging he is unable to continue eating, and setting the firm limit to help him wash up.

When stress or old conditioning comes out and I react with anger, I always make certain that I apologize sincerely afterward, or in the moment, if I can catch myself. I openly talk about how I'm still learning to use kind words when I'm upset or frustrated. Though not ideal, I know they understand the *overarching message when I hear them stand up for themselves: "Mama, you need to practice using your kind words and voice right now. I am not listening to you until you stop being angry." Oh, right. I forgot. Sorry.*

Setting and holding loving, strong boundaries for our kids, while staying unruffled, rarely feels "easy." But my husband and I are starting to see that all our imperfect attempts at this have made a difference in how secure our children feel inside our firm boundaries, even as they push against them with all their might!

WEEK 16

ENDLESS POSSIBILITIES
Spontaneous play, flow, and imagination

WHEN CHILDREN FEEL RELAXED and safe, there is lightness in the way they move. The natural joy so often regarded as part of childhood emanates from them, and lights up the world. When children play freely, without direction from adults but merely by interacting with their environment in creative ways, they drop in and out of flow, and there is usually a component of imagination involved. The element of imagination added by the child naturally trains the mind to go beyond what is tangible in their concrete environment and pretend-create exactly what a child wants.

Children from all cultures curiously explore and manipulate their environment using the items they find to create their personal imaginary world. While completely focused in the here and now, they spontaneously practice the art of creative imagination. When playing with blocks and pebbles, a city may be imagined. When playing with dolls, a family or school situation may be imagined. When crafting an object, its purpose or character is imagined before or while it is created. Free play is the child's perfect practice to connect two foundational ways of perception: The ability to see *what is,* and the creativity to change it to *what could be.*

During hands-on play, the tangible world naturally forms the foundation for the imaginative world to emerge. This anchor in the tangible world provides the necessary grounding for children to remain connected to the reality of earth. Only the practice of such a grounded way of imagining during childhood assures that children learn to feel comfortable in their bodies. They learn to accept the needs, characteristics, and vulnerabilities of the tangible world. From this place, imagining *what could be* is wholesome, empowering, and powerful. Imagination, in conjunction with hands-on play, becomes our ability to invent, renew, and create, within the grounded context of what already is. The skills involved in exploring one's environment and changing it to one's desire empower children throughout their lives to change situations to their liking, rather than feeling like a victim of their circumstances. Some adults may fear that these skills translate into children who are unable to exist without everything conforming to what they want. However, emotionally secure children become adults who are able to empathize and consider other people's needs, even as they work to create a personal vision. It also develops their skills for devising wildly creative solutions to seemingly insurmountable problems, which is a highly sought-after skill in modern companies who set themselves apart through their innovation.

Today's headlines often tell about young people who invented or discovered a solution to fix serious problems, which up to that point seemed impossible to solve. Nineteen-year-old Boyan Slat invented a sun-powered floating device that removes plastic debris from the ocean; fifteen-year-old Param Jaggi created a small device that removes almost 89% of the carbon dioxide from a car's exhaust and transforms it into oxygen; fifteen-year-old Jack Andraka created a new diagnostic test for cancer; braille, a reading system consisting of small raised dots that allows blind people to read, was invented by fifteen-year-old Louis Braille in 1824. This creative thinking would not be possible without the opportunity to play, experiment, and learn in flow.

IN FLOW, CHILDREN LEARN TO DISTINGUISH
BETWEEN REAL AND IMAGINED

When children have regular and consistent experiences in the natural, tangible world, they are clear about the difference between real and pretend. They intuitively know what *pretending* is and will tell you when they are "just pretending." So many times I have witnessed interactions such as these:

Mom: "Please, don't hit the doll!"

Daughter, age four: "Mom, don't worry, I'm just pretending!"

However, because of their limited experience in the world at large, children need our help in discerning reality from fiction when they hear stories, watch movies or shows, and engage with online content. For example, I once realized that a three-year-old girl was afraid of a big tree in the play area at our school. To my careful inquiry, she responded that she had seen walking trees in an episode of a *Smurfs* cartoon and she was scared the tree would move. She needed me to calm her fear, clarify that trees don't walk, and assure her that the idea of walking trees was something that had been imagined by an adult.

NOTE: Already over hundred years ago, the educator Maria Montessori scolded adults for scaring children with horrible stories about witches and monsters who would come and punish them if they weren't "good." Let's not create imaginary monsters to help us raise children, but instead build a trusting bond with them, so they will respect instead of fear adults.

A THOUGHT ABOUT SANTA CLAUS
AND THE EASTER BUNNY

Instead of simply letting children believe in Santa Claus and the Easter Bunny and risking their disappointment when they "find out," we may consider playing these magical, traditional games together *with* the children instead of *for* them. For instance, when we tell the story about how Santa Claus comes down the chimney to bring gifts, we could share with children that "some people believe in Santa Claus but most adults don't; everyone can decide for themselves if they would like to believe in this story. We can both pretend to believe it to have fun!" This way we explore magic in our lives together with a child. Instead of an adult who secretly "knows what's up," we become a companion who is willing to explore, have fun, and be in awe together with the child. This shared wonder offers a truly magical chance to strengthen the bond and trust between child and adult. In addition to letting children in on the fun of magical traditions, some also choose to make the magic of generosity part of their celebration. For example, you might spend time creating and delivering holiday gift boxes with children, letting them help to choose which toys, clothing, food and other items they'd like to contribute. The real magical feelings that come from sharing help children develop generosity towards community members in need.

We may also consider sharing with children about the "real" magic of life, the unseen world that is increasingly researched in science; for example, that plants react to our communication; that trees and fungi can communicate over long distances; that flowers make their nectar sweeter when they "hear" bees buzzing nearby; that we are all connected; and that the earth is a living organism. Many children recognize and feel this energy and will be grateful to find understanding adults who confirm their inner knowing.

TRY THIS
Enhance your child's play

This week, when you see your child play, think of how you can support them to continue playing in a way that ensures *you* feel comfortable. Enhance their play by providing items for them to use in play as much as they like.

In this way, you create a play environment that feels safe for children and adults—the child knows they are safe because the adult is comfortable, and each of you are free to enjoy the play. This can be accomplished with forethought and preparation by the adult, or when necessary, by interrupting a situation that makes the adult uncomfortable (for instance, messes or broken valuables), and providing an alternative environment that allows for the desired play. For instance:

Your child starts playing dress up with your clothes: Give them a place with a mirror and the clothes you don't mind being played with.

Your child starts pouring water back and forth from glass to plates at the table: Create a simple water play station in the bathroom or outside where you offer one or two buckets with water and childproof containers for them to play with as much as they wish.

Your toddler takes out everything from the lower drawers: Prepare some or all the bottom drawers with materials you don't mind being taken in and out, such as rags, socks, or toys, and help the child to play that game. Use childproof locks on the drawers you don't want to share; if it's a dresser, make sure it is safely mounted to the wall to prevent it from falling onto the child.

THE HEALING POWER OF IMAGINATIVE PLAY
Children "play out" what adults talk out

JUST LIKE MANY ADULTS benefit from talking about upsetting thoughts, emotions, and experiences, many children spontaneously "play out" what creates tension within. During their spontaneous play, children tend to create pretend settings that express their inner world, and where they can safely re-experience anything they perceived as confusing, upsetting, or threatening. Through creatively revisiting what happened and imagining what could have happened, children relax, open up, and regain their inner serenity.

In flow, children transform from being passive recipients into active participants. The feeling that one has some kind of command over their situation, and the act of giving it personal meaning, are very healing. Something deep inside of us relaxes when we become co-creators. Unless experiences are extremely traumatizing, children are quick to let go of tension through their own self-healing play. This applies not only to preschool-aged children but also to elementary grades and beyond.

Inner tension can stem from challenging real-life events such as the loss of a pet, or a visit to the doctor, or virtual events, like watching movies that have large amounts of action and other adult themes children may need to process through play. (The significance of pretend play in connection with screen time is explained in Week 22.) During child-led pretend play, a doll becomes a patient, two puppets become a mom and dad fighting, or a teddy bear becomes a suffering pet. The surroundings become imaginary backdrops, and suddenly children are at the doctor's office, a family reunion, or grandfather's house. Pretend play and role-play (referring here to play where a child takes on a role) provide many opportunities to recreate in the three-dimensional world what a child has internally experienced. When difficult emotions or threatening situations are explored in a safe, self-chosen context, inner balance is naturally restored. Non-directive play therapy enhances this extraordinary self-healing power of the child. We can use some tools from this approach (such as a sand table) at home and in schools to offer children restorative play opportunities.

TRY THIS
Set up a sand table for healing play

Sand tables are used in non-directive play therapy for children to play out their inner world. The intentional pretend play on the sand table allows children to express their inner world with and without words. Conscious and unconscious elements are brought to light while children create landscapes and play out scenes in the sand. You can create a simple sand table by placing a box or tray with raised edges on a table and filling it with fine sand. Clean, fine sand can be purchased in crafting stores.

On a shelf near the sand table, place a variety of figurines, such as moms, dads, caregivers, and other family figures, pets, firefighters, doctors, and other professions, fairytale figures, mythical creatures, dollhouse furniture, cars, bridges, houses, trees, and the like. The important part is that these elements ignite the child's imagination. Children are invited to choose any of the figurines and create a mini landscape or backdrop for whatever event they would like to play out. Sometimes the mere creation of the setting is enough for the child to feel complete and healed.

WEEK 18

NATURE BEFORE CULTURE
Facilitate a gift that keeps giving

AS YOUNG CHILDREN, when we feel safely bonded with adults, we eagerly strive for greater independence, as we become more and more interested in our surroundings. Natural environments, such as beaches, forests, and meadows, are ideal places for children to be in flow and create their own healthy identity.

Children deeply connect with nature during their non-directed time outdoors. They thrive when they can contemplate, explore, inspect, build, collect, and pretend-play, just as their heart desires. They love to tinker with natural elements such as water, sand, pebbles, and sticks. They take their time to observe ants marching in line, river water bubbling over rocks, and the cloud formations in the sky. They are usually very interested in learning wilderness skills such as wild food foraging, animal tracking, fire making, and water finding. They are excited about creating shelter and little homes where they pretend to be living independently in nature. These games nurture and strengthen our innate connection to nature.

When growing up connected to nature, children learn to feel comfortable there and experience it as a place where they can always go for adventure, joy, and rest. This way, children learn about the cycles of nature and how these relate to their own lives. They develop patience for slow, organic growth, and learn to feel comfortable with the ebb and flow that exists in all areas of life. This in turn leads to intuitive environmental awareness. We naturally feel protective of what we learn to love in childhood. Littering, destroying natural habitats, or thoughtlessly harming animals, and exploiting the earth feels barbaric to those who love nature.

In his seminal book *Magical Child*, Joseph Chilton Pearce describes the anxiety that is instilled in the child who doesn't have the opportunity to connect to nature before culture. Many children prematurely learn about their culture to discover that it is full of uncertainty, injustice, and violence. Without nature as a refuge and counterbalance, this weighs heavily on a child's mental health and leads to symptoms of "nature deficit disorder," a term coined by author Richard Louv, co-founder of the Children and Nature Network. Our ever-changing culture, including our relationships, jobs, and homes, fail to provide a complete foundation for children. They process and heal deeply during time spent in the natural world. If nature is known as a nurturing place in childhood, as adults we will more likely find comfort there, both as a regular practice of joyful reconnection, and during times of personal and cultural crisis.

TRY THIS
Lead children to nature

Think about how much time your child can spend in nature freely exploring, just being a child. Ponder whether it is possible to have a regular time when your child can be in nature nearby. Don't leave your child completely alone, but create a way to see them from afar or check in with them regularly to make sure they are safe.

If a child spends a lot of time playing computer games or watching videos, help them transition away from it by replacing screen time with nature time. The slowness of nature can't initially compete with the fast action gameplay and attention-grabbing sounds. Begin with something to do to in nature: "Let's collect colorful pebbles," or "Let's do this nature scavenger hunt together," or "Let's see if we can find this bird in the field guide." Include the screen in a healthy way, such as using an app that recognizes plants or bird songs. Attend a child-geared nature class where you and your child will receive some guidance in exploring nature.

Children love and benefit from wilderness skills classes where they learn simple survival skills. Learning that nature provides for survival is calming for the nervous system on a very primal level.

STEP INTO THE RIVER
Flow from birth to 18 and beyond

MANY EDUCATORS AND PARENTS have realized that quite a few traditional ideas about raising children no longer apply. As children, we aren't empty vessels to be filled, waiting to someday be adults. We are whole personalities at each stage of our lives, and during all transitions. Each developmental stage, fully lived, prepares us perfectly for the next stage. A seed is a complete seed and doesn't need to practice being a plant; it will be the best plant possible by being a healthy seed, a complete sprout, and a sound seedling, which all hinge upon a healthy environment at each and every stage.

Intuitively aware of their own dignity, children often intensely rebel against rules that don't make sense to them. They often aren't intimidated by punishments and rewards, and they "stubbornly" (or bravely, depending on one's interpretation) seek to fulfill their genuine needs, struggling to remain their authentic, whole selves.

Children continually surprise us with perspectives and behaviors that do not fit our previous understanding of where they "should" be at their age. This is why the summarized archetypal stages of child development (below) aren't connected to specific ages; instead, they describe interwoven periods in the life of a growing child that help us recognize corresponding needs and respond to them. We can learn to work with children's age-typical, self-centered views in one moment, while remaining open to often surprisingly mature behavior in the next. The natural stages of development remain significant throughout our lives. Using our imagination, we can travel back in time to previous stages of development and make up for lost time. The author Tom Robbins (in his book *Still Life With Woodpecker*) wrote: "It's never too late to have a happy childhood." Even as adults, we can invite ourselves into moments of joyful presence (like an infant and baby), we can live as carefree explorers in the garden (like a toddler and preschooler, a young child), and we can connect to our primal soul (like an older child). We can re-learn and practice seeing the world with awe, and noticing as it looks back at us in wonder as well.

STAGES OF NATURAL CHILD DEVELOPMENT

The following glimpses of natural child development include research from Rebeca Wild, Maria Montessori, Jean Piaget, Joseph Chilton Pearce, and Bill Plotkin, as well as insights from the European Rebeca Wild based schools.

AS INFANTS AND BABIES
WE LIVE AS A JOYFUL PRESENCE

From the first breath we take, we live as a joyful presence. We learn best when we feel protected and relaxed in a cozy, safe nest. Even though we utterly depend on our caretakers and cannot yet move around on our own, we have strong impulses to learn independently in flow. Dr. Emmi Pikler (1902-1984), founder of the Lóczy orphanage in Hungary, Magda Gerber (1910-2007) founder of Resources for Infant Educarers (RIE), and Janet Lansbury, a California-based parenting expert in the same tradition, have all dedicated their lives to raising awareness about the value of self-initiated and self-guided activity from the earliest age.

As infants and babies, we gradually become accustomed to our bodies, and through self-directed movement we learn to move our limbs and muscles at will. We learn about the material world through sucking, touching, smelling, tasting, feeling, hearing, and seeing. Simple activities such as grabbing and letting go of items, throwing something on the floor, and bringing something to our mouth, are powerful learning events, and must be respected as such.

We need a warm, soft, peaceful place where we can connect with our significant adults through eye-gazing, soft language, and touch. We thrive when our significant adult is fully present with us during caretaking. Through loving attention, touch, non-verbal and verbal communication, we learn that we are separate beings but bonded with others.

Our existential question is: *Can I trust the world?*

AS TODDLERS AND PRESCHOOLERS
WE LIVE AS EXPLORERS IN THE GARDEN

Once we start walking upright, as young children, we become explorers in the garden —the safe environments that our significant adults prepare for us. At this age, everything is wondrous, mysterious, and exciting. Spontaneous learning is our nature, and we playfully acquire new skills every day: new words, new movements, new foods, new textures, new sounds, new songs, new stories—everything is a learning opportunity.

As toddlers and preschoolers, when we do any activity, we don't necessarily need results—we learn through the *process*. What we are interacting with is not as important as the information we gain from that encounter. We learn through sensorial experiences and movement, and we naturally want to touch, feel, see, hear, and taste everything in order to know it. We start to deduce patterns from our sensory experiences and learn to make sense of our environment.

Yet, we strive to feel safe in this exciting world. That's why we love repetition and structure. For example, we like to hear the same story or song many times, and we like morning and evening rituals that announce the beginning and end of a day. Even though we completely depend on our significant adults for love and care, we have a natural inner drive to become an individual.

This is the age when we learn to say "no" and are delighted by our own power. When a toddler disobeys you next time, observe the incredible courage it takes for a young child who dares not to cooperate with the one source that gives them food, shelter, and loving care. Help a toddler experience their individuation as a positive process. Instead of getting into a power struggle, reflect and acknowledge, "Yes, I can hear you say 'no,' you do not like this." Sometimes you may be able to yield to a toddler's wish, and sometimes you cannot, but even then, you can agree to disagree. The simple act of receiving genuine recognition of their perspective helps this person feel seen and feel respected, even at the youngest age.

Our existential question is: *Is it okay to be me?*

AS CHILDREN
WE LIVE AS PRIMAL SOULS, AND EMOTIONAL ACTORS

Once we grow adult teeth, we want to experience our primal self as well as intense emotions just like an emotional actor. Our primal self thrives when we get to playfully develop survival skills, such as learning how to make fire, which berries to eat, and how to build shelter. This provides us with a profound feeling of being safe on earth.

Our inner playful, emotional actor-self is nurtured when we have opportunities to *feel deeply*. As older children, there are still times when we overflow with passionate emotions. Intense sadness, fear, anger, guilt, and joy are often unrelated to actual events. Often, it is not an outer circumstance that triggers these intense emotions, rather it is an inner impulse. Safely experiencing these intense emotions helps us to develop empathy. With this understanding, adults can provide children with pretend and role-play opportunities where these emotions can be experienced without further consequences, in a safe space, within healthy boundaries. This stage simply requires a healthy exploration of these deep feelings. If children don't find this chance through make-believe, they unconsciously look for opportunities to experience these strong, passionate emotions, which can lead to misunderstandings (children overreacting) and negative experiences (adults getting confused and upset).

Our existential question is: *Is it okay for me to move, to feel, and to be an active participant?*

TRY THIS
Three existential questions for you

Think of your childhood and ponder if and how it connects to your present life experiences with children. Can you trace any correlations between the three existential questions of childhood, how you learned to answer them, and how you may contribute—as a significant adult—to your children's inner answers? One by one, contemplate these questions:

1. Can I trust the world?

2. Is it okay to be me?

3. Is it okay for me to move, to feel, and to be an active participant?

Being Authentic with Children

Susanne, FLOW TO LEARN's parenting expert, shares about the benefits and subtleties of being authentic with children, even during stressful moments:

I feel it's of utmost importance that I talk with my children about my authentic feelings in a careful way. I know they might feel nervous or scared when they see their parent upset or sad, so I make sure we process such events together (in the moment when possible, or later if necessary) and transform them into deeper, authentic connection. Rather than hiding my experiences, sharing my feelings in careful ways has become a chance for me to model how to communicate even when it's hard to do so. Even anger can be expressed when we are able to do so in a way that guarantees safety. Amazingly, it is possible to express anger quietly. If I can do it, I know most anyone can!

After all, children who aren't yet capable of expressing emotions in careful, loving ways need to see repeated examples of how that can happen. It could be as simple as "Ouch! That hurt when you threw the block at my face. I don't want to you to do that again, please," or more complex, for example, "I'm feeling frustrated that you dumped your oatmeal on the floor, because I worked hard to make it for you and the place for our food is on our plates. Please, tell me with words what you need instead of throwing your food."

I remind myself often that it's totally okay to be imperfect – even our mistakes are opportunities to model how fundamentally human it is to misstep. We must be gentle with ourselves as we allow our children the freedom to make sense of their world through play and testing boundaries. Children, as young scientists, push outward toward all the limits to find out where, exactly, those boundaries are and what happens when they are tested in the most impactful or sophisticated way a child can muster. This is in every child's job description!

Emotional transparency in parenting is a relatively modern concept gaining traction around the world. As UK-based mom and author Katherine

Thornalley, aka Mrs. Mombastic, states in her popular online blog on parenting and fitness:

"If halfway through disciplining your child, you realise that you are perhaps overreacting, it is ok to stop. It is okay to tell them "sorry". It is ok to admit that you overreacted and tell them you've had a bad day, or feel tired, or unwell causing a knee jerk reaction. It doesn't mean you've failed. It is in fact a valuable lesson in itself. It is showing your child that you can admit when you're wrong. That you can talk about your feelings. That even as the parent you have good days and bad days. It's never a defeat when you stop viewing parenting as a battle of wills."

The stakes are high for me: I know that when I take responsibility for my actions and behavior, make efforts to repair and reconnect, communicate respectfully even as I share my hard feelings, forgive my children, and practice self-forgiveness, I model for them the keys to thriving inside the challenging interpersonal moments of life.

WEEK 20

WHAT A YOUNG MASTER NEEDS

Tending to your child's body, mind, and heart

CHILDREN FROM ALL CULTURES have similar basic genuine needs. Anything that is crucial to a child's emotional, mental, and physical health can be considered a "genuine need." In addition, each child has individual genuine needs that they reveal over time.

Children instinctively strive to meet their needs through their preferences, behavior, and self-chosen activities. They communicate needs verbally and non-verbally. The ongoing fulfillment of genuine needs calms a child's nervous system and relaxes body and mind, so they can remain open for curiosity, flow, and learning. Too many unmet genuine needs cause myriad behavioral and health problems in addition to preventing age-appropriate, inner-learning processes.

The significance of meeting *genuine* (as opposed to *replacement*) needs cannot be stressed enough. If genuine needs aren't met over long periods of time, addiction becomes a real threat for children. Consistently unmet genuine needs create internal pain, and children unconsciously try to soothe that pain with activities and substances that temporarily alter the body's chemistry in a way that feels good, in either relaxing or exciting ways. In any case, the goal is to divert attention from the pain of unmet genuine needs, such as not enough time in nature, not enough quality time with significant adults, or not enough movement. As we see in the RWB schools, the more children's genuine needs are taken care of when they are little, and the more they are encouraged to take care of their own needs, the more empathy they develop over time. It has been beautiful to witness how the RWB high school graduates confidently meet their own needs as young adults while also showing highly empathic skills as team players.

The fulfillment of *genuine* needs defines a child's health, happiness, and developing intelligence. Children's emotional and physical genuine needs must be met to a crucial degree for them to be drawn to learning in flow.

GENUINE NEEDS VERSUS REPLACEMENT NEEDS

Children, as well as adults, can learn to recognize and fulfill their own genuine needs (as opposed to replacement needs) when they discover how satisfying it feels to have their genuine needs met, and when they are provided with a safe environment in which to *practice* (which means learning through making mistakes for a while). To distinguish easily between genuine needs and replacement needs, observe the feeling that remains in a child after a specific activity. If a genuine need was met, a child is usually happy, peaceful, and fulfilled.

However, a replacement activity most often leaves the child with an empty, unsatisfied feeling. For example, after running around in nature, a child is comfortably tired; after solving a jigsaw puzzle, a child may feel accomplished and satisfied. Eating candy or playing addictive video games typically leave a child grumpy, uncomfortable, and wanting more, even though their body has had enough.

When you feel a child is overly attached to something addictive and misbehaves in the context of wanting more (for example more sugar or digital media), then help wean them from those habits and moderate their intake or use. Often "I need my candy!" or "I want my tablet now!" can be translated as, *I need to feel alive! I need to be engaged! I need to learn! I need comfort! I need your attention! I need nature!*

Steadily provide more wholesome activities, such as trips into nature, crafting projects, and rough and tumble play. Supply more naturally sweet foods such as fruit. Help them understand the *why* behind reducing unhealthy activities in terms they can understand, for example, "Screen time takes away the chance for you to have your very own thoughts, and we need to make sure you get lots of time for that."

When genuine needs are fulfilled, the addictive "something" will lose its attraction over time, and the child can rediscover their inner balance. When children start to feel emotionally safe and bond with adults again, they dare to communicate what they really feel, and they are able to return to flow states more frequently, slowly but surely. The more children are able to practice identifying and meeting their true, genuine needs, the better they will be at taking care of themselves, and at recognizing the value of others' genuine needs, throughout their entire lives.

We must provide a multitude of fulfilling situations for children and for ourselves, because to find out what our genuine needs are, we need to experience having our genuine needs met. Nothing can replace a warm hug, or a deep conversation, the feeling of timelessness during a fulfilling activity such as cooking or making a craft, or the feeling of accomplishment after making a mud pie when these experiences are meeting a genuine need. Nothing compares to the inner joy of just doing without being afraid of making mistakes. Nothing holds up to the feeling of being part of nature, being able to climb a tree, or eating a tomato grown in your own garden.

When we do something that *feels just right*, we are at the right place at the right time, and all the cells in our bodies light up with joy! *That is flow*, and that is what we need to support in children. The easier it is for a child to access their flow state, the more misbehavior will simply dissipate.

A SUMMARY OF CHILDREN'S GENUINE NEEDS

Physical and emotional genuine needs build the foundation of a child's well-being and must be met before or at the same time as intellectual needs are met.

Children's emotional needs

☆ Being sincerely seen, heard, and valued for what they say, feel, experience, or imagine

☆ Time to bond with adults, nature, and culture

☆ Staying in touch with their inner world

☆ Loving attention

☆ Kindness

☆ Predictability, order, and beauty in the environment

☆ Respect for a child's body autonomy and personal belongings

☆ Alone time

☆ Help with learning to be friends with peers

☆ Contributing to community

Children's physical needs

☆ Healthy nutrition

☆ Drinking water

☆ Free movement

☆ Resting and sleeping

☆ Nurturing touch

☆ Weather-appropriate clothing

☆ Learning to take care of personal bodily needs

Children's intellectual needs

☆ Following natural interests

☆ Spontaneous imaginative play

☆ Self-directed activities

☆ Sensorial, hands-on learning

☆ Stories, puzzles, rhythm, rhyme, and poetry

☆ Contemplation and boredom

☆ The feeling that "there is enough time"

TRY THIS:
Reconnect with your own genuine needs

As children, we depend on our caretakers to fulfill our basic genuine needs. As adults, we must take care of ourselves as well as possible. Parents usually have to place their own needs second to their children's needs, so caring for children necessarily becomes a path of sacrifice, patience, and compassion. Many of us often don't know what we truly need, because we have lost touch with our genuine needs. Instead of deeply inquiring within, we come up with all kinds of harmful behaviors, including addiction, self-medicating, fighting with our significant others, or internally withdrawing, to name a few. Even when we are clear about a genuine need we have, it can take great courage for us to ask that our need be met, or to meet that need ourselves.

What might an adult's genuine need look like? Slowing down? Taking a day off? Devoting time to creating music or art? Being less "productive" so we can get more sleep? Skipping an event or gathering because we are feeling exhausted? Recognizing our emotional needs, and asking for help from a partner or a counselor?

Exploring your own genuine needs will help you attune to children and their unique responses to the world. In fact, your own body and nervous system are still very much connected to the child you once were. The exercise below will help you tune in to your body's genuine needs; it is best done in private. Done regularly, it will help your awareness to more fully inhabit your own body. Soon you will experience the difference between fulfilling a genuine need or a replacement need. Experiment with this simple three-minute self-awareness exercise:

☆ Sit quietly and bring your awareness towards the different areas of your body. From top to bottom, what do you feel?

☆ If you feel a need arise fulfill it as best as you can.

☆ Are you thirsty? Then drink.

☆ Are you craving a specific taste? Go for it!

☆ Do you need to burp, spit, or yawn? Do it!

☆ Do you feel tension? Lightly touch or rub that area, your jaw, belly, arm, or feet. Move exactly how it feels right to you.

☆ Do you feel alone? Hug yourself and speak to yourself like a loving mother or father: "I am always with you and I take care of you, as best as I can." Positive self-talk is a powerful mental health tool.

WEEK 21

STRIVING FOR A HEALTHY IDENTITY
Understanding your child's perspective

AS YOUNG CHILDREN, we instinctively love ourselves. We spontaneously honor our own needs, still innocently unaware of the impact we have on others. We are focused on ourselves to make sure we learn how to survive and thrive as individuals. This age-typical, self-centered worldview is a natural, legitimate part of growing up. It is essential to forming a healthy identity, helping us to identify preferences, talents, and boundaries. At this young age, we are often simply not capable of understanding another person's viewpoint, and this is why we need adults who try to understand us.

A child's egocentric view of the world is commonly misunderstood as entitlement that needs to be corrected. However, children's egocentrism is –at its essence– a pure expression of innocent self-love. This pure self-love can be nurtured by allowing children to safely experience their negative emotions. For instance, we can allow children to be frustrated, upset, envious, jealous, irrational, or greedy simply by witnessing and empathizing, and letting them know that everyone feels like that sometimes.

When we guide children through their negative feelings until they come out on the other side, we help them avoid hasty or desperate actions that might hurt another or themselves –actions that might be interpreted as revenge or out of spite yet in reality are cries for help because a child feels alone and scared.

As children, we need to be allowed to feel egocentric within healthy boundaries in order to learn self-care, self-respect, and empathy. There is almost always a way to allow these feelings while keeping a child and others safe. When we are allowed to first have empathy for ourselves, we more likely develop empathy for others. When we are respected for who we are and we continue to feel loved during challenging moments, then our behavior naturally softens over time. This is beautifully expressed in the Tao Te Ching: "If you want to shrink something, you must first allow it to expand. If you want to get rid of something, you must first allow it to flourish."

Even though children's inflated concern with themselves may cause discomfort at times, usually there are no long-term negative consequences when they are allowed to express their uninhibited views within a safe space. Here are some examples: A four-year-old girl has a temper tantrum seemingly because she is not given a toy; a five-year-old boy is angry and yells because he feels treated unjustly; a six-year-old girl judges a younger child harshly because he cannot sit still at the table; a seven-year-old does not want to share his chocolate bar; an eight-year-old excludes another from a playground game; a nine-year-old is unforgiving and feels insulted by his grandfather's remark; a ten-year-old plays a punishing father in a role game; an eleven-year-old has a fight with another eleven-year-old because he copied his painting. These youngsters' behaviors have little long-term influence on the wider community. If it's allowed, it can dissolve. However, when suppressed, shamed, and punished during childhood, these urges become unconscious, underlying patterns for our behavior even as adults. As adults, these behaviors do impact the community through serious, far-reaching political, legal, economic, and social decisions and actions.

Instead of scolding, shaming, or punishing, we can let young children know that it's better not to act on negative emotions. Rather guide them in how to let the emotions pass by, like a storm. You can say, "Uh-oh. I see a storm is coming. Let's sit together, and please tell me all about your storm." Allowing and reflecting back feelings is incredibly healing. When our children feel seen and heard, they rarely need to continue with the "storm" of emotion. For instance, "You wanted her to stop saying that. It was really bothering you. I won't let you hit her, but I think I do understand how hard this is for you." You will find that—if supported—it is often easy for children to deeply feel an emotion and let it go in no time, going back to playing as if nothing had happened. (For more persistent emotions, you can also try some of the tools explained in Week 11.)

With older children who experience their deep emotions through intense social interactions, it may take time to find a way to talk with them about what happened. As difficult as it may be for a parent, inviting these feelings to be expressed and supporting the child without judgment toward reflection, trust, and empathy will build a strong foundation of trust. Traditional punishments aimed at producing a "respectful" child have the potential to and often do backfire. Strong emotions do not go away when suppressed, but instead grow until they find a way out. No matter the age of the child, feeling "seen" by a caring adult does wonders for nourishing their changing sense of self.

THE CHILD'S SELF-CENTERED PERSPECTIVE
FULFILLS TWO MAIN DEVELOPMENTAL NEEDS

1. Becoming an individual: Through being innocently self-centered, children experience themselves as individuals. They realize their emotions, thoughts, and physical needs are not necessarily the same as everyone else's.

2. Learning to take care of personal needs: Children's self-centered perspective is developmentally useful because it pushes them to learn to fulfill their own needs during the rapid, intense changes of growing up.

When egocentric behaviors are suppressed and a child is scolded, punished, shamed, and deprived of love during negative states, tension is stored; what's worse, a child's self-love and self-esteem is diminished. In addition, whatever we suppress gets stronger: A scolded, shamed child may develop defense or attack behaviors. In adulthood, these behaviors may be expressed as unconscious patterns with the potential to hurt other people severely or hamper a person's ability to maintain long-term, loving relationships. Observe eight- or nine-year-old children who often have already replaced the young child's natural love for themselves with self-doubt, low confidence, suspicion, or defensive behavior. Older children, teenagers, and adults often find it easier to appreciate someone else but are unable to appreciate themselves. This may be in great part because their surroundings as younger people were not equipped to understand, and therefore did not support their age-typical, self-centered perspective. Moreover, challenging adult behaviors reflect to a large extent the level of empathy offered to, and modeled for, a person during their childhood.

Children need to relate positively to their own individuality in order to respectfully relate to others. Only as well-defined individuals with the ability for empathy can we intelligently relate to others without projecting our emotions, opinions, and attitudes on them.

Please know *it is okay* that children are not yet wise, compassionate, responsible members of the community. We can trust that they will naturally learn from the empathy we show them. In this context, *modeling* is the best way to teach.

TRY THIS
Learning from indigenous cultures

In *Voices of the First Day: Awakening in the Aboriginal Dreamtime*, Robert Lawlor describes how parents in the Australian indigenous culture used to raise their children. In their tribes and extended families, a sense of relatedness was unanimously considered the most important thing to preserve. Children's age-typical drive for play, including their unfettered, self-centered behavior, was considered appropriate. They were allowed to spend their days freely following their instincts, needs, wishes, and desires, and they were allowed to express their emotions fully.

Adults patiently let the children play around them and even allowed them to climb on them and tease them. Over time children were introduced to the obligations of society and they proudly found their place in the tribe. As a result of this natural maturation process, adults were extremely relaxed and mild-mannered; they did not harbor the repressed emotions that produce defensive parenting behaviors such as yelling and punishing.

Since we live in a very different culture, we may not always be able to let children express themselves fully while accompanying them with loving attention. The reasons are many: sometimes there is simply not enough time; sometimes the space (such as a grocery store or a restaurant) is not appropriate; and sometimes children's emotional expressions make us extremely uncomfortable, or they may trigger us into our own challenging emotions. All we can do is become aware of our behavioral patterns and aim at reducing to a minimum the situations in which children's authentic selves are not welcome while increasing occasions where children are entirely welcome to be who they are.

WEEK 22

THE CHILD AND THE SCREEN
A love-hate story

I'M NOT ADVOCATING A ZERO-SCREEN policy. Instead, I encourage parents and teacher to use screens to everyone's benefit: use technology and let it enrich you and your child, but *don't let it take over.* As a rule of thumb, increase the quality of screen time and decrease its quantity. The incredible high-tech tools we have at our fingertips can be educational, entertaining, and can even help families bond but only when used intentionally and in moderation. Watching a beloved movie, using an educational app, or playing a sophisticated video game can be entertaining and instructive. Even in schools, if used with purpose and sparingly, screens can be valuable learning tools (more so from middle school onward). For younger children, however, very little screen time is enough.

Once in a while, child-friendly, sophisticated programs can be exciting for children and supplement their own imagination. Make sure programs for young children are short, move at a slow pace, have no violent content, and tell a positive, uplifting story, such as *Mr. Roger's Neighborhood* and *Sesame Street.*

As you probably know, books are a great alternative to screens. They also keep a children engaged, yet allow them much more control over their experience. With a book, children can stay with an impression for longer (as long as they need). The individual, often slower pace of reading or looking at still pictures, and the lack of stimulating audio, gently inspires the mind to create its own imagery. There is enough time to associate a story or image with a personal experience, which leads to deeper understanding and easier integration of the new information.

A story watched on the screen can place itself like a thick layer on a child's inner world and can be very hard to integrate. When a story is told or read by someone, children can use their own imagination. Self-generated images are rarely too scary to handle, and they easily are shaped internally until they fit into a child's personal cosmology.

It takes very little action-packed, plot-driven screen time to replace a child's innate creation of original storylines; not because children are weak, but because these art forms are captivating, penetrating, and highly sophisticated stimuli. Children do not yet possess the filters or life experience required to separate their reality from one presented to them on-screen: their physiology literally obligates them to incorporate these experiences into their baseline reality. In this way, screens can override a child's individual drive to create original play themes. If this occurs over long spans of time, their myriad skills used for spontaneous and self-driven play can decline.

Too much screen time or frightening content can take over a child's inner world, sometimes leaving less or very little room for individual formation through direct experience, and instead implanting narratives and ways of seeing the world that are someone else's ideas. This can override the innate resources and insights a child would otherwise be developing through their own experiences. Let's give the screen its proper place and make screen time an exception, not the rule.

SCREEN TIME REQUIRES PLAY TIME

Even if children were learning while watching a screen, their bodies have separate needs that must be fulfilled. Allowing children to be as active as they need after screen time is essential for them to properly process it. Taking the time of day into account to plan for ample tension-release time through movement and play is key. For example, expecting a child to sit still at the table for a meal directly after watching a screen will undoubtedly create difficulty for that child, who nearly involuntarily must move their body, and will not be able to meet an adult's expectations. Conversely, if a child is allowed to move after screen time, the compulsive need for movement related to their passive viewing experience will dissipate or be completely resolved for that session.

Screen time, including age-appropriate, child-friendly movies and games, often obligate children to "play out" what they have passively observed. "Playing out" activities such as pretend play and role-play are age-typical ways of processing information and impressions, as explained in Week 17. It is common for children to imitate or create their own storylines of something they have seen on the screen, possibly for days or even weeks afterward.

For the trained eye observing children it is very easy to tell which young children watched an action-packed show the day before, or even days before, and who did not: the quality of spontaneous play is quite different between these two groups. Children who have recently and repeatedly viewed shows have a strong inner drive to "play out" its characters and scenes in order to digest it. Children who haven't watched it will play along, much less driven and much more open to playing out or incorporating experiences from their own lives, such as their last doctor's visit or their relationship with their parents.

THE SCREEN'S ADDICTIVE POTENTIAL

Children need significant help with responsible use of the screen because of its addictive potential; in general, less is better. There is an extreme draw for children to focus on the screen; for many decades, well-funded research teams have intentionally engineered its irresistible attraction. Apps and computer games evoke a state that is very similar to flow and that is extremely comforting and exciting at the same time. However, *it is not flow as described in this book*. Unfortunately, if overused, screens drain a child's life force, deprive them of important learning opportunities in the tangible world, and may interfere with social skills development.

Yet, there is evidence that not all content is created equal. Faster-paced games, cartoons, or even social media can create substantially greater detrimental effects on brain development. For example, the more frequent gratification is achieved, even within educational games, the more often the brain releases dopamine, and thus the more often it craves that additional dopamine release. The brain literally can become addicted to its own chemicals, and young children have no defense against this.

We can allow more screen time as children get older and have a stronger connection to their bodies, other people, and nature. Only a rooted connection in the tangible world, built up over years of meaningful, playful experiences, provides a safe foundation for excursions into the computer-generated world. Imagination that has not been rooted in the tangible world disregards vital factors of our human reality.

HELP YOUR CHILD PLANT ROOTS
IN THE TANGIBLE WORLD

One the greatest teachings of childhood is vulnerability. When children wander too early into the virtual worlds on the screen, they miss many opportunities to learn about the sensitivity, slower pace, gentleness, and genuine needs of their own body and being, as well as others. Children may become talking heads; they may miss the chance to become embodied. The virtual world cannot replace what is felt and experienced in a human body. For instance, contrary to what is lightheartedly presented in many movies and computer games, people are truly hurt and insulted when they are victims of pranks, are yelled at, are lied to, or are neglected. Falling, attacking, fist-fighting, and shooting all damage, hurt, and devastate in real life. Some children may be more able to tell the difference between imagination and reality—others may not. Observe your child closely when they play computer games. Only through bruising our knee do we learn that the body is resilient yet delicate. Only through interacting directly with friends do children see how they can get hurt. Only through countless real-life experiences do children understand what it means to be human and to create one-on-one friendships.

Sitting and participating in a virtual world for hours on end prevents children from having sensory experiences with the real world. In order to develop an appropriate perspective of the world, children need experiences with concrete objects that can be handled, weighed, touched, smelled, manipulated, changed. They need the "wholeness" of physical experiences in order to learn to use all their senses and to connect their inner world to the earth. Through experiences with nature, children learn to love nature. The aliveness of climbing a tree, diving into water, and smelling flowers cannot be replaced by technology. When respectful human interactions, play, and nature experiences occupy the most space in a child's life, the virtual world can become a wholesome addition.

LET GO OF TECH FOMO (Fear Of Missing Out)

There is no need to worry that children may not catch up with learning how to use technology. By the time these children are ready for jobs, the computers we offer them today will likely be outdated. What we *can* give to children, and what they will need for certain, is learning how to learn, a strong connection to their own body, knowledge of how to access and spend time in nature, and the ability to communicate with people of all ages and stages. Simple things such as looking up from a screen, giving one's full attention, making eye contact, and friendly conversation with people are not a given—these are skills that need to be cultivated every day throughout childhood.

TRY THIS
Balance your child's screen time

Every child reacts differently to screen time. Some children can handle it better than others. Observe your child and develop a plan based on what you've noticed regarding how much screen time is enough for your child and consider stopping short of that limit. Consciously curate your child's screen content. The American Academy of Pediatrics (AAP) offers the following guidelines on their website:

Parents should co-view media with children to help them understand what they are seeing and apply it to the world around them. Occasionally pausing the content to clarify, discuss, ask children questions or simply allow everyone to take a breather offers children the opportunity to reconnect with themselves briefly, stepping out of the virtual reality even if for a few minutes. Parents also should designate media-free times together, such during meals or driving, as well as media-free locations at home, such as bedrooms.

— For children younger than 18 months, avoid use of screen media other than video-chatting.
— For children ages 2 to 5 years, limit screen use to 1 hour per day of high-quality programs.
— For children ages 6 and older, place consistent limits on the time spent using media, and the types of media consumed. Make sure media does not take the place of adequate sleep, physical activity, and other behaviors essential to health.

Growing Healthy Technology Habits

The research is clear—the less time children spend in front of a screen, the better. However, integrating this ideal into daily life and all its challenges may not be as straightforward. FLOW TO LEARN's parenting advisor Susanne describes how her family deals with the influence of technology on their lives:

When my son was a toddler, I was vigilant around his exposure to screens, because I'd read so much about how they impact children's brains. As he became more active and after our daughter was born, our reasons for turning to technology expanded—being at our wits' end on next to no sleep, faced with a messy house and dinner to make, needing to do farm chores unsafe for children, were those moments when I felt Mr. Rogers would do a better job being with our children than I could.

I experienced a lot of guilt as our screen time increased. I kept thinking maybe life would slow down enough for us to become a screen-free family. Eventually, however, I had to accept this as an unrealistic goal for our lifestyle. My husband and I made a pact: we would carefully walk the line between the serious health risks technology poses and the inspiration, delight, and educational discovery it offers. We set up the following guidelines for how to model and practice healthy interactions with technology in our day-to-day lives:

1. *All media is carefully curated by us as parents and may be turned off at any time we deem necessary.*
2. *Screen time is an occasion, not a given, and can change based on stress levels, health, or schedules.*
3. *School nights are always screen-free.*
4. *Free time should follow screen time so our kids can move their bodies and process what they've seen.*
5. *We pause for discussions on scary or sticky elements in media and reflect afterward on the parts we liked or didn't like and why, to encourage critical thinking.*

6. We take regular, extended breaks from all screen routines and remind the kids why this is important.

7. We limit our phone use around the children.

8. Media may not be used to avoid challenging interactions, emotions, or experiences that are naturally part of living together. It's okay for us to enjoy the escape that entertainment provides, but not at the expense of healthy family dynamics.

9. Exceptions to these guidelines must be based on a true need that we have as parents. (In other words, not just because turning on a show would be easier.)

The way we enforce our ground rules around technology could be summed up by a quote from Janet Lansbury, a prominent voice in the RIE community: "An important element of respectful discipline is that it requires us to find that sense of certainty in <u>ourselves</u> as loving leaders for our children." For me, that means that I'm at peace with whatever feelings my children have about the limits I set before they come out of my mouth. When I treat our tech ground rules as non-negotiable, I stay calmer and more able to accept our children's (at times, really big) feelings, and perhaps calmly remind them of the reasons behind the limit in language they can understand, if they seem receptive.

Our children often need help to "restart" themselves after screen time. One effective tool we've found to help us all transition away from visual media is to listen to creative songs and vivid storytelling. When it's a new song or story, we actively engage to stimulate our imaginations, paying close attention to plots, characters, and lyrics. We try to make out instruments; we tap out rhythms; we substitute with silly words; we marvel and reflect aloud; we dance together. On the other hand, when we choose an old favorite, a relaxed energy permeates our space, and typically, we all drop into our respective flows.

Clearly, the influence of these songs and stories goes far beyond their role as "in between" media to help us switch gears after screen time. When the kids are in their own quiet flow, they'll often create their own rhythms, rhymes, songs, or stories. For us, this practice is a fun way to hone our listening skills and a deeply enriching source of bonding and individual expression.

 Alas, the kids (and their parents!) still want to sit and be entertained. We hope our practices around healthy technology usage help them understand that the screen is but one small thread in the vibrant, enlivened fabric of our world. After all, most of the best stories we know and love as a culture were conceived in the wild imaginations of someone who was unplugged, fully present, and tuned in deeply to the genius of their own flow. Even Mr. Rogers knew this, asking us openly, "Do you ever grow anything, in the garden of your mind?"

WEEK 23

FLOW AND FRIENDS
Creating a healthy social identity

THE GAMES GROUPS OF CHILDREN CREATE for themselves differ fundamentally from the games adults create for them. In RWB schools (see Glossary), there is great emphasis on creating environments of emotional and physical safety, and as such children ages three to eighteen can play as their hearts desire. We observe that underneath all the spontaneous (often seemingly irrational) interactions between one another, all children have a genuine need to include and feel included, to understand and be understood, to treat and be treated justly, and to compete in friendly ways. In order for these interactions to become sustainable learning experiences, they must be supported by highly observant, sensitive, and caring adults.

When children have ample time to play freely with peers, they often drop into role-play. In the RWB schools, we have found that children who feel secure create unending, fascinating social and educational opportunities for themselves. As they play and interact with each other on their own terms, they have learned they can say "stop" if something doesn't feel right or step out of a game anytime. When adults create a safe space for children's self-organized, imaginative role-play and help them solve potential conflicts, it becomes a natural way for children to learn empathy.

When children feel emotionally safe, their human potential for empathy is free to develop throughout their childhood, into adulthood. Like every skill, it takes practice, and we all continually improve these skills throughout life. A child's capacity for empathy, fully activated over time, forms the foundation for a healthy social identity.

Sometimes adults assume that it's enough to let children play by themselves for them to learn and mature. However, children left without adult guidance tend to reinforce each other's age-typical, self-centric views of the world. Children are just learning to respect or even perceive another's boundaries, and they don't yet have the necessary comprehension and empathy to solve their own conflicts peacefully without help. Without adult mediation and modeling healthy exchanges when disagreements escalate, children may remain stuck in their egocentric childhood perspectives, and more likely grow up to be survival-oriented, easily feeling threatened even when their surroundings are safe.

Before they play, children often go through elaborate processes where they establish the rules of their pretend world. For instance, "let's play circus," "let's play bank," "let's play marketplace." "I will be the circus director, what would you like to be?" "I will be a clown." "I will be a merchant." "I will be a mom." "I will be your daughter," and so on. Even at this initial stage, adults need to make sure that no child is pressured into taking on a role they don't like. When in doubt, ask a child if that is the role they would like to play.

Already during this time of preparation for the role-play, children experience authentic social interactions where they take on various roles that inform them what it feels like to be the one who has an idea that the group likes, to be the one whose idea gets rejected, to be the one who helps realize another's idea, or to be the one who just doesn't fit into that game—the disappointed one, or the one who disappoints.

With empathic and empowering adult guidance, children build an inner resource and memory bank for empathy and resilience. Experientially, they learn to play together, to work in teams, to work on a common goal, to share feelings, to get along, to respect each other's wishes, to be flexible, and find solutions that work for all. They learn to recover from not being chosen, from their ideas not gaining traction in a group, or from a serious disagreement. With the ongoing reassurance of an adult whenever it's needed, they can learn to let go and move on, even when it's hard.

In addition, this kind of play allows children to embody archetypal roles of the human experience within a safe container. They can experiment with being a dangerous character or creating a scary scenario, without actually being in danger or hurting another. This way, empathy and resilience can be developed through how it feels to be the ruler and the ruled; the boss and the employee; the teacher and the pupil; the warrior, the hunted, the protector, or the victim. Children intensely experience the emotions that arise while taking on these roles, and intimately get to know what it feels like when the roles are taken on by others. If allowed, children will love to role-play all the way into their middle school years, or beyond.

Parents can invite one or more of their children's friends over and accompany them with whatever healthy boundaries need to be set as the group comes up with their own ideas for role-play. Schools can offer time and space for accompanied, child-directed role-play as part of their programs and reap the benefits of children developing authentic, empathic social skills. Positive results can be observed when children consistently spend time role-playing in these emotionally safe environments.

TRY THIS

Offer role-play for several children

Ideally, offer a room, part of a room, or an outdoor area with some empty space dedicated to role-play. Take out items you don't want children to use and offer things that may be used freely in their play. Children often don't need much to create a role-play for themselves. You will see how your children react to the space you create and, accordingly, you can add more or less. Fewer props may allow for more imagination and creativity.

To begin, add a table, chairs or bench, a shelf, and a blanket for play on the floor. Add simple elements such as colorful shawls for dress-up, a mirror and combs, shoeboxes, paper, crayons and tape, and some special toys such as dolls and stuffed animals. With practice, you will become adept at knowing what to add or take away as needed. You might invite children to the space by offering an introduction, for example, "This is where you all can play 'let's pretend' whenever you like."

For now, you can be a quiet observer and see what happens, or you can make suggestions. Children may pretend play scenarios set in a circus, TV show, school, doctor's office, hair salon, castle with princesses and knights, grocery store, zoo, restaurant, home, dragon's lair, and whatever else they imagine.

NOTE: If a child has never experienced the opportunity to free-play with other children, or has not spent much time with other children, they will most likely need an adjustment period during which a trusted adult remains very close by, or even involved in the role-playing.

WEEK 24

FLOW AND PRACTICAL LIFE SKILLS
Help me do it myself!

AS YOUNG CHILDREN, learning is simply exhilarating! We receive extreme pleasure from learning in flow, doing things for and with ourselves, and feeling ever more empowered in our small world. We constantly rearrange our inner landscape according to new discoveries. Learning is our way of life.

Already as infants and toddlers, we find profound pleasure in becoming more and more independent and functional in our environment. Consider that as infants we find ourselves in a state of utter helplessness and dependence upon our caregivers. Increasingly, however, things don't just happen to us–*we make things happen!*

We delight in experiencing ourselves as the cause of things. Splashing water, rolling a ball, and picking up a toy: each small step toward more independence is a great conquest and a victory! We learn step by step, need by need, desire by desire, and this needs-based way of learning will continue happily throughout our lives if supported by our environment early on. Needs-based learning allows us to continue to choose what supports us throughout our lives, rather than succumbing to an environment chosen for us. This is how innovation happens. Many problems cannot be solved from within the problem—one must rearrange reality in order to solve them. And that is exactly what children are masters at doing.

As we grow, we naturally learn practical life skills that soon become automatic and turn into body memory such as opening drawers, blowing bubbles, and turning book pages. With an untamable willingness to practice, we learn numerous things every day. Suddenly a child can open the door, sing a song, and even read! Classes and teachers aren't always necessary when a child has regular access to an environment that provides learning opportunities.

Our impulses for independence get stronger as we grow and as soon as we can communicate, even non-verbally, we let adults know that we want to do things on our own. Courageously, we follow our inner drive to become a "stand-alone" individual while still needing so much care. Think about the incredible courage it takes for a child to follow their inner impulses toward authenticity! Daring to say "no" to a significant adult who has considerable power over them takes nothing less than heroism, especially when their impulses for independence aren't regarded as positive.

The revolutionary educator Maria Montessori fully grasped this instinct for independence and valued it as a significant part of growing up healthy. As mentioned in Week 6, she coined the phrase "Help me do it myself" to help adults understand that children try to say, "Give me independence but don't leave me alone." When properly understood, many of our children's actions demand supported independence. Montessori empowered children to directly connect to their environment: to engage with it, change it, and improve it. Traditional classrooms offer little opportunity for such interaction, and children often become passive observers and receivers along with a feeling of "there is nothing I can do about it" or "it's not my responsibility."

Based on her observations of children, Montessori's innovative schools consisted of child-sized environments and learning materials that allowed children to independently, playfully learn practical life skills. For instance, children would find (and still do today in many Montessori schools) child-sized sinks or water buckets in which to do their own dishes; basins and pitchers with which to ceremoniously wash their hands; places to wash their own clothes; and trays with several beautiful glass containers to learn pouring tea or rice into. She offered a great variety of refined toys to allow children to practice opening and closing rows of buttons, tying ribbons, or braiding. She identified a series of activities to help children prepare their hand for writing. During these playful activities, children practiced the muscles needed to hold a pen in a relaxed way without cramping. Furthermore, children were supported in learning to take care of their bodies, including cleaning their noses, brushing their hair, and putting on their shoes.

At home, this can be a bit challenging for adults who want or need to get things done quickly. Children often do things more slowly, a bit clumsily, and not as neatly by adult standards. Every time we can set up tasks where we can welcome their participation, and then have patience with their processes, we give a child a tremendous gift. A prepared environment can really help a child learn practical skills for daily life.

TRY THIS
Making chores child-friendly

If your young child is interested in daily life chores, ride that wave as long as it lasts! Let them help you, let them imitate you, let them surprise you with their fervor. I have seen many children vigorously cleaning floors, handwashing their shirts, and polishing mirrors.

Consciously change the cultural conditioning around household chores being a burden. Activities such as cooking, cleaning, and making order can be seen as a satisfying contribution that connects the family as a functioning unit. Let children grow into that notion from a young age onward. Make it a habit that certain times each week are set aside for housework; times for upkeep where you do things together, side by side.

Doing chores together can be a time of connection and bonding. Experiment with doing the routine tasks of your home mindfully and with calm focus, so children observe how chores can be enjoyed. In doing them this way, they may become more pleasurable for you, too. In your home, contributing to the family's needs can be valued as a sign of maturity and co-determine whether a child is ready for more responsibility. If necessary, take time to explain to your child that everyone contributes to the family in different ways, and you will help them find a way to contribute that works best for them, which might change over time. This may sound unusual, and it is. I hope you will find that it works and uplifts the whole atmosphere at home. It certainly does at the RWB schools. Here are a few ideas for some simple ways to elevate chores:

☆ "Chores are *us*-time: we do it together." Put on special music and a special apron to signal this is our time to maintain our clean home, as a family.

☆ Make a game of chores. When cleaning the surface of a table or sweeping the floor, provide childproof cleaning supplies such as warm water with a few drops of mild, natural dish soap or a child-sized broom. Have your child imitate your moves and vice versa. Narrate each step of your activity such as, "Now I'm sweeping back and forth." Invent or do an internet search for simple songs or rhymes, such as "Clean and bright, day and night, we make it shine with all our might!" or "This is the way we sweep the floor, sweep the floor, sweep the floor. This is the way we sweep the floor. This is the way, yay, yay!"

☆ Add a stepstool to a sink where your child can imitate you and practice all kinds of things such as washing their hands, brushing their teeth, or handwashing their own shirt.

WEEK 25

CONNECTING WHILE PLAYING
Delight children with your playful side

CHILDREN LOVE TO PLAY with their significant adults. The full attention they receive while playing is healing and uplifting. The beautiful moments during play, when all hearts are open, are moments of deep connection; moments that show children they belong. Many adults don't like to play with children or don't really know how. It's totally okay not to play when you don't want to, or when it feels boring, or too much. But if you never play with your child, you might miss out on some wonderful ways of connecting. Lawrence Cohen shares in his book *Playful Parenting* how play can become a bridge to a deep emotional bond between parent and child, and how it can ease the stress of parenting.

GAMES WE CAN PLAY WITH CHILDREN
Due to the many physical and cognitive differences between grown-ups and youngsters, not all games work well for all ages. Below are some ways you can connect through play with children at various stages of development.

PLAY WITH YOUNGER CHILDREN
Let your child be a pretend pet or wild animal: If your child wants to engage or play with you, but doesn't really know how, ask them if they are a cat, a dog, a wild lion, or any other animal they know or love. The child will

probably tell you what animal they are, if they are friendly or wild, and then you can engage with them under that premise. Perhaps the cat likes to be pet on their head, and curl up in your lap; perhaps the lion is going to roar out loud, and you can admire or run away from them; or perhaps, the dog wants to play fetch with you. Engage on your child's terms, and let them keep informing you on how the play should develop; perhaps saying, "You can tell me what to do" or "What happens next?"

Be a car, airplane, horse, or rocket ship: If you are strong enough to lift your child up high, carry them piggyback, or fly them safely in the air, you might truly delight your child. Play an airplane that comes in for landing and let the child hop on board for a short flight; play a school bus (or another transportation they know) that comes to pick up your child and ask if they want to hop on the bus; play a friendly horse that the child can pet and ride on. Be sure to be gentle, keep tuning in with your child, and assess if they are still happy with this game.

Nursery rhyme games and hand clapping games: There are many wonderful traditional and modern nursery rhyme or song games as well as hand clapping and finger play games that you can play with a child. Find the ones you like by asking around or doing an internet search. Below are some fun examples:

☆ Paddy Cake
☆ I Have Ten Little Fingers
☆ One Potato, Two Potato, Three Potato, Four!
☆ The Itsy Bitsy (or Eensy Weensy) Spider
☆ Hickory, Dickory, Dock
☆ Twinkle, Twinkle, Little Star
☆ Miss Mary Mack
☆ Down, Down, Baby

Pretend play with children: If children allow you into their pretend world, know that it is an honor; it means that a child trusts you. During pretend play, you can experience the child's imagination, and participate in non-directive ways. Let the child take the lead and respond in friendly ways. If you are being served pretend tea and mud pie, of course, you can kindly pretend drink and eat. If you are assigned a role (dad, magician, cat, servant, monster), and you feel comfortable with it, ask if this character is friendly or wild. As a rule of thumb, you don't need to do that much, just be present with your full attention, and let the child play around you, and at times with you.

PLAY WITH OLDER AND YOUNGER CHILDREN

Roughhousing: Roughhousing, such as rolling around on the floor and play wresting, is important play for all children, not just for boys. Even though it may include play fighting with your child, for children it has nothing to do with aggression or competition (nor should it for the adult); its purpose is pure delight and joy. And it is a fertile ground for socio-emotional learning. During roughhousing, children experience their own strengths and limits and they learn to balance it in interaction with their playmate. They also experience that their parent is much stronger, and they learn from that play, (just like their parents) to hold back their strength at times, regulating it in order not to hurt. Read below play expert O. Fred Donaldson's wisdom on how you can safely play with children.

Ball games, playing catch, and other movement games: When you play games with children where you both are in movement, keep in mind that you are much taller, faster, and stronger. It's okay to adapt to your child's skills, play more softly, and play in a way so it is fun and uplifting for them.

PLAY WITH OLDER CHILDREN

Play games where luck is a main component: When we play games based on luck, such as dice games, then everyone has an equal chance to win. There are dice games ranging from simple to complex, and children may invent their own. For instance, everyone takes turn to throw one die again and again and add up all numbers. But when they throw a 1, then they must stop. See who can get to the highest number.

Play cooperative games: Cooperative games are games in which you and your child are on a team together. A simple cooperative game is to build a block tower together that is very high. There are many modern, cooperative board games designed to have participants work with one another instead of competing.

When you play competitive games: When you play competitive games with a child, such as chess, where you as an adult have a clear advantage, explain to the child beforehand that you may win, because you are older and have more experience because you played this game many times. Let your child know that if they continue to practice, they may become as good as or better than you at this game, and so your winning is not a demonstration of your superiority but an inspiring example of what can be done with practice.

Hands-on activities are best done side by side: Most hands-on activities, such as cooking, crafting, or playing with Legos are best done side by side, where each person works on their own material. You might work on a common goal together, such as baking cookies. As part of this common goal, each person contributes what they can or like. For instance, you might measure the exact amounts of ingredients and your child might shape the dough into heart cookies.

TRY THIS
Safe roughhousing with your child

For safe roughhousing, you need an empty floor space. If the floor is cold, cover it with a rug, blanket, and some pillows. The main concern during roughhousing is that children (and you, of course) feel safe at all times and never get scared or feel attacked by the adult. During safe, heart-based roughhousing, the bond between the generations is strengthened, as children do not need to develop defense mechanisms but can relax and trust the safety and strength of their elder. They know, "Mom or Dad is not going to hurt me, no matter what I do." Use "stop" or another safety word for everyone to use when it's too much for them. Make sure to immediately respect this request to stop in order to model to your child how important this word is.

O. FRED DONALDSON'S ORIGINAL PLAY

If you would like to study roughhousing further, perhaps even introduce it into a play-based program for groups of children, look into the work of contemporary play expert, O. Fred Donaldson. He has studied physical play with children, adults, and animals for over four decades. He observed that children, just like animal cubs, yearn for their significant adults to touch them and play with them. He developed a respectful, non-invasive way for adults to engage in physical, spontaneous play with children. His philosophy and guidelines, called Original Play, are described in his books *Playing by Heart* and *Playing for Real*.

In his own words: "From children and animals I rediscovered that authentic play is: A gift of Creation, not an artifact of culture; it's a sharing of two gifts: you're lovable, and there's nothing to be afraid of; it's a relationship of kindness and belonging that is in Nature and in our nature; characterized by love, trust, kindness, touch, wonder, joy. It is belonging to and being in touch with a world that is in touch with us."

WEEK 26

A CLOSE LOOK AT BOREDOM
Why children get bored and what to do

WHEN A CHILD SAYS, "I am bored," or you can see that they are passive, listless, and unable to engage with their immediate environment, take that as a signal to look deeper. There are many different shades of boredom, and this child might need your understanding and support. Often boredom is a necessary part of the creative process, a precursor to an activity that is born from within. Below are descriptions of several different kinds of boredom and what you can do about them, if in fact you should do anything at all.

SIMPLE BOREDOM

Simple boredom is a passing state. It is easily recognized merely a short interruption in a child's otherwise industrious day, especially when they are immersed in an interesting environment. It is almost like a break for reorientation, a necessary gap that may not feel comfortable but is needed in order to discover what is next.

What you can do: When a child reaches out to you with "I am bored" or you can tell they are bored, and really do need some help, come closer and be curious about this state together with the child. Unless a child is unable to recover on their own (as we will discuss next), avoid offering activities, instead simply acknowledge, "Yes, I can see you are bored." And try to ask friendly questions such as: "Do you want to tell

WEEK 26 | A CLOSE LOOK AT BOREDOM

me about it?" "How does it feel?" "Where in your body do you feel this?" "How would you feel if you weren't bored?" or "What would you do if you weren't bored?" Or simply state, "I can sit here with you until you aren't bored anymore." Your presence and warmth will help a child accept this uncomfortable state. A child will know you aren't here to "fix" this. Instead they experience that this feeling is okay, that *they are okay*, that they are strong enough to feel this, and move on from this state when the time is right. Soon enough, they will feel a surge of energy, an internal impulse that leads them to their next self-chosen activity, "Oh, I'm going to do this now!" And off they will go to their next adventure.

BOREDOM FROM DISINTEREST

If a child is repeatedly bored and disinterested in their surroundings, the environment may simply not be inspiring enough; it may not offer the kinds of activities a child currently needs. Even prepared environments such as schools often lack activities that respond to developmental needs. This can lead to all kinds of behavioral issues, and these children may increasingly shut down over time. As best as you can, try to supplement inspiring activities at home.

What you can do: Experiment with a variety of changes in the environment as suggested in this book. Bring your child to nature, help them explore fauna, flora, weather patterns, let them experiment on their own with art supplies, instruments and sound-makers; or let them try art, music or dance classes. Offer interesting items such as an old telephone or typewriter to play with or take apart and offer inspiring books. Let your children speak and play with interesting people who you think could become role models. Change the environment before trying to change the child.

170   PART TWO | YOUR CHILD: A YOUNG MASTER OF FLOW

DAYDREAMING

Children who are "daydreaming" may look as if they are bored, but they are actually in a valuable, pleasurable internal state that is necessary for good mental health and integrating new information. Even in the most inspiring environment, children can momentarily detach from their surroundings and focus their attention inward. During what we call daydreaming, children may be in natural contemplation, allowing thoughts, visions, and feelings to arise and dissipate. They may playfully tackle problems important to them. And, they may not think at all, which gives their mind an important break during which sudden insights may occur, which is so well described in Guy Claxton's book *Hare Brain, Tortoise Mind: How Intelligence Increases When You Think Less.*

What you can do: If you notice that a child is "staring into space" and not participating actively I anything, try to find out if they are in a pleasurable state. If they are, simply smile, nod, and let them be. Don't interrupt. If a child trusts you, they may tell you about their internal journey afterward.

BOREDOM FROM INNER PAIN

If you see that a child rarely plays with toys, art supplies, or other games, if they cling to their significant adults or withdraw frequently, even though the environment is interesting, this child may be experiencing some deep internal pain. Emotional pain needs to be addressed before a child can be active and self-motivated.

What you can do: Try to find out what is weighing the child down: Is it a conflict with peers? Is bullying involved? Is it a stressful situation at school or at home? Are they afraid of something? Whatever it is, do your best to listen and acknowledge what the child is going through and take whatever measures are in your power to support the child. Sometimes this may involve mediating between children, talking to their teacher, or helping the child apologize and make amends for something they did. Or, you may need to apologize for something you did. All of these are natural challenges and as long as a child sees they are not alone, and there are things they can do to heal with our support, we are giving them valuable tools for future challenges. You can also offer the suggestions for tension release described in Week 11.

BOREDOM WITH THE WORLD OFF THE SCREEN

Children who are used to being entertained by a screen might easily get bored with the world when the screen is off. Natural things are usually slower and clumsier; they don't light up, vibrate, or give instant points for progress. Conversations with real people are much more complex and might not be as exciting as computer games. When a child gets bored with the real world and wants to go back to the screen as soon as possible, they need our help with reincorporating natural or human elements back into the fabric of their day-to-day lives.

What you can do: Make the off-screen world attractive! For instance, let a child be in touch with animals,—get them a pet, or take them to a farm; go camping with them and hike to a spectacular waterfall; help them make friends, perhaps with children who are also used to the screen— offer them physical activities, so they can commiserate and heal together.

TRY THIS
Dare to be bored

If you and your child are always busy, you will never get bored. Even though boredom is not very comfortable, it is informative and, ideally, it leads you and your child to an activity that is truly in alignment with your inner world in that moment, rather than a distraction or another part of this week's schedule. So, this week, announce an experiment you'll do with yourself or together with your child. Create time with absolutely no agenda. You don't necessarily have to play together, just be side by side, each doing what feels right. This is your time for timelessness where you have absolutely no plans, no chores, and no screens. Only you and your children in your own home that is more or less prepared for comfortable rest and activity. Let go of anything you would like your child to do, or anything "better" you should be doing. If thoughts such as "I need to do something useful," "This is ridiculous," or "I'm wasting my time," come up, simply accept them, and know that this is conditioning. If you or your child feel inner pain expressed as boredom, try using the suggestions above and provide that extra support for yourself and your child.

You absolutely have the right not to do anything that you "ought" to do sometimes. Keep looking around in your environment with the intention to be, feel, play, tinker, and create until you find an activity that feels perfectly right and that you love. This space that you consciously allow naturally connects you to the world of children. It is like a reset button and a break from business as usual.

Welcome whatever feelings, conversations, or ideas may arise during that time. There may be some confusion, some contemplation, some tinkering, some doodling, some wandering around aimlessly, some daydreaming... maybe it's time for a nap. You may miss your phone, or see what needs to be cleaned, but this is not the time for screens or chores. Whatever arises that is not part of the to-do list is good, authentic, and fair game for exploration. All of this is part of eventually dropping into flow. Trust that "Doing nothing often leads to the very best of something." as A. A. Milne writes in Winnie-the-Pooh.

They Don't Always Need Me

I learned from Susanne, FLOW TO LEARN's parenting advisor, that she often informs her children (three and five years old) that she is working at the moment, and she trusts they have the creativity to find their next project on their own. Or, she insists that they go outside because she can sense that their energies inside have run their course, and a change of venue is really all they need to be reinvigorated. She jokes that 95% of the time she is effective at ignoring her children into their creative play-flow when they are bored. Here are some of Susanne's thoughts about her children's boredom:

I deeply love the time my kids and I play together, and of course it's essential to their well-being and secure attachment. Sometimes to transition away from our special time together, they need me to "ignore" them intentionally but in a respectful way, for example, "I am still working, I can play with you in (xx) minutes. I'll set a timer; would you like to press 'go?' Okay, see you in (xx) minutes!! Have fun!!" When it sounds decisive, this often compels them to gather their inner resources and make something of the moment, instead of depending upon me to navigate it for them.

It might take a few exchanges like this to convince them I will not be providing entertainment or be pulled away from my work. One or both might protest loudly about what they want me to do with or for them. Though it seems counterintuitive at first glance, what they really need is for me to say "no" and mean it. I know from experience that if I indulge in the age-old "one more time," they'll continue to ask for many more "one more times," and at its conclusion the "but I'm bored" or "but I need you" cycle starts all over again, because they love spending time with me and with their Dada. It's a lot like a friendly dare— I dare you to help yourself on this one. Are you ready? Want to try? No? But look! I am not available. It is a bit like a mother bird insisting her baby step out of the nest. And more often than not, no matter how grudgingly they start out on their own, they soon joyfully spread their wings, freely exploring and adventuring. Of course, if either child feels truly needy, sad, tired, or otherwise unable to take command of their own focus, I do my best to respond in a loving and accepting manner as soon as that's clear (usually it's immediately after they try their best and are obviously unable to continue). In this case, I might help them get started by playing with items I know they love and involving them as well, or by meeting whatever genuine need they have.

I couldn't possibly count the number of times that both children have become immersed in their self-chosen activity for long stretches of time—even hours—after this type of exchange with me. It might seem like unsupportive parenting at first, but after a few occasions of a child exuberantly experiencing their ultimate flow state, it becomes clear how beneficial it can be to stand up for the benefits of boredom!

PART THREE

THE ZONE

CREATING FLOW
ACTIVITY STATIONS

*In a universe in which everything
must move and flow in order to exist,
only ability to interact with that flow is of value.
This is what the child intuitively knows
and strives to maintain.*

—Joseph Chilton Pearce, *Magical Child*

*The fact is that given the challenges we face,
education doesn't need to be reformed—it needs to be transformed.
The key to this transformation is not to standardize education,
but to personalize it, to build achievement on discovering the individual
talents of each child, to put students in an environment where they want to
learn and where they can naturally discover their true passions.*

—Sir Ken Robinson, *The Element*

A MASTER NEEDS A DOJO

Change the environment, not the child

A DOJO IS A PREPARED ENVIRONMENT, a training hall, for martial arts practitioners—created with the explicit purpose for them to be *in the zone*, which is another expression for dropping into flow. *Being in the zone* makes clear how significantly the flow state is connected to a suitable environment. Flow requires a specific space where flow can happen. A tennis player needs a court, a swimmer needs a body of water, a carpenter needs a woodshop, a musician needs a quiet place, and children need nature and a variety of flow stations. Flow stations are prepared environments in which a child can experiment with a multitude of skills and discover their innate talents.

Whatever your home and whatever your budget, you can rearrange just a few things (or many things) to help your child feel more welcome and find places to fully experience flow. Even one small, well-prepared place can have a positive effect on your child's well-being and behavior. Ideally, you unleash your own creativity and have fun creating learning wonderlands. Do not hesitate to remove elements at any time that don't seem to work and dare to experiment with inventing new flow stations. Take clues from your child; for instance, if they are fascinated with ice, create a place where your child can experiment with a big bucket of ice cubes, and add a towel and watercolors, and other things they may need.

Children need places where they can be the creators of their own reality, where they can pretend, build, craft, play, tinker, and talk to themselves as they wish. When a child has regular access to flow stations, they can settle down and venture into their own world. As a result, they almost always become happier, more relaxed, more accessible, and more collaborative.

Flow stations make it easy for children to choose an activity and focus on it. They provide access to a variety of toys, hands-on materials, and age-appropriate crafting supplies that allow a child to explore and discover activities that suit their development in the moment. Depending on your relationship, you might like to spend time with your child in the newly created places until they feel comfortably connected with you and can focus on their own activities. A flow station can have highly beneficial effects on your child and the atmosphere in your home. Many power struggles may disappear because in this place your child can feel powerful. Clinging may diminish because your child will feel at home. Whining and boredom may decrease because they will have interesting options to pursue on their own.

In RWB schools we also welcome children who had a hard time fitting into standardized education. When these children feel safe and can relax into an activity they choose, their behavior dramatically improves, and they become willing to collaborate and make friends. Instead of trying to modify a child's behavior through reward, punishment, and medication, let's first change their environment and see if their behavior changes naturally.

At home you can dedicate a complete room or nooks and corners to your child; ideally, there is also an outdoor space. Create these places so *your* child loves to spend time there. Different children need different elements. The simple action of creating special places for your child is a profound act of love. It shows your child that you truly care, that they can trust you, that they matter and belong, and that this is also their home.

We can't control the world at large, but we can be in charge of our own home. Your home can be a sanctuary for you and your child. In your home, you decide which influences you allow and what must stay out. Consciously create healthy boundaries around your home so it remains a place where you and your family can recover, relax, and be creative. Children don't need *all* the flow stations presented in this book (even though it would be wonderful, of course, to have a place such as an RWB school that offers these and more). Even one prepared space in your home will have a positive impact on your relationship with your child and on their behavior.

TRY THIS
Set up a makerspace

A makerspace is a place where children (and adults) find supplies for experimenting, creating, crafting, tinkering, exploring, and learning as their hearts' desire. Some makerspaces may offer tech tools such as complete woodshops, 3D printers, special loose parts, or laser cutters. Simpler spaces (private or public) may offer arts and craft supplies and inexpensive tinkering materials.

The maker movement has long been advocating for more hands-on learning in education. There are makerspaces and maker faires around the world where children and adults meet to share their knowledge, craft together, and together go "from consumption to creation." We can use one of their simplest and finest tools—creating an arts and crafts tinkering table—in homes and classrooms.

STEP BY STEP TO YOUR OWN MAKERSPACE
Choose or add a table, suitable for the child's height, in a welcoming, well-lighted place in your home or classroom. Next to it, add a deep, low shelf that is easily accessible. On the shelves, in clean and sturdy open

boxes, baskets, or trays, visibly offer a variety of open-ended tinkering and crafting materials. Allow the child to use them as they wish for their self-directed crafting experiments. For older children who have learned to use crafting materials responsibly, you can add a great variety of supplies. It's okay to offer a limited amount of supplies (for instance, 25 buttons, instead of hundreds of buttons) to prevent overwhelming children and to facilitate responsible use of supplies. However, make sure each child has enough supplies for their projects. You can also provide a sewing machine, crafting books, instruction guidelines, and examples of crafted items. You can offer non-invasive introductory lessons (as explained in Week 47) for more complex activities such as knitting.

START COLLECTING MAKER SUPPLIES

Office supplies such as pencils, glue, tape, scissors, paper clips, hole punchers, and rulers.

Recycled materials such as paper rolls, shoeboxes, egg cartons, wire, rubber bands, bottle caps, ice-cream sticks, plastic spoons, and wine corks.

Nature materials such as pinecones, pebbles, seashells, flower petals, leaves, and wood pieces.

Art supplies such as construction paper in all sizes and colors, knitting and other needles, yarn, thread, wool, buttons, zippers, fabric scraps, crayons, watercolors, and clay.

Old gadgets to take apart or play with such as cameras, flip phones, and typewriters.

You can expand a basic makerspace over time and offer various crafting opportunities on different days such as water coloring, clay work, looms for weaving, and felting.

WEEK 28

ACTIVATING THE ZONE
Let children's life force flow

ENVIRONMENTS DIRECTLY INFLUENCE what and how children and adults relate, think, and behave. For instance, children often spontaneously learn to read when they are immersed in a literate environment and play with early reading and first-reader books. Children are likely to climb when there is a tree and play with water when there is water access. Interesting, welcoming, activity-inviting environments inspire creative thought and action. Uniform, rigid surroundings common in many standardized classrooms are more conducive to boredom and passivity. Creating intentional beauty and warmth can be achieved in any space, and the outdoors is always full of engaging activities that children enjoy.

By being aware of this immediate connection between environments and learners' thoughts and activities, you can partially shape and predict what your child will do in the places you create. Let your environment become your ally, and the child's teacher.

A flow station allows children's energy to expand while simultaneously allowing adults to relax, because they are relieved from managing another (or multiple) person's moment-to-moment choices, activities, reactions, interactions with others, and the interplay of all these. The unnecessary weight of over-managing even one child is huge. It leaves very little room for an adult to relax, accomplish things they would like to do, be authentic, or observe the true nature of a child emerging.

Flow stations that allow for a child's optimal learning state create a serenity that, once experienced, will grow its own momentum through the positive feelings it evokes. The idea that an adult does not have to be "on" every moment when caring for one or multiple children is a welcome revelation and a healing experience for adults who introduce this into their lives and those of the children they care for.

The life force of a child is like water—it's in movement, it's alive, and a flow station gives it a place to be. Sometimes adults are wary of this force because it can be an intense energy, like a big wave. And just like waves of water, a child's life energy needs a channel, where it can follow its natural pattern. When a river is restricted into too narrow a path, it is likely to overflow its banks and spread out in a flood, but when the river water is allowed to meander and change over time, it is a source of nourishment for the whole area.

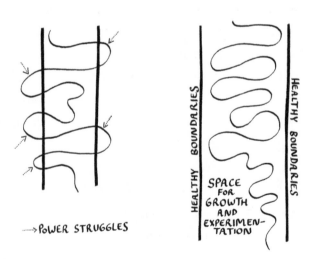

When children's life force is continuously suppressed, it turns into tension revealed as behavioral and emotional problems that may even develop into disease. In traditional school settings, where children can engage in moving their bodies only during recess or physical education, their movement often consists of mostly tension release. The most impressive example of this is children getting loud and chaotic as soon as the teacher leaves the classroom. In the RWB schools, there is no such behavior. When children are allowed to move anytime, they don't store up the same tension. Instead, they naturally experiment with their physical skills whenever they feel the need to move. They learn to move gracefully and with awareness of their environment.

In your home, you can offer your child places for movement, tension release, rest, play, and whatever works for you that *they* love to do. You can *activate the zone* for them. You can create an environment for your child's energy to expand within the healthy boundaries that you carefully provide, and (crucially) that you gently hold firm. It needn't happen all at once, require large purchases of many specific items, or involve a complete overhaul of your home. Small changes can make a huge impact in how a child feels and interacts with a space.

A FLOW STATION IS A "YES SPACE"

As explained in Week 27, a flow station is a dojo, a prepared environment in which a person—no matter how old—can experience flow. In a flow station, you can say "yes" far more often than "no." "*Yes*, you can take this off the shelf, *yes* you can touch this, *yes* you can explore this, *yes*, you can play with this, and you don't have to ask me for permission." In this way, a flow station is also a yes space.

The term yes space was coined by RIE parenting expert Janet Lansbury. While she was writing a post in 2010 for her website describing the benefits of Magda Gerber's 100% safe spaces, she created yes space as a term for the place where babies and toddlers could freely explore without hearing "no, no, no." As Magda wrote in *Dear Parent: Caring for Infants with Respect*, "By safety, I mean an environment which is so totally safe that, even without any adult supervision, the infant or toddler would be totally safe."

The way flow stations are prepared largely determines to what degree a child can play and tinker without adult supervision. The materials should reflect a child's readiness for using them independently. If you offer materials such as an expensive microscope or a sewing machine that need an introduction or your help, put it out of reach of very young children, confirm with older children they understand the rules for using that item, or mark it with a red dot, so they come get you if they would like to use it.

In the yes space of a flow station, your child feels welcome, safe, and protected. You may see your child take things out, touch and explore them, and move right on to the next thing. Let that be okay and help them recreate order at the end of that exploratory process. You may observe your child start several projects and not end them until they find an activity that captures their interest in a deeper way. That is also okay. Don't force your child to finish what they started.

For a child, and even for adults in flow, *now* is all about the process, not about the result. If a child doesn't find anything interesting over a longer period of time, make sure the environment truly offers activities that inspire. Inquire more deeply and see if a child's other genuine needs for physical health, connection, belonging, healthy empowerment, and emotional safety are being met.

It is possible a child will need to spend time at the flow station with their trusted adult before they feel safe to move forward on their own. This type of "checking in" within a secure attachment is common. For example, younger children at a playground often play on their own for a bit, then return to their parent or caregiver to briefly connect, if only to see or touch them and feel their loving presence. Then they happily run off again to their self-chosen activities.

REDIRECT THE CHILD'S ENERGY
INSTEAD OF BLOCKING IT

Children's life force needs space. Sometimes it is big and intense; sometimes it is gentle and vulnerable. If it feels like too much at times, instead of trying to block it, try to help them move their energy to a place where it can be allowed. Ideally you can offer various kinds of environments, so you can guide your child to an appropriate place for their activity, instead of merely saying "no." Here are some examples: "You won't find peace reading your book here with everyone around, but I created a cozy reading corner in your room." "I won't let you climb the bookshelf, but we can go to the monkey bars on the playground." "You need to be loud right now and that's okay. Let's go outside so you can keep being loud, and I will go back inside to finish my phone call."

BUT WHAT IF YOU HAVE TO SAY NO?

Even in well-prepared environments, there may be instances when you need to say "no." Saying "no" is not easy but can be absolutely necessary: sometimes for safety, sometimes because you can't give something to a child, sometimes because things got out of hand and you don't feel comfortable anymore. *Children need us to set boundaries.* A child may not know when they went too far. Often only by overstepping limits do they become aware of them. In fact, pushing limits is one of the spontaneous ways to find out where limits are, thus it's natural for children not to simply accept boundaries.

Here is where our patience and compassion for children as a learners is crucial. When necessary, gently remind your child of a boundary without getting into negotiations. Make eye contact, use a soft voice, and get down to their level whenever possible. Practice saying "no" without yelling at your child. Learn to insist on a boundary without withdrawing your love and connection. Avoid saying "no" and leaving them alone with the pain of rejection. If you can, stay with your child until they feel better. Accept all emotions, as they arise. Listen to their complaining and protesting with an understanding and open heart. Allow tears to flow and assure your child you understand that they don't like that "no," but sadly you still need to insist on that "no."

In RWB schools, when a child is upset about a boundary we need to set, such as "I won't let you throw pebbles at the dog," we allow them to be upset. We say things like, "I understand that you are upset. I see you would like to throw these pebbles at the dog, but the dog doesn't like it at all, and I won't let you do it. I'm sorry you are so upset, but I still won't let you do it." We might give an alternative: "You are welcome to throw pebbles into this bush over here." We might explain, "The dog might get hurt, and I protect him, just like I would protect you, if this should happen to you." Often, to keep everyone safe, it's necessary that we step in to set a boundary in a way that is non-negotiable. If we must communicate a boundary to a child from a distance, and the child is unable to heed the request, it is essential that the next communication be made from right next to the child, with eye contact and gentleness, as well as a readiness on our part to enforce the boundary. This way, at RWB schools, children feel secure that what is being said is true and does not need to be further tested, since a child's only method of knowing whether it's true is to test.

We stay with a child until they feel better, until they integrate this experience. The empathy we provide makes all the difference. The child feels heard and seen, and the experience becomes a practice of resilience—"even if I can't have what I want, even when I make a mistake, I am learning, I am surviving and I am still a good person, *I am ok*ay, and my parent or my teacher still loves and respects me."

From this place of emotional safety, incidents like this can become profound learning experiences and they become learning memories. If emotional safety is not offered during a boundary being set, the child will likely return to push that boundary again, and possibly in a stronger way next time, in order to find out how to achieve connection together within the boundary. This is their fundamental charge as young people learning to navigate their world. And once these learning memories reach a satisfactory completion, children simply move on to the next activity. This approach helps children create an inner framework of experiences that will inform them in future interactions. They will more likely feel empowered to say "no" with firmness and gentleness when they don't feel comfortable with something, because they experienced repeated examples of how to say "no" without punishing, hurting, or shaming someone, and without feeling guilty about it.

The above are some ways that teachers deal with saying "no" in the RWB schools. In Susanne's Parenting Insights and in the Resource pages at the end of this book, you will find more in-depth information on setting limits at home.

TRY THIS
Create a weather station

A weather station is a great way to play scientist with your child and show them how to collect their own data instead of relying only on other sources. Your weather station can be on the balcony or in the yard. Offer a simple station for a younger child and one that's more complex for older children.

For younger children simply provide a bucket to measure rainfall, a flag to detect the wind direction, and a stick to trace the movement of the sun via the shadow. Put a drawing pad nearby to take simple notes or check a multiple-choice sheet, every day or once a week.

For older children, also provide thermometers, barometers, precise rain gauges, a windsock with compass, a wind vane, a sun dial, and the like. If your child loves this, they can document their observations independently in a weather observation book, perhaps a sketchpad, an unlined notebook, or a three-ring binder with blank pages. You can also provide and draw weather maps with your child and play weather forecast. Also offer weather books on cloud formations, winds, and precipitation, and perhaps poetry, songs, and even jokes about the weather:

☆ What happens when it rains cats and dogs? You might step in a poodle.

☆ What is a tornado's favorite game? Twister!

☆ Knock knock! Who's there? Lettuce. Lettuce who? Lettuce in, it's freezing outside!

FREEDOM WITHIN STRUCTURE
Safely fostering child-directed movement

THE MORE FREEDOM WE ALLOW, the more structure we need to provide; this includes upholding structure and order in the environment as well as providing healthy boundaries for children (as explained in Week 30). The better your home is prepared for child-directed activity, the more you can relax and allow your child to take the lead. Create an atmosphere where your child feels confident being an explorer and learner. This includes eliminating distractions while nurturing and enhancing the learner's spontaneous activities that lead to flow. Flow experiences where children visibly learn and thrive cannot be forced or rushed. They naturally happen when the time is right, and all we can do is continue to create suitable conditions. Below are some simple ways to create structure that allows more freedom:

Childproof each area.

Make sure each flow station is childproofed. Here are some suggestions: cover electricity outlets, take everything potentially dangerous out of reach (matches, medication, toxic cleaners), cover table corners and edges with edge guards (especially for toddlers learning to walk), and outdoors make sure the area is safe in all ways, ideally even safe for walking barefoot.

Select specific toys and learning materials.

Often less is more. It's easier for a child to focus when there are a few thoughtfully placed things that invite them to engage, instead of a lot of things that don't give a specific, direct invitation. For instance, instead of a big pile of puzzle and board game boxes, only leave a few select puzzles and games out at a time. You can choose them together with your child or make the decisions and curate the materials yourself ahead of time. In order to avoid accumulating piles of toys and cluttering the space, experiment with a one-in, one-out rule for toys in the storage space.

<u>Create simple systems for order.</u>

The simpler your system for order is, the more likely it will be used over time. Create *a home* for things, so you can say, "the crayons live here" and "the watercolors live there." Here are some ideas: Provide big, open boxes, or baskets for various toys, such as a box for blocks, a basket for stuffed animals, another basket for toy cars, and a box for Legos. Offer board games and instruments on separate open selves if possible. Boxes and trays can be labeled with words or images, so it is clear where things go.

<u>Provide structure in the space.</u>

Define play areas to prevent an activity from taking over the whole room or home. For instance, offer a nook for block building and another area for arts and crafts.

Indoor Spaces can be defined through..
— Area rugs and small portable rugs
— Table, chairs, shelves
— Moveable walls, curtains, moveable shelves, tables on wheels
— Naturally-defined spaces using the architecture of a room

Outdoor Spaces can be defined or enclosed through..
— Blankets on the ground
— Ropes on the ground
— Natural landmarks, such as trees

— Outdoor furniture, such as tables and benches

— Living fences, such as bushes

— Gardens with clear borders

— Elements on the ground, such as logs and rocks

Give mess a place.

When we allow children to explore and play, naturally there will be periods when it gets messy, and that's okay. It's part of the process. But don't let it get so out of hand that your own nervous system suffers. Think beforehand how much of a mess you can handle and empower yourself to stop a child's self-chosen course of action if it feels too much. You are the guardian of the home. Try to allow some messes to be okay during an activity and then you create order together with the children afterward. There may even be an area in your home where you don't mind a mess and where your child could leave a construction site of blocks, Legos, or other toys overnight or longer.

Provide a time structure.

If necessary, give your child a time structure and help them keep it by letting them know how much time for play is left. Hang a big clock on the wall and teach them how to read it. Give gentle reminders before time is over ("In 10 minutes, when you see this on the clock, it's clean up time," or "In 2 minutes it's clean up time.") and let them know what is next, such as transitioning to dinner. Older children may enjoy setting the timer themselves, as a way of taking responsibility and developing time-management skills. Most children will go through periods when they are unable to stop a flow activity. Gently help them transition out of their flow state as explored in Parenting Insight #8.

Be a flow companion.

Be close to your child and give suggestions, support and inspiration until they feel comfortable to go about their own activities.

"Reset" the flow stations regularly.

Each season, or whenever you notice children lose interest in one or all of the flow stations, create a clean slate and offer a new start in the environment. You can take "stale" toys, crafting supplies, and learning materials away, and add different ones. You can move some furniture or relocate flow stations. Many parents notice this gives children a boost of energy and a greater ability to self-start projects.

TRY THIS
Bonding while putting things back in order

Transform the task of putting things back in order (sometimes seen or felt as annoying) into a time for bonding with your child. Instead of, "You need to put things back after playing," offer assistance: "I see you've finished playing. May I help you to put things back in order?" This way, making order is not the dreaded thing to do after playing, but a way of reconnecting with the surrounding world after a timespan of focused activity. Ask, "How did you like this game?" or "What did you discover?" and receive important information on the inner world and progress of your child.

If your child would like to keep being in flow, even though it's time to put things away, try to understand their point of view and help them transition to dinner or bedtime or whatever is next by reassuring them: "It's okay to be upset about having to put the toys away now. The time to go to bed is in 10 minutes, so we will put the toys away together. I can help you put them away. I think I understand how you feel. It's okay to feel upset. You wanted to finish. I hear you."

Sometimes a child is too exhausted to help pick things up. You might say out loud, "I will pick these blocks up now because it's time to put them away. I would love it if you helped me!" but allow a child not to participate, trusting they will grow into the appreciation for picking up when they are ready. Power struggles around cleaning up rarely work for very long. Some parents choose to wait until the following day, when everyone is rested and feeling positive, picking up as a group before anything else is taken out and played with. Find what works for your family and develop a dependable routine around it.

You might invent a simple pick-up song that fits your family. Most children adore coming up with rhymes and songs. Susanne, parenting advisor for FLOW TO LEARN, was so kind to share their family's song:

"Picking it up to put it away, makes it more fun next time we play / When we pick up our toys for the day, tomorrow we play without delay!"

WEEK 30

THE FLOW ZONE RULES
Boundaries give safety

IMAGINE YOUR CHILD WALKING through a forest with no paths. At first it might be fun for them to go anywhere their mood and instincts take them, but after a while they'd find themselves in the midst of the unknown, not knowing where to turn next and how to get out of there. They would be confused, anxious, and scared. For a child this is how frightening it can be when everything is possible and there are no paths, railings, or boundaries to guide them.

Having too many choices overstimulates a child's nervous system. What's more, your home is not a free-for-all. You are the guardian of your home and that means you can create gentle and clear paths for your child to follow. Your child can choose which path to take and enjoy freedom within a framework safe for them, for you, and for your home.

Before you invite children to use a flow station, use the station yourself as intended. Notice whether everything necessary is there or whether you could remove unnecessary items. Decide which boundaries are needed to keep the supplies and children safe. The better a flow station is prepared, the less children will need you. For instance, using your makerspace (as explained in Week 27), try to craft a simple pencil holder from a paper roll and flat cardboard. To see this through from start to finish you might need: paper cores, cardboard, scissors, crayons, stapler, glue, decorative beads, stickers, inspirational crafting books, perhaps a real-life model, photos showing each step, or other materials you are inspired to use for the project. Do you find everything you need to finish? If something is missing, add it before children play there by themselves. Determine any requirements, limits, or special allowances your child should know about before using this flow station, such as wearing aprons or safely handling scissors. Each flow station is best introduced separately with its own possibilities, rules, and boundaries. Let children know that each activity has three stages:

☆ Preparing: Choose an activity and take things out.

☆ Working and playing: Play, work, craft, move, engage, and flow.

☆ Cleaning up: Put things back and, if you like, celebrate.

BASIC RULES OF A FLOW STATION

Some limits, such as the three rules mentioned below, need to be communicated before children play at a flow station. Introduce each child personally to these rules, and write them on a poster to hang next to the flow station. These rules are agreements you are asking each child to keep before they start playing. More agreements and variations on these agreements might emerge as children use a flow station.

1. Handle materials with care.

Show children precisely as many times as necessary how to handle each object, so that it doesn't break, and so no one gets hurt. For instance, show children how to handle scissors safely and how to play an instrument without breaking it. Stay nearby to verify the skills have been acquired and be prepared to review the rules calmly when accidents happen.

2. Help children focus on their self-chosen game.

Children can choose if they would like to play on their own or with others. If children want to play on their own, help them have the space they need to do that alongside others, or help them move to a station farther away if necessary. Often, the focus of flow requires individual space; often siblings need space from each other. As needed, explain to a child not to disrupt another's flow; instead, model and encourage asking if another child wants to play. If the response is "no," give emotional support to the asking child, who might perceive this as a personal rejection, which will not always happen; I have observed many interactions where the "rejected" child simply accepts a "no" and moves on to the next game.

3. Put things back in order after playing.

Include making order as part of the process from the very beginning. Take your time for this important, tricky part of the flow process. Of course, children want to go on to the next thing once an activity is finished. Creating order can become a pleasurable and satisfying habit that needs to be formed together with children over time. Games and songs are wonderful additions to this process. Rewards are discouraged, since this develops a replacement need of receiving external rewards after cleaning, which does not happen in the real world, as adults well know. The reward of order is a clean slate where a new game can begin again.

ADDITIONAL LIMITS YOU MIGHT NEED TO SET

Other limits you might discover only as children explore or test them, and then you can patiently set those limits whenever needed. If a child starts shooting rubber bands and playing table soccer in the makerspace, consider whether this is still okay for you or if you need to provide another, safer space for these games. Remember, redirecting energy is usually better than blocking it. For example, "I won't let you shoot rubber bands in the makerspace. But if you'd like to keep doing it, you may go outside and shoot them at the mud kitchen wall, but never at people or animals."

When multiple children are using a flow station, adult flow companions are often needed in order to maintain emotional safety for everyone. Make sure to intervene when a child is clearly talked into doing something they'd rather not. At a flow station, everyone can make their own choices, as long as those choices do not negatively impact others' physical and emotional safety. Be aware if a child is laughed at, ridiculed, teased, or startled by another child. It is okay to stand by when there is a conflict if it seems the group might be working it out respectfully. Be ready to step in and process the incident together with the children. Ask each child what happened, how they are feeling, and what they could do differently next time.

TRY THIS
Create a place for treasures

Create a place where children can keep their most treasured objects. Offer one or more appealing spaces where children can display their treasures. As we honor the items children love, as well as our own, we model gratitude and we show that we can give things personal meaning and value. There may be special things your child finds in nature, favorite books, photos of family members, meaningful items from your heritage, flowers, rocks, crystals, toys, photos, art works, pictures of animals, vacation memorabilia, figurines —in short, things that delight your child's heart.

Thriving During Transitions

The intensely positive emotions that come with being in complete command of one's actions, and the pure joy of being in a flow state, may create difficulty for children when they are interrupted and asked to transition to another activity. FLOW TO LEARN's parenting advisor Susanne reflects below on what she brings to these moments with her two children:

If my children aren't ready to stop playing when it's time to switch to another activity, I try to get a clear answer from them about when they can finish. Although hollering from another room is quite tempting, especially when I'm involved in my own activity, ideally, I will go to them, gently make eye contact, and let them know it's time to transition to what's happening next.

Working with Carmen, I have learned that a deep flow state feels like a different reality to a child. They can become so engrossed in flow that they might hear a voice, but it might seem far away, and they may not realize they're being asked for a response, even when the person asking is close by. I've often wished I could hear the inner workings of my son's flow state when I'm right next to him, speaking directly to him, but he doesn't hear me. I used to feel certain he was ignoring me in these moments. Now, I can clearly see that when this happens, he's aware of me and knows I am talking to him, but he appears to be "finishing his thought" deep inside his flow state before he's able to be present and ask me to repeat myself. To a parent who is unaware of this level of focus like I was, it might seem that a child is purposely disregarding them, which could be taken personally and lead to a frustrated parent.

Understanding this, when my children (five and three years old) are deeply in flow, I might get close to them, touch their backs or arms gently, and ask them calmly or in a fun way to make eye contact. A sing-song voice works wonders in this context, as it creates an inviting way for them to make the shift (I'm not always able to muster the sing-song voice, and that's okay too). Once we're all in the same world, I will offer the advance notice: "In 15 minutes we'll be cleaning up. Are you at a good stopping point? No? Okay, please find one soon. Would you like to set the timer?" When the timer rings, if they haven't finished (usually, no one has), I take a deep breath and remember their job is to push back, and that it's never personal.

Time and again it's been clear to me that how I'm feeling and the state of my own inner world are inextricably connected to my children's sense of safety (and thus, their behavior). If I approach a transition like this with the stress or worry from the day in the forefront of my mind, chances are it's going to affect how I interact with the kids, even if I do stay calm. I try not to take this on as additional pressure to be the perfect parent, but instead use it as a gentle reminder to check in with my own mood before interacting with the kids. I might breathe deeply and set my energy as squarely within a respectful parenting approach as I can. If I can't set the stress aside for a bit, I might ask for help.

I have also noticed that if I anticipate a tug-of-war over transitioning away from flow activities, I'm more likely to get pulled into that energy. On the other hand, when I take a few moments to ground myself as their confident leader, think of what I love about them, and interrupt as gently as possible, my job becomes easier. I'm better able to listen. I'm more able to express clearly and calmly the rules that must be followed in that moment, even if I think they should know the rules by now. I'm better able to speak quietly as I let them know there is no chance of negotiation and that I will help them move their bodies if they cannot do so.

Staying calm when it's loud and emotional is not easy for me, and I am so grateful for all the times I tried using the RIE (Resources for Infant Educarers) approach based on my faith in the evidence, without first seeing any proof that it would work for us. Even though I've been practicing RIE for many years now, I am still amazed by how the kids can go from full, soaring emotions one minute to truly contented and relaxed a short time later, when they feel safe, and when they feel seen. There may be tears, messes, and upset along the way. It will never be a perfect process or become miraculously effortless. But when I meet our kids where they are, with respect and support, honoring their world as important too, they can let go of the bliss of flow states and move into the next phase of the day within a space of emotional safety, and with their dignity intact.

WEEK 31

KEEP IT SIMPLE

Places for infants, toddlers, and children

CREATING FLOW-FRIENDLY PLACES is a process that will take some time. You don't need to offer *all* the various flow stations suggested in this book. Instead, choose the ones that you think your child will enjoy and that will work for you, your family, and your space. Keep it simple. There is no need for a big budget or major renovation. In fact, it's almost better not to spend a fortune so the pressure is off and it's not a big deal if something is unused or gets broken.

Be willing to experiment and adjust over time. Your child is growing, and will develop different needs and interests, so your flow stations need to grow with your child. Infants, babies, toddlers, and young children all need different types of flow stations, all with the same goal: to give them the opportunity drop into flow as often and for as long as they like.

Infants and babies are so vulnerable, and it's easy to consider them as wholly dependent upon their parents to provide everything for them, including mental stimulation. However, babies are truly self-learners by nature. They are born masters of flow. If we as adults try to entertain them, move their bodies for them, or repeatedly interrupt their flow state, we inadvertently stifle their natural abilities to build sophisticated networks of learning that last from early infancy into adulthood.

When these little people can move freely within an environment that's been set up for their success and safety, including appropriate risk-taking, then we can relax and trust them to discover on their own terms. This way, they develop a precise self-awareness of what they're capable of safely doing. This also provides very young children with the invaluable feeling of being trusted by the adults in their lives, creating an atmosphere of emotional safety for them at their earliest stages. See the Resources section of this book for many sources of in-depth information on how to support infants, babies, and toddlers in developing strong habits of safe, independent play.

A FLOW STATION FOR BABIES AND TODDLERS

As soon as children crawl and walk, they need bigger areas for movement in flow. Offer a protected floor space with stable, childproof furniture for them to hold on to as they move their bodies in the way they need to (babies know exactly what their bodies need to do next). Offer simple play objects such as nesting cups, felt shapes, or blocks. Provide safe obstacles such as firm pillows and wooden ramps low to the ground for practice with balancing, crawling, and navigating movement over different levels. Mount a mirror close to the floor so your child can become more aware of their body. The "yes" space of a flow station for babies and toddlers who are mobile should be enclosed so that the child cannot independently move to an area that is not childproof. In this 100% safe environment, babies and toddlers can develop long periods of discovery, immersion in their flow state, and exploration uninterrupted by an adult telling them "no." As with all flow stations for young people, the adult should remain nearby to ensure the children's genuine needs are met.

MANY FLOW STATIONS
FOR YOUNGER AND OLDER CHILDREN

Your preschoolers and school-aged children benefit from additional and larger flow stations. Yet, all you really need is some empty floor space, a child-sized table, chairs, and accessible shelving that can hold an endless combination of age-appropriate supplies. Such a place can be used for all kinds of flow-friendly activities. In addition to this basic flow space, you can offer all or some of the flow stations suggested in this book. Be sure to take your child outside of the home as well, to playgrounds and nature spaces. Ideally, you can find an accessible play-based school that offers additional play, stimulating materials, and movement areas. Your child might love to help with the set-up of their flow stations. Setting up environments together can be a wonderful bonding experience, allowing everyone to feel more involved and connected to the space they helped create.

TRY THIS
Create a water play station

A water play station can be indoors in the bathroom or, ideally, in a shaded spot outdoors. If the water station is set up inside, be sure you set children up for success by ensuring they can't accidentally ruin the area by spilling water where you don't want it to go. A simple station may include a low bucket on the floor with containers of various shapes and sizes for filling, emptying, and pouring back and forth. You might add containers with water tinted with natural food coloring, so your child can mix colors. For older children, add measuring containers and tools such as pipettes, funnels, tubes, and waterwheels. Your child might also craft boats for a bucket-lake or experiment with items you provide in order to see what sinks and what floats.

OPPORTUNITIES TO EXPERIMENT
Activities perfect for flow experiences

ALMOST ALL WHOLE-BODY MOVEMENTS and hands-on activities can lead to flow experiences. All activities that give direct, real-time feedback, when each step naturally flows into the next step, are suitable for alert, deep focus. Children are experts at experimenting with how their bodies move, work, balance, feel, and perform in different environments and will explore these interactions repeatedly, internalizing the results, when given the opportunity.

It's understandable when we adults perceive that certain skills like playing an instrument, learning a sport, or mastering a craft are more valuable than, say, a child perfecting walking across a tree trunk on the ground without falling off or carefully balancing a stack of beach stones. However, playful experimentation like this is ideal for fanning the flames of a child's interest in any skillset. Their experiences "practicing how to practice" are essential for helping children develop the self-discipline required in any field of study.

Before signing a child up for an expensive class or purchasing a precious instrument, find ways to allow them to experiment with what will be taught. You can ask a teacher or workshop organizer if your child may try one class before you make a longer commitment. Many music schools offer trial lessons, which could allow your child to experience the material. Perhaps you have a friend, familiar with the material or the instrument in question, who would allow your child to get to know it to see if they could imagine spending a lot of time pursuing that particular instrument.

Self-discipline comes much more easily if a child really likes the activity. Introduce each activity playfully, without any pressure for succeeding or getting it right. For example, playfully shoot some hoops with a child over an extended period of time before encouraging them to join a basketball team. Tinker on the piano or work with clay just for fun several times before signing them up for music or art lessons. Before getting a dog, allow your child to experience playing properly with a neighbor's or friend's trusted dog (always review with a child the correct and incorrect ways for them to interact with pets, even if the pets are friendly, as certain actions may be interpreted by an animal as aggressive when they are not meant to be). Once the dog is comfortable around them, they might be encouraged to help with feeding and cleaning up after the dog, so they understand the responsibilities they would be signing up for.

Like all of us, children do not know what they like and what they can handle before they experience it at least a little bit for themselves. Even after these initial experiences, allow them to change their mind. If you see your child is becoming unhappy with an activity or a class, you may ask open-ended questions, allow them to take a break, go more slowly, or do the same activity in a more playful way. Ideally, children's flow activities have the following characteristics:

— Involve the whole body or at least the hands.
— Connect the inner world with an activity. For instance, measuring exactly 6 inches on a wood block while feeling the cold of the metal ruler and the warmth of the wood.
— Provide hands-on intrinsic error feedback. For instance, it fits, or it doesn't fit; it holds up, or it doesn't; it's the right result, or it's not.
— Connect to tangible items through a symbolic link such as an agreement that a blue bead is worth 10 units and a red bead is worth 100 units (as used in Montessori math materials).

IDEAS FOR FLOW LEARNING MATERIALS AND ACTIVITIES

☆ Open-ended materials and crafting materials such as cardboard, scissors, buttons, ribbons, feathers, and crayons.

☆ Clay work with kids' modeling clay that you can purchase, or natural earth clay purchased or collected in nature.

☆ Woodwork on a wooden bench, or simply tinkering with a few boards, nails and hammer.

☆ Needlework such as sewing, knitting, or crocheting.

☆ Block play with pretend play materials to create miniature landscapes

☆ Drums, sound-makers, homemade instruments, Orff instruments, and child-size musical instruments.

☆ Food preparation, including measuring, weighing, chopping, stirring.

☆ Gardening, including sowing, planting, watering, measuring growth, and harvesting vegetables, fruit, nuts, seeds, and flowers.

☆ Play with natural elements, such as mud, sand, and water.

☆ Montessori and other hands-on learning materials.

☆ Board games such as chess, Scrabble, and Connect 4.

☆ Science activities, such as simple chemistry and physics experiments (you can find plenty online), naming plants and animals, creating a weather observation station as suggested in Week 28.

☆ Language-based activities, such as reading, writing, singing, poetry, rhymes, listening to stories, storytelling with or without puppets.

☆ Time with a pet (with younger children, this should be adult supervised to ensure the safety of the child and the pet).

☆ All movement (non-competitive, at least initially) such as dance, gymnastics, ball play, balancing, and climbing.

☆ Movement-based kids' games such as hide and seek, and Simon Says.

☆ Long-distance walking, such as a distance that is usually driven in the car, in order to learn about time and distance.

☆ Purpose-filled activities such as stacking wood or gathering sticks for kindling, pulling weeds, raking leaves, or hanging laundry on a clothesline outside or an indoor drying rack.

☆ Toys that deeply engage both sides of the brain, such as puzzles, kaleidoscopes, mazes, labyrinths, modular marble tracks, and the like.

TRY THIS

What were your favorite childhood activities?

Remember your own childhood and create a list of the pastimes, games, and activities you held dear. There are so many classic childhood games that children love; many are being forgotten around the world and replaced by screens. Think of ball games, running games, games with props like jump ropes, tin cans, or string, pretend play, songs, rhymes, and toys from your childhood that you could share with your child. If you can't remember them all, find printed or online collections of traditional games and activities to look through with your child—you might find some new ones you can all enjoy playing together!

WEEK 33

SYSTEMS THINKING IN YOUR HOME
Go for gentle impact

THINK OF YOUR HOME AS A SENSITIVE system. Be aware that all members of your household are connected in many complex ways and form a unit. Everyone has habits, preferences, and needs. A change in the environment may affect other members in your household. Before you introduce new flow stations for your child, make sure everyone is on board and no one's space is being infringed upon. Talk about your plans with all who use the space and find what works for all. Nothing you do is set in stone. You can always respond to feedback, share brainstorming sessions, and rearrange flow stations.

Be aware that flow is not a given. Flow needs to be invited, cultivated, and celebrated—otherwise even children forget about it. Human beings are easily distracted, especially when there is a screen or a smart phone nearby, and children are extra sensitive to these distractions. You can help your child find their flow by setting the tone for deep, focused activities in your home.

As a parent and flow companion, you are the guardian of your home environment. You can give purpose to each room, floor, and outdoor space—of course, also designate places for adult purposes only, such as an office. You can create different kinds of atmospheres in different areas, some suitable for quiet activities and individual creativity, and some more suited for movement, collaboration, and louder play.

It's possible to integrate flow stations into the rooms that everyone in the family shares, such as the living room, the kitchen, the bathroom, and outdoor areas. In addition or instead, dedicate a single room or several rooms to your child's flow activities. There is no need to let your child's play take over the whole house. It's essential that you as a single parent, or you and your partner and all other family members also have the personal zones you all need. In a well-prepared environment, with consistent, clear, and gentle communication, children and adults can do flow activities side by side.

The way you set up flow stations and the way you move within these environments strongly affect your child. Include your child in the setup process, ask them if, how, and where they would like to have a flow station. If their answers are not practical or otherwise will not work for the space in question, discuss this matter-of-factly and with compassion, perhaps offering options that provide a similar station that works for everyone. Below are some additional suggestions to help you set the tone for flow.

Setting the tone for quiet activities:
— Remove everything that creates unwanted clutter or noise.
— Choose the time for quiet wisely, for example, while an infant sibling naps or an older child is at school.
— Avoid calling across the room, instead walk over and speak in a quiet voice while making eye contact.
— If you don't want your child to run in a room, put furniture in the way; wide-open, empty spaces are an irresistible invitation for children to run.

Setting the tone for collaboration and being in flow side by side:
— Place a child-size and an adult-size table and chairs side by side.
— Provide large, comfortable seating areas around a childproof coffee table.

Setting the tone for pretend play and movement:
— Create a large empty space for your child to run and move freely.
— Assure your child that here it's okay to move and be loud.

TRY THIS
Puzzles for everyone

A simple puzzle station can be fun for older children and adults alike. Puzzles give our minds food for thinking and our hands practice with fine motor skills. Solving puzzles can be a great way for practicing flow. Dedicate a big table to a jigsaw puzzle that can be solved over several days where everyone can work on it. Over time, you can rotate various kinds of puzzles, brainteasers, and interesting toys that can be solved by whomever is in the mood. You can offer crossword puzzles, riddles, math problems, Sudoku, Rubik's Cubes, kaleidoscopes, tangram, Montessori materials, spinning tops, stacking and sorting toys, dominoes, mazes, Russian dolls, mosaic tile toys, and whatever else you and your children find inspiring.

If there are very young children in the home, classroom, or other space, these will most likely need to be put out of reach at times. Large baking or breakfast trays, totes, or other storage options that can contain a game or activity that is in progress will help older children more easily cope with the idea that their project is unavailable for a time. This mobility also allows for a pause in the activity with the ability to pick it back up later, after lunch, a nap, outside time, or other interruptions.

You can kindle curiosity through the environment by adding a puzzling element and see if your child will notice; for example, lay out a puzzle that is obviously wrongly assembled or bring an unknown object into the environment, such as a tape recorder...yes, a tape recorder!

WEEK 34

SIZING UP YOUR SPACE
Look through your child's eyes

IMAGINE BEING YOUR CHILD in your home. Take a close look and consider where you could create some flow stations. Get down to your child's height and let your eyes wander around the rooms. What do you see from this perspective? How does it feel to be at your child's height? Which are the places you are drawn to?

<u>Walk through your home with the below questions in mind.</u>
Which areas are suitable for play and flow? Is there space and furniture you could use as is, or could you create additional or more inviting spaces by moving, removing or adding furniture? Consider the following possible elements: a whole room, corners, shelves, table and chairs, a floor area defined by a rug, or a work bench.

<u>Assign purpose and function to each area.</u>
Try to find places for:
— Sitting at a table for a hands-on activity
— Play on the floor with puzzles, blocks, cars, dolls etc.
— Being comfy cozy to rest, read, and contemplate
— Louder indoor play with more movement involved
— Things to get a bit messy, or really messy
— Outdoor movement, balancing, climbing
— Ball play and other sports

<u>Draft a layout.</u>

Draw a simple sketch of your home that shows the essential elements as they are currently and play around with adding new elements you choose. Consider making copies or laminating the page to try out options you can erase over and over. Here is an example draft of an apartment layout with added elements for flow stations:

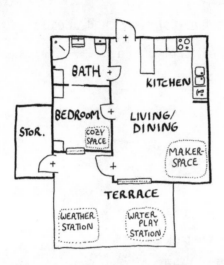

MANY IDEAS FOR FLOW STATIONS

Below you will find more ideas for flow stations. You might come up with additional ones or do an internet search for play spaces. Use the basic principles of FLOW TO LEARN to prepare all flow stations safely and effectively. The possibilities are endless.

<u>Indoors</u>

☆ Floor space for block and pretend play

☆ Table for a makerspace

☆ A clay/ molding dough station

☆ Sensory exploration space

☆ Table for a puzzle station

☆ Nature science table

☆ Table or floor space for board games

☆ Dress-up and role-play for several children

☆ Floor space for movement, rough-and-tumble

☆ A place for instruments and sound-makers

☆ Sand table for sensory and healing play

Outdoors (balcony, porch, yard, playground, or park)

☆ Sandbox with a variety of containers

☆ Water play station

☆ Weather station

☆ Potting station

☆ Mud kitchen

☆ Trampoline

☆ Bike-riding

☆ Space for ball play

☆ Nature play areas in park

☆ Outdoor adventure play

TRY THIS
Arrange a nature science table

Naturalistic intelligence, the ability to find patterns and relationships in nature, was identified as one of the nine intelligences by Professor Howard Gardner (refer to Week 8). His ideas lead us away from the notion that intelligence can be measured only with traditional IQ tests that mostly measure only analytical and logical-mathematical intelligence.

A simple nature science table can offer a space for specimens your child collects from nature and reference books to identify them. With younger children, you can collect leaves, flowers, and seeds on a nature walk, arrange or display them at home, and look them up in encyclopedias. You can match up (store-bought) crystals and rocks with their entries in books to find out about them. Your nature science table can change with the seasons and display typical items for each period of the year, such as seasonal fruits, herbs, spices, vegetables, and other plants.

For older children, you could also add a monthly calendar, moon phase calendar, geographical and geological maps, a globe, and informational materials on the planets and their movement. You can offer a flower press, magnifying glass, binoculars, a microscope, or a telescope.

Another nature table activity is to plant seeds in a glass container, so the growing roots can be seen as you observe or document their growth over time. If you would like to incorporate screens, there are apps that identify plants, insects, bird songs, and star formations. Anything that might excite the spirit of a nature scientist in your child (and yourself) is suitable. The natural world offers endless avenues for exploration, so you are unlikely to run out of options.

OCTOBER

WEEK 35

INDEPENDENCE = DIGNITY
Design your space to meet genuine needs

YOU CAN HELP CHILDREN LEARN to meet many of their own needs by preparing environments where they can independently find what they need. When you arrange a flow station, make sure your child finds all the necessary tools for the proposed activities. If appropriate, provide an introduction, and model for them how to use this flow station. Show them everything they might need. For instance, clay work needs a table, a chair, a tray with clay, a bowl of water, shaping tools, an apron, and clean up materials. Set them up for an independent experience, so they don't have to go find you to continue their work.

Helping your child maintain a sense of dignity builds the foundation for self-respect and respect towards others. Treating each other with dignity elevates our human interactions and makes everything more pleasurable because it brings about a sense of safety and belonging. Though acting with dignity might bring royalty to mind, dignified behavior doesn't need to be formal at all. Dignity is preserved through being kind and generous to one another, to allow each other basic freedoms, authenticity, and consent. A big part of protecting a child's sense of dignity consists of enabling them to meet their own needs. Here are some elements that allow children to meet physical needs independently:

Designate a place for water.

Have drinking water available always in the same visible, accessible place.

Choose a place for a snacking tray.

Provide simple healthy snacks, such as fresh fruits and veggies, without your child having to ask for them.

Practice independent access to the restroom.

For very young children, you may provide portable child potties close to flow stations, inside or outside, to encourage children's initiative to use the potty more frequently and as the need arises. Your child will learn how to use the restroom independently over time, and you can encourage that by making it easy for them to go on their own.

Provide access to body care essentials.

Patiently teach your child how to take care of their body. Give them chances to "do it by myself," knowing that the occasional evening of imperfectly cleaned teeth is well worth a child's interest in brushing their teeth and desire to continue learning that skill. Songs and games that children can incorporate into their practice help make the activity fun and memorable.

Provide access to clothes.

Help your child learn to get dressed and change their clothes independently; have a drawer with a few clothes, socks, etc., accessible at all times. On days when it's possible, allow them to pick out their clothes on their own, ensure there is plenty of time for the process, and then honor their choices, even if they seem silly or inappropriate for the weather.

Design sleeping and resting areas.

Offer a very low bed, even a mattress on the floor, so your child can get in and out of bed independently. If that is not possible, consider putting a sturdy, safe step or other aid for them to use to easily get into and out of bed.

TRY THIS
Prepare a sensory play station

Sensory play stations offer activities that help children refine their senses. These include the five senses of sight, sound, taste, touch, and smell, as well as our ability to balance, sense weight, and notice temperature. Here's an idea for a big, fun sensory play station: On a protected floor, or on the ground outside, offer a series of trays or buckets with a variety of contents inside, into which children can step barefoot. One bucket might contain flower petals, the next one rounded pebbles or dry beans, the next one fine sand, the next one velvet fabric, the next one paper balls, and so on. You can use the same concept with shallow totes on a table, welcoming children to insert their hands into the sensory-stimulating contents. You can do the same game blindfolded.

Meeting Children's Physical Needs

Learning to meet their physical needs independently is crucial for children's well-being in flow states and beyond. Susanne, FLOW TO LEARN's parenting advisor, shares how she helps her children become more aware of those needs when they are deeply focused in play:

Seeing or hearing my children in flow is one of the best feelings I experience as a mom, so I've avoided needlessly interrupting their flow states since they were infants. However, sometimes they're so deeply engaged, they forget about their physical needs. This is a juggling act we all try to master as parents: ensuring our children's physical needs are met, supporting them to make their own decisions, not bombarding them with reminders, and staying positive through the mistakes of their learning process.

How does this work for us in practice? Usually my son (five) and daughter (three) can freely access snacks and water to satisfy their hunger and thirst on their own. However, if I see the time of day and know that snacking will interfere with their ability to eat at mealtime, snacking ceases to be an option, and I let them know we'll be eating soon. Or, if I notice it's time for a bathroom break, I might say, "Time for a potty check!" or "Do you need to take a bathroom break?" If their answer is "no," often they'll go to the bathroom on their own a few minutes later. This way, they maintain their body autonomy and also get a cue from me that might help them notice their physical needs (before it becomes an emergency). Over time, their awareness has increased, and they've needed less support.

Some days, however, a physical need that my child has long since mastered becomes impossible for them to manage while in flow. This used to catch me totally off guard, because I would get accustomed to that skill being "checked off the list" of things I needed to be watching for. I tried harder to be more flexible and accommodating. Yet I found myself on edge, unable to grasp the reasons behind the unpredictability. My aha moment came while reading an article by parenting expert Maggie Dent of Australia, in which she discusses children's "energy cup" and how subtle signs of a child's energy levels can look very different from one child to the next. As a parent of two children who could not be more different from one another, this helped me look more closely and see how each of them responds to feeling unbalanced in their energy levels. Now, I feel naturally more supportive when my kids can't handle meeting or communicating their own physical needs in flow.

For example, my extroverted daughter often responds to overstimulation by ramping up her energy and getting ever sillier. If she appears to have tons of energy after school, I could easily assume it's normal and that she'll burn it off through playing. Upon observing more carefully, however, I might notice that instead of simply needing to release what's pent up, she is wired and tired simultaneously. This means she'll be more likely to have trouble processing a physical need that arises when she's deeply engaged in flow. Equipped with this knowledge, I can be more sensitive to helping her without hesitation and without the fear that I'm "babying" her. If she says she's thirsty and her water bottle is empty, instead of encouraging her to fill it herself like she normally does, I'll simply help her do it. This gives her a feeling of comfort and relief that I see she needs extra support, and I offer it to her, no questions asked.

My son's personality is more introspective, so when I see him staring into space on the way home from a playdate, I naturally assume he's contentedly lost in thought. Looking closer, however, I might recognize signs that he's quite drained. If I don't have time to connect one on one with him right away, I know playing in flow is the best place for him to recharge as much as he can. While he's happily in that deep, focused flow, I might observe that he looks flushed and way too hot, with too many layers on. When asked if I can help him take some off, he'll probably nod, and that's the extent of his extra energy beyond what he's using for play. Clearly, the benefits of his time spent in flow far outweigh the value of my reminding him that he's fully capable of taking off his own sweatshirt. I know he can do it, because normally, he does! This shows him I'm paying attention to his needs, even if he can't explain himself in that moment. Soon my children will be capable of meeting their own physical needs in flow, and everywhere else. In the meantime, I'm grateful for all the tools that help me make their learning process as empowered and supported as possible, so they feel fully accepted right where they are.

WEEK 36

OFFER OUTDOOR ADVENTURE PLAY
Balance between protection and safe risk

MANY CHILDREN THRIVE when they can be outdoors moving in flow, just as their heart desires. Children need to move their whole body; to feel their muscles, physical ability, and the freedom of taking responsibility for their own movements. The small risks involved in climbing a tree, balancing on a log, or stacking big branches are exhilarating to a child's spirit. Outdoor adventure play is deeply fulfilling and connects children to nature.

Minor injuries, such as scratches on their knees or light bruises from falling, help children refine their gross motor skills and learn to see and evaluate risks. Children are very unlikely to be hurt during self-guided play, especially when flow companions keep an eye out for them daring each other to do things they are not ready for. Most children understand, and are guided by, their own capacities and limitations. They know exactly when they are ready to take a risk. If you notice a child is too dare-devilish, help them assess an activity for safety before they start to play. Ask open-ended questions ("What do you notice about this piece of wood?") and offer pointed observations about the potential dangers and possible consequences of a risk ("Have you noticed these scissors are very sharp?"). Of course, preventing a serious accident or injury is always appropriate.

If a child continuously hurts themselves or others, take a closer look: Is this child insensitive to pain? Does this child have adequate physical function regarding sight, hearing, and balancing?

Outdoor adventure play has the power to help children who have behavioral issues inside classrooms made for sitting. There are many anecdotes of strong, highly intelligent children (almost all boys) who transferred to RWB schools because they were disruptive in standardized classrooms. All these children were allowed to play as much as they wanted at the RWB grade schools. Without exception, they chose gross-motor activities such as digging deep holes in the ground, building wooden structures, and moving heavy objects. All of them made friends with adults and peers and developed outstanding social skills. One of these boys (who was my student) is now age 24 and running his own successful tree removal service, still thriving in his self-chosen environment where he can climb tall trees.

You can offer outdoor adventure play in parks that allow children to go off trails. Or, you can create a small *adventure playground* in your backyard. Adventure playgrounds are supervised areas created for risky play. They offer things such as dirt piles, boards, paints, tools, zip lines, and uneven climbing structures. You might initiate the creation of an adventure playground in your neighborhood. There are good examples that can be seen on the internet from around the U.S. and the world, using different approaches and materials.

If a child has a habit of relying on external feedback for whether their choices are safe, they may need additional supervision during the transition from looking externally for what to do next, to knowing what they are capable of physically. For example, if an adult holds a child's hand at all times to prevent falling as they learn to walk, that child may develop a false inner sense of safety and try stepping down stairs versus cautiously crawling down backwards one stair at a time. Or, it could cause them to be too afraid to try anything without holding onto an adult's hand or a prop like a walker. If this is the case, the child should be supervised while they recalibrate their instincts to the reality of what their body is capable of.

Open-ended questions help children reconnect with these instincts, for example, "You climbed up onto the wall and now you're up high—what is your plan for getting back down safely?" Below are some elements to keep in mind when offering adventure play.

Inspect the area before play.

Before you offer any play space to children, inspect the area thoroughly to see if it is a suitable place. Remove anything that is obviously harmful such as broken glass, litter, and rotten branches on a climbable tree.

Provide protection.

Children should never be left all to themselves over longer periods of time. Sometimes a child may get overly scared or need to check in with an adult about their choice. Just in case, always be available. This will make sure a child feels protected.

Allow group role-play in nature and remain close-by.

Children may spontaneously start role-playing in nature. During their role-play and physical play, they may experience intense energy and adrenal highs when they play games such as pretend fleeing from a hunter, hiding from a bear, looking for a secret cave, or pretend attacking another group of children. This is healthy play as long as each child knows they are pretending within a protected space, and that they can stop anytime (Refer to Week 23).

TRY THIS
Protect children from damaging influences

Naturally, parents want to protect their children from harm. However, risky outdoor play is not at all a real danger compared to other damaging influences in our culture. Children desperately need our protection in this world, but not from risky outdoor play, once their innate risk assessment has been reestablished through experimentation. What children are not equipped to weather is the onslaught of damaging influences that have become normal in our physical and digital environments. Here are some modern dangers to mental and physical health from which children need our protection:

— Screen addiction and information overload
— R-rated movies, shows, and computer games
— Cyber-bullying and bullying
— Abusive adults
— Junk food and sugar
— Consumerism
— Unrealistic beauty standards
— Overfull schedules with little to no "down time"
— Too early or unhealthy academic pressures

Helping Children Keep Themselves Safe

Susanne, parenting advisor for FLOW TO LEARN shares about her journey to trust her children as they learn to use risky items:

The idea of allowing children to take appropriate risks (for example, a toddler using scissors) might be foreign to parents and other adults. Yet many parents and teachers realize that we do children a great service by allowing them to safely learn how to handle potentially risky objects. It's a good idea to avoid leaving a child alone with a risky item until you're confident they've learned to use it carefully.

If you see a child handling an object in an unsafe way, try to stay matter of fact and even positive, when possible. Get close to the child, try to make eye contact (For example, "May I see your eyes, please?"), and state clearly or do what's necessary for everyone to stay safe. With a one-year-old I might use language from the RIE approach such as, "You're hitting the table with the ceramic bowl. That could break the bowl, so I'm going to take it for now." I welcome any emotional reaction with empathy and steady leadership without wavering on the boundary. The child may have big feelings that I validate, for instance, "You really wanted to keep using the bowl."

This response changes as toddlers grow into children. As my children have grown older, I've learned to check in with them (verbally or non-verbally) without saying "be careful." This well-meaning, common phrase often adds fear without offering guidance and interrupts a child's focus. Open-ended questions, such as "Have you noticed how slick the moss made those rocks?" help children better develop their awareness of how to manage possible danger.

My son (five years old) and daughter (three years old) showed me they were more aware of risks than I imagined when they played with straight pins at an early age, sorting them into colors or sticking them into the carpet in creative patterns while I worked nearby. I would gauge their choices unobtrusively and speak up when a line was crossed, for example, "I don't want you to stick pins into the mattress, please." Incredibly, they always respected my limits in this context! They loved the added feeling of risk, the responsibility of handling adult tools, and knowing their parent trusted them to play safely with a sharp object.

Still, it can be a challenge for me to let go of the instinct to control their choices from a place of concern. One of my consistent sources of encouragement to trust my kids comes from Teacher Tom, an expert in early childcare based in Seattle, Washington. A well-known teacher, blogger, and artist, he has spent nearly 20 years as the preschool teacher for the Woodland Park Cooperative. In his blog entry "Fifty Dangerous Things," in which he references Gever Tulley's important book Fifty Dangerous Things (You Should Let Your Children Do)*, Teacher Tom offers guidance that calms my overly vigilant leanings: "At some point, if a child is going to ever learn to drive a nail, he will hit his own thumb. That's how everyone learns to use a hammer and it's going to hurt no matter when we do it. One could argue, in fact, that young children with their low to the ground bodies, flexible bones, quicker healing times, and shorter memories are designed by nature to learn exactly these lessons now, rather than later when falls are from a greater height, bones are easier to break, wounds slower to mend, and emotional recovery time longer."*

Of course, adults shouldn't challenge children to take risks or try to influence them into "being brave" if they haven't already decided to try something on their own. Simply watching the process and being ready to step in if they ask for help is enough. For example, during a visit with extended family my daughter, then two years old, climbed onto a chair and stood up. Upon seeing her do this, many of the adults instinctively lunged toward her. "I think she's okay," I said, asking them to wait. I then checked in directly with my daughter, who was holding on and beaming with satisfaction. "You climbed onto the chair. Do you feel safe?" She smiled and nodded emphatically. The other adults still seemed concerned for her safety, but soon everyone accepted this radical act of trust. When she was ready to do so, my daughter climbed down and ran off to play somewhere else. This may be an incremental journey for many parents who are understandably afraid for the safety of their children. Though the idea of supporting them in taking risks may be a scary leap of faith, my direct experience and that of countless other parents, teachers, experts, and caregivers recommends that we take this leap on behalf of the children we care for. Children, like all people, will consistently rise to our expectations! I have learned that through trusting my children and helping them process their missteps without lecturing, I actually worry less, because I know that their intuitive sense of what they can safely do is strong. I know it will stand them in good stead as they take exciting risks throughout their childhoods and beyond.

WEEK 37

EXPAND YOUR VISION OF TOYS
Through the eyes of a child-centered teacher

WHEN PLAY IS RECOGNIZED as a child's main way of learning, instead of being seen as simply amusement or a way for children to occupy themselves, then all play objects become valuable learning materials. Through the eyes of a child-centered teacher, everything a child explores with hands, body, and senses has educational value. Learning materials include traditional toys such as blocks, pretend cars, dolls and board games; modern toys such as Lego sets, magnetic tiles, and brain teasers; tools from the household, garden, and woodshop such as scales, shovels, screwdrivers; as well as materials made to teach specific concepts, such as the Montessori math materials.

Child-centered teachers, who give priority to the needs and interests of a child, create learning materials from everyday items such as egg cartons, napkins, and measuring cups. For instance, Maria Montessori developed a series of exercises with everyday items like tweezers, pipettes, and pouring containers (the "practical life materials") that prepare a child's hand for holding pens and pencils.

Let children know that some materials are more expensive and rare than others, and some are available in abundance. Point out materials that children can use however they wish (unstructured and open-ended) such as the materials in the makerspace (Week 27), and spend more time introducing materials that need to be handled in certain ways, such as board games, breakable items, or toys with small pieces.

IDEAS FOR TOYS AND OTHER LEARNING MATERIALS

Unstructured, open-ended materials: Art and craft supplies (as described in Week 27), all kinds of building blocks auch as Kapla, Wedgits, Lincoln Logs, DIY milk carton blocks, marble runs, magnetic tiles.

Circus equipment: Juggling toys, diabolos, hula hoops, silks, yo-yos, poi, staffs, unicycles, and balls.

Transformed daily life items: A tray with tweezers (unless they are blunt or wooden, these can be accompanied by an adult for younger children) arranged to pick up and sort colorful beads; a tray with a peeler and carrots, an orange squeezer and oranges, scales and various items to weigh, or bowls of tea or rice to pour; cardboard boxes, clothespins, ice cream sticks, and bottle caps as crafting supplies and building toys; a chocolate box or egg carton turned into a sorting tray; a shoebox as a dollhouse; and glass jars as scientific tasting jars with salt water, sugar water, and rose water (often seen in Montessori and Reggio Emilia classrooms).

Learning materials for babies and toddlers: Chewing toys (avoid soft plastic other than food-grade silicone), squeezing toys, wooden spoons, stuffed animals made of natural fibers, balls, rattles, big puzzles, stacking and sorting materials, and stainless steel bowls.

Board games: Chess, Mastermind, Reversi, Halma, Scrabble, Tangram, Risk, Mancala, Go, Backgammon, and Mill. You might also offer some of the new cooperative board games such as Stone Soup, A Beautiful Place, Amazing Illusions, Aunty Ruth's Apples, and Hugs and Tickles.

Pretend play materials: Dolls, doll houses, toy cars, (Schleich or other non-toxic) animal figurines, Waldorf dolls and felted toys, dress-up clothes and mirrors, big cardboard boxes to sit inside and play airplane, truck, and ship, a table, chairs and some props to play grocery store, post office, school, and the like.

Montessori materials: Montessori math materials allow children to playfully learn the complete elementary math curriculum. Through working with these hands-on materials, math becomes a practical tool, connecting multiple parts of the brain (instead of an abstract mind game on paper). Check out the following Montessori materials:

☆ **Golden beads:** A visual, touchable representation of the decimal system, the golden beads allow children to develop a firm understanding of quantities (1,10,100, and 1000 bead-units) and place value.

☆ **Stamp game:** As the next logical material after the golden beads, the stamp game represents the decimal system in a more abstract way: 1 is a green stamp, 10 is a blue stamp, 100 is a red stamp, and so on. Perfect for deepening addition, subtraction, division, and multiplication.

☆ **Multiplication beads:** Created to play with numerical patterns and to easily memorize the multiplication tables.

☆ **Square root board:** A wooden board with holes for beads that allows children to easily understand the patterns of growing squares and their square roots.

☆ **Bead frame:** An abacus that allows children to add, subtract, and multiply with numbers up to millions.

☆ **Fraction materials:** Circles and other geometric shapes divided into equal parts give children a hands-on experience of fractions.

TRY THIS
Prepare a potting station and mud kitchen

A simple, wooden, child-size table in the yard can easily become a potting station or a mud kitchen when needed. Offer clean potting soil (100% free of chemical additives), seeds and seedlings, pots, seedling containers, and a small watering can. Together with your child plant some seeds and watch them grow. At other times, allow your child to freely play in the mud kitchen. Offer a variety of containers, maybe even an outdoor enamelware tea set, pots and pans, a water bucket, and sand. Many young children have a blast in this environment and drop into flow while baking a mud pie and serving flower petals tea.

WEEK 38

WHERE DO THE CHILDREN PLAY?
Finding play space in an adult's world

CURRENTLY, THERE ARE FEW ENVIRONMENTS in our cities and suburbs where children's genuine needs can be easily fulfilled. Looking around, most children are constantly in settings made for adults: chairs too tall, food out of reach, and little space to run and play freely apart from playgrounds. Stores, offices, public transport, restaurants — all of these spaces are based on the needs of grown-ups. Even schools are mostly based on our adult needs for children to be a certain way, not on a child's natural way of being.

In adult-based environments, where there is nothing for a child to engage with, children are constantly trying to find an activity that is acceptable. They try this and that, participating in the adults' conversations (often in spite of admonishments not to interrupt) or playing with the salt and pepper shakers on the table. Often, nothing children do seems to be welcome, unless they are being quiet and still while adults go about their activities. It's common for adults to offer them a phone or tablet to occupy their attention. Although this may result in short-term gratification, the child's genuine needs have not been met. Flow stations give children a place to be and keep themselves busy with activities that are in alignment with their developmental needs.

Fortunately, some businesses and public places offer kids' corners, so children can feel welcome. Sometimes we see small chairs, toys, and books at hairdressers and in waiting rooms. Restaurants might provide coloring paper and crayons. My advice is to reduce as much as we can the time children spend in purely adult-based environments. If such an environment is unavoidable, remain bonded with your child during that time and smile reassuringly at them often. Bring play objects from home that can be easily accessed, and gathered back up quickly. Use these to create a little space, a temporary flow station, where your child can find an activity. Here are some suggestions for being out and about with children:

Prepare a ready-to-go flow bag.

It's wonderful that many parents already do this. When they leave home, they bring a "flow bag," a backpack or tote with little toys, books, stuffed animals, portable puzzles, and other comforting items for their child. Many parents also add snacks, water bottles, and additional clothes. Wherever you go, a flow bag can help to create a more pleasurable experience for your child, and for you.

Create a tiny, temporary flow station at the restaurant table.

Bring paper and crayons, drawing books, portable puzzles such as magnetic jigsaw puzzles or other easily transportable play objects.

Get creative to include your child in grocery shopping.

If you need to take your child to the supermarket, if possible, give your child (depending on their age) a small amount of money, perhaps a few dollars, and let them choose an item in that price range. If you don't have much time and need the child to ride in a cart, engage them in the process by asking for their help holding onto non-breakable grocery items, and helping place the items on the counter during checkout.

Prepare for car rides.

To make car rides easier, have books, portable puzzles, and soft toys ready in your car. Listen to a sing-along or story. Bring a pillow, a cozy comforter, a stuffed friend, and a water bottle.

TRY THIS
A place for instruments and sound-makers

Music is part of our innate drive for self-expression and doesn't need to be taught solely in lessons. Many instruments allow children to experiment and improvise on their own and intuitively create rhythms, sounds, melodies, and dance movements. You can offer simple sound-makers such as rainmakers, bucket drums, marimbas, bells, and rattles. You can provide Orff instruments, such as xylophones, metallophones, and glockenspiel. There may be various drums and even a percussion set. You can also inspire children to create their own sound-makers by filling containers with sand or pebbles. Classic instruments such as flutes, violins, and the like may be placed there as well, but usually need at least a basic introduction and supervision around young children until they are ready to use them responsibly. But after the introduction, children should be allowed to improvise, not only expected to play following along or using the correct technique. Children benefit from both technical instruction and lots of time to experiment on their own.

Think of a place in which children can make music without disrupting anyone else in the household. If there is no such place, put the instruments in a basket and bring them out only at specific, suitable times.

"Musical intelligence" is the understanding of rhythm and sounds, and the ability to understand, create, and compose music. It is one of the nine intelligences identified by Harvard psychologist and author Howard Gardner (as mentioned in Week 8).

WEEK 39

CREATING FLOW LEARNING CENTERS
Flow stations for multiple children

WHILE IT IS TRUE THAT CHILDREN often experience flow states during individual activities, it also possible for multiple children to drop into flow side by side or while playing together. Centers for flow are designed for groups of children. They are flow-friendly environments that can serve as after school programs, and with thorough preparation, also as replacements for traditional school settings, as we have done successfully for decades in RWB schools.

Flow learning centers such as RWB schools offer learners a great variety of prepared, hands-on learning environments. Often, a big family home is transformed into a wonderland for discovery and learning, and each room is dedicated to a specific purpose. There usually is a room for hands-on math with Montessori and other math materials, a language lab, a fully accessible kitchen for cooking projects, pretend play areas, library, woodshop, indoor and outdoor movement opportunities, and gardens.

In flow learning centers, countless learning opportunities naturally emerge: learning to work in pairs or teams as well as focusing on oneself while others are around; learning to solve conflicts peacefully; observing others doing an activity before starting oneself; learning from peers; teaching peers; and learning to say a wholehearted "yes" or "no" to play invitations. These and many other social-emotional as well as intellectual learning opportunities emerge when children share flow-friendly environments.

Louder flow activities need to be set up in a separate space from more quiet activities, so children don't disrupt each other. Help children find a suitable place for their games, so the rooms dedicated to quiet, focused activity and study remain quiet, and children who need to be louder have other spaces in which to freely express themselves. Make sure there are enough materials for children to play side by side. Help maintain order, cleanliness, and beauty in the rooms and refine your system of order over time as you see what works best.

In addition to a well-prepared environment with a variety of flow stations, your presence as a flow companion is needed (see Week 40). Help children respect one another's flow processes and when you suspect a conflict arising, come closer to the children and sharpen your awareness to see if adult intervention is needed or whether the children can reach a solution on their own. If not, signal your willingness to help them find a solution.

When a child expresses intense emotions, be there for support, and if necessary, spend some time alone with them until they feel balanced again. In movement areas, let children know not to dare, cheer on, take away another's discovery by "showing them how," or otherwise comment on each other during focused activities, so each learner can calmly experiment with their abilities. As you spend more time with children in a flow-friendly environment, you will increasingly know when to step in and when to allow situations to take their natural course.

Over time, as children get familiar with the house rules and healthy boundaries, they naturally work in harmony side by side, forming a self-organizing collective. The busy children (ages five to fourteen) in the RWB schools in Italy and Austria often reminded me of the self-organizing flight patterns of a flock of birds or a school of fish, where each participant finds their place spontaneously, without premeditated plans. Very often learners will find their place in accordance with their nature, without interfering with anyone else, instead modeling for others ways to find their own inspired flow activity.

ELEMENTS OF FLOW STATIONS FOR LEARNERS AT ANY AGE

The basic structure of a flow station remains the same for individual and shared flow stations and for learners of all ages. All flow stations are..

☆ Prepared environments with healthy boundaries within which learners enjoy freedom

☆ Safe to use

☆ Attractive and inspiring

☆ Yes places

☆ Emotionally safe for both flow companion and learner

☆ Designed to enable learners to be independent and active

☆ Full of hands-on activities, with toys and learning materials freely accessible at the learner's height

☆ Meet genuine needs through the environment

☆ Spaces adapted to the learner's needs, interests, and preferences.

TRY THIS
Your role in a flow learning center

Once you have created one or several flow stations at home or a flow learning center, where children find a variety of flow stations and can choose what they would like to do, you can truly be a flow companion. It's much easier to be relaxed in an environment prepared for play as opposed to a place where you constantly need to say "no" to a child's self-chosen activity (and point them to other activities). Below are some simple guidelines on how to be available for children in flow-friendly environments:

Be aware of your body in the environment.

Breathe deeply and realize that in many ways your presence sets the tone for the children to be relaxed or insecure. If you are experiencing a negative emotion for any reason, try sharing it out loud in a simple way to ensure that the children do not have to guess why you seem different that day. For example, "I want to let you know that today I'm sad because my friend is sick" is transparent, normalizes the wide range of human emotions, and provides a "check mark" for children's innate sense of the energy in their environment, so they will not need to spend any time on exploring whether they are safe.

Find a place where you have a clear view.

Be visible in a place from which you can see a child and they can see you.

Observe with loving attention.

Show interest in a child's activity but let them take the lead. Observing children in flow will help you trust the intelligence of natural learning. As you reconnect with this trust, you pave the way for your own personal healing and learning processes.

Be active in the flow environment in non-invasive ways.

When you feel confident that the children in your environment do not need your full attention, you might rest or do something that you love to do, or even something that you need to do, like household chores, while keeping an eye and ear out for them. Talking on the phone, even if you feel you are still watching the child, would not be an example of being active in the flow environment. Children will hear your side of the conversation even if they appear engrossed in their activity and will likely be distracted from their activity as a result. Depending upon the proximity of your own workstation, you may be able to do household chores, reading, or computer work. This must be evaluated on a case-by-case basis, using observations about how it affects the child's ability to stay in flow. If they are able to go to you, ask questions, get reassurance, and easily go back to their activity without missing a beat, this may be a combination that works in your home. Always be aware that our actions are models absorbed by children, so limiting your own screen time around children when possible is an important aspect of encouraging their hands-on flow states.

Let children participate in your task.

Allow children to participate somehow in your task, if that is what they want, or help them find their own activity by your side. A child may like to join you for a while, be next to you, or watch you. Often, children will move between their own self-directed play and interest in your activity, which imbues their flow state with a precious combination of safety, connection, and self-direction.

Step in when you feel it's needed.

The more we observe children, the more we develop the sensitivity to know when we are needed. When you sense a conflict arise, step closer to the children and, if needed, accompany the conflict with simple mediation. You can also step in with kind offers: "May I help you put things back in order?" or "May I bring you some more water?" However, be clear as to whether you truly wish to ask a question, or if you want to communicate a genuine need you have that is not up for discussion. Then, instead of a question, you might say, "I really need things to be put back in order now, and I'm willing to help you." In this way, you can remain calm and keep the environment safe, while respecting the children's needs and your needs.

PART FOUR

YOU

A FLOW COMPANION

Again and again, we realize
that each arrival of a child on this earth
is an invitation for us as adults to perceive
what has been considered "normal" with new eyes.
This means that we renew our contact
with the origin of our own lives
and ask ourselves why we are on this earth.
Love is the force that allows all creatures
to interact with a new environment,
thereby creating the neurological networks needed
for a meaningful life on planet earth.
It is the adult's responsibility to create environments
suitable to the stages of development of children,
adolescents, and other adults.
Learning environments must be relaxed enough so that everyone
can remain in contact with their own developmental needs.

—Rebeca Wild

The most sophisticated people I know,
inside they are all children.
—Jim Henson

WEEK 40

ADULT AND CHILD
You can be a flow companion

AS A FLOW COMPANION, you prepare the safe, inspiring space for your child to play and learn in flow. You provide loving attention until the child is happily busy with their own activity, in their own world. You will find that amidst the complex dynamics of relationships between the generations there is the sweet simplicity of moments in which a grown-up and a child enjoy doing something side by side.

As an adult and flow companion, you can do so much to help children build awareness of their inner resources, and thus, help them find purpose and joy in themselves. In some cases, this can also provide direction regarding their profession, not just their hobbies.

Your thoughts, emotions, intentions, and expectations directly influence children. As a flow companion, you support the children in your care by internally holding space for the highest potential of each child. Scientifically referred to as the Pygmalion or Rosenthal effect, the expectation teachers have of their students profoundly influences the students' performance.

Let's train ourselves to perceive children's willingness to connect and learn, so we become increasingly aware of their innocence and natural intelligence and we can encourage them to unfold toward their optimal potential. In general, a child's pure intentions consist of learning how to fulfill personal needs while being accepted and loved by others. As children grow, they also naturally want to learn how to fulfill other people's needs.

I have witnessed children of various ages whose parents completely believed in them and supported their natural pace of learning, and therefore they thrived at the RWB schools. Conversely, children whose parents doubted the potential of child-directed learning often felt insecure in the school environments and continued craving reassurance from adults.

Observing children with loving attention and genuine interest is a powerful way to help them learn. *Loving attention is a catalyst for learning.* As a flow companion, your role is one of complete support: you are ready to assist when you are needed, and you become a friendly observer when children are engaged in their activities. Observing with loving attention means witnessing children without judging them, and being a friendly, non-invasive presence. This is one of the important features of a stress-free, emotionally safe environment.

A flow companion's trust that children will learn everything they need to know in their own time directly enhances the learning progress. Children benefit immensely when we let them know once in a while, "I believe you can do it!"

Especially when they face challenges, a flow companion's inner knowing that children have the capacity to solve their own problems will help them move through obstacles and find solutions. Here is an example from my experience: A six-year-old girl was trying to put a thread through a needle. She was getting impatient and was about to give up. When she asked me if I could do it for her, I said, "Would you like to try it a bit more? I will sit here by your side and hope that you can do it. If it doesn't work, I will do it for you." Within a few minutes, the thread was in the needle and the girl was very happy. Through my loving attention and belief in her ability, I provided an optimal field for learning for her.

When adults are respectful and non-invasive, they are welcome companions in the children's world. Children want us to be close to help with potential challenges or with conflicts, and yet they must be able to trust us not to interrupt their games unnecessarily.

Of course, all children are different in how they handle frustration, and there are moments when life's challenges feel too difficult to tackle head-on. The inner world of a child is just as complex as that of an adult, and although it is extremely flexible, there are times when life circumstances can feel overwhelming. As children integrate social, emotional, and intellectual changes in their lives, they might have a "cranky" or "blue" day, and their self-confidence may fluctuate. What works to support them one day, or one month, may need to be adjusted according to their individual needs or external circumstances, and the adult's needs as well.

The ability of a flow companion to allow a child the same flexibility of "being human" that we offer adults is an important part of our role. Knowing a child can do something and encouraging them, consistently empowers them to believe in themselves. But there will always be moments when above all else, a child needs connection. What could this look like for a flow companion? The child may simply need to be held, or perhaps helped with something they had already mastered, or they might need a gentle but firm boundary against which they feel safe to push, allowing for a release of pent-up stress or emotion. In this way, "holding space for their highest potential" can mean providing them the space in which to fall apart safely.

Given the opportunity, children regularly and deftly process stress within deep flow states. However, not all stress is equal. A good cry, in a safe environment with an adult they trust, can clean the slate for the next steps of their healthy intellectual, emotional, and even physical growth. Children do not yet possess the language to describe what's going on inside. A child cannot say, "I'm not sure why, but I feel stressed and I need a good cry. Would you please just listen for a while?" Rather, it's the role of the flow companion to recognize and respond to the often hidden messages in a child's behavior.

Remaining present for an emotional release may not be easy for an adult who is new to such an experience. It may be loud. It may be difficult to stay present with a child's discomfort, woe, sadness, or pain. We may be conditioned to try to stop a child from crying, to fix their pain or problem, or to encourage them to feel better by distracting them from their emotions. Though well-intentioned, these responses will simply postpone the inevitable release of stress. If a child does not have a space in which they can consciously release built-up feelings, then the feelings or stress may come out in disruptive ways. The sooner the adult can embrace this process as a normal, healthy, and necessary part of a child's development into their greatest potential, the more effective the release will be. It is often a non-negotiable boundary held lovingly by a caregiver that provides a setting in which a child feels safe enough to completely "lose it." A quiet, witnessing presence is often all that is needed. As long as you keep yourself, the child, and others safe, it can be a sacred honor to be trusted with a child's most vulnerable state of being.

Seeing children once again dive deeply into the joy of their life after they have been allowed to release their emotions is rewarding and reaffirming for any adult caregiver. Children often rocket forward in their development when freely allowed to practice self-care in this way. By developing a habit of releasing stress rather than internalizing it, a child builds the foundation for lifelong health and forward momentum, to indeed fulfill their greatest potential.

TRY THIS
Allow time for self-correction

When mistakes can be self-corrected over time, they become an empowering part of the learning process and may make it even more interesting. Instead of correcting mistakes immediately, you can give children a chance to learn by doing. Within healthy boundaries, you can allow them to find out what went wrong and draw their own conclusions.

Hands-on activities often provide immediate error feedback and alert a child in case of a mistake. However, even if a child does not immediately self-correct but continues with their activity, direct intervention is rarely necessary. Most mistakes will be naturally corrected over time.

The practice of judging and immediately correcting mistakes has created generations of adults scared of making mistakes and therefore shying away from trying new things. Growing up in a cycle of judgment and perfectionistic thinking creates an adulthood that follows the same patterns. At schools and in homes, children and adults have been shamed, ridiculed, and even punished for their learning attempts. Many adults are afraid of public speaking, conversing in a foreign language, sharing their personal art, dancing, singing, music, math, or writing because of their childhood experiences. Those fears at times keep people from exploring their talents, even in their private space.

Not correcting mistakes may be hard to imagine for some of us, because we grew up believing that mistakes must be immediately addressed; otherwise the correct way of doing things will be lost. What our well-intentioned teachers and parents didn't know is that very often, instead of remembering the correct way of doing something, children remember feelings of inadequacy.

Let's experiment with trusting children's capacity to self-correct over time, and only correct mistakes when an injury can be prevented, or we can safe a learner considerable time and hard work. The opportunity to make mistakes and learn from them in an emotionally safe environment is one of the most powerful ways to develop independent thinking.

WEEK 41

YOUR POWERFUL INNER CHILD
Revisit your childhood to understand children

IN EVERY MOMENT OF OUR LIVES, our inner child is present inside of us and influences our being, even when we don't know it or cannot feel it. The way our parents and teachers took care of us as children is reflected in the way we take care of ourselves today. The voices from significant adults we heard in our childhoods have become part of our inner voice that reflects what we think of ourselves and how we hold ourselves in high or low esteem. Our internal self-talk may echo the comforting voice of our mother, one moment, or the critical words of a teacher the next.

Undoubtedly, our environments shaped our behavior as children, because as all children are, we were extremely open to conditioning. In an environment that allowed us to unfold with authenticity, our inherent goodness was nurtured. When we felt accepted, loved, and part of a community, we naturally opened to flow and learning, which led to lasting self-confidence.

On the other hand, if we were uncertain of our caregiver's benevolence, we would, at times, hide our authentic selves, contorting our behaviors to bring us more acceptance, comfort, and our desired bond with adults. We might have become louder, quieter, invisible, or even aggressive. We developed all kinds of creative and apparently unrelated coping strategies to feel more accepted or at least to be noticed because being "invisible" can be equally painful for a child as being abused. The coping patterns we developed in our childhoods still arise at times in our adult lives in stressful situations, or in more severe cases, as our primary inner voice that must be healed in order to feel safe to be our authentic selves.

Since we are part of a lineage of generations, these patterns were not only transmitted to us as children—now, we are the ones who potentially transfer them to our children and students. Our own childhood experiences influence our connection with children and students so much that unless we bring awareness to them, we contribute to similar patterns or wounds in our sons, our daughters, and our students. The ability to be our own loving parents and teachers endows us also with a natural ability to nurture children. As we learn to comfort and trust ourselves, we naturally become a comforting, trustworthy presence for children.

There are many ways we can bring awareness to our conditioning and heal what keeps us from being present, joyful, and kind with children. The first steps to becoming a flow companion include journeying back into our own past to comfort and love the child we once were. We can do that in the here and now by becoming extremely kind to ourselves, even pampering ourselves, relaxing, playing, and giving ourselves repeated permission to make our *now* enjoyable whenever we can, as much as we can.

The more we become aware of our inner child and patiently include it in our daily lives, the more we feel its beneficial power; and this process often goes hand in hand while spending time with children. Slowing down daily life for children also relaxes our inner child, and thus our whole nervous system. Playing with children delights our inner child. Wholeheartedly laughing with children can elate your inner child! Once the inner child feels cherished, its magic will steadily unfold. At the very least, you will see how life becomes more pleasurable, and in best-case scenarios, your inner child becomes your superpower!

TRY THIS
Remember yourself as a child

Find a picture of yourself as a child, put it in a beautiful frame, maybe even a frame you crafted, put it in your most precious place at home, and invite your inner child to be part of your life.

When you are ready to go deeper, explore how your childhood memories may influence the time you spend with your children or students. If this process becomes disruptive to the balance of your current life, it's important to take your time, or even take a break. You might find a supportive adult like a counselor and/or a trusted friend to talk with or read a book about recovering from childhood wounds and thriving as an adult. I recommend the book *Home Coming* by John Bradshaw, Lucia Capacchione's work, and other books which you will find in the Resources and Bibliography. The most important thing is that you accept all feelings that come up for you throughout the process, allow it to take as long as it takes, don't give up on your own potential to live a life that includes your own joyful flow.

Explore if the following quote by Carl Jung feels true to you: "Nothing has a stronger influence psychologically on their environment and especially on their children than the unlived life of the parent." This week, take some time to ponder the following questions..

— As a child, how did you feel about your significant adults?
— Which are your favorite childhood memories?
— Which are your worst ones?
— Think...what would you have needed from your parents and teachers? What do you wish you had had, but did not have? Is that something your children may need or want?
— Did you feel connected to your parents?
— Did you feel they were always there for you?

— Were you afraid of your parents?

— Could you talk about your fears to your parents?

— Were you punished?

— Were you shamed?

— How do you feel thinking about your parents and teachers? Do you smile? Do you contract? Are there memories that need deeper healing, maybe with the help of a therapist?

— Were you forced to do things you did not enjoy? Which of these things do you think were necessary? Which of these things created unnecessary suffering? Do you see this show up in your life with your own children and students?

— What do you remember regarding school content and subjects? Why do you remember specific subjects, while forgetting others?

— How did you learn best?

— Who were your favorite teachers? Why were they your favorite teachers? Because of what they taught or because of how they taught?

— In what ways (if so) are you repeating patterns you observed in your parents and teachers?

— How might you be able to learn from your own memories and provide better experiences for your children and students?

WEEK 42

RE-PARENT YOURSELF—REINVENT YOURSELF
Letting go of negative conditioning

MANY OF US RECEIVED negative conditioning from parents and teachers who themselves had received similar conditioning when they were young and vulnerable. If unexamined, the judgments we received as children may turn into harsh criticism towards others and ourselves. These discouraging inner messages can be damaging to our health and to our children, and they simply take the fun out of life! Let's break the generational chain of conditioning and give our children and ourselves the greatest gift possible: unconditional support.

Negative conditioning is softened every time we catch it and question its truth. At first, it may seem nearly impossible to notice thoughts that stem from deep conditioning, since they can happen so fast. Just the intention to begin noticing them and staying open to the process will allow the healing to unfold. The following beliefs influence many of us at every turn of our lives; however, as soon as you learn to practice seeing yourself and children with compassion, you will realize they are untrue.

"Something must be wrong with me."
This subtle yet powerful sentiment, which many people have about themselves, is the result of not having received the necessary affirmations of belonging and contributing with authenticity. In truth, nothing is "wrong" with anybody! We are all living the human experience, and everyone is different. Everyone is made to bring something *new* into

the world. In the eyes of close-minded people (who were conditioned to fear their own unique gifts), the *new* may seem wrong, off, strange, out of place, weird, unhealthy, or even frightening. In the eyes of open-minded people (who were accepted as children or have healed from their childhood conditioning), that same *new* may be original, inventive, creative, imaginative, inspired, artistic, and resourceful.

"*I am not good enough.*"

In addition to being stated directly, this message can be given through a judging look or a slight disapproving shake of the head. Adults also communicate this message by being impatient and saying, "Let me do this for you." This message pushes children toward self-doubt and mediocrity. When children give their best and the result is not good enough or even harshly judged, it hurts so much that often they are resigned to being mediocre. Mediocrity is preferable to revealing their best and having it not be good enough. Their best is kept secret, until perhaps it is forgotten. Instead, let yourself and children know, *you are safe*, and your best is *always* good enough. Instead of adapting to systems and institutions that make human beings feel "not good enough," we can start creating places—whether in our own hearts, our homes, or our schools—where we are not only good enough but also shine brightly!

"*I should be doing something else right now.*"

This attitude can arise when, as children, we are frequently interrupted in our focused activities. With their pre-made agenda and curriculum, lack of awareness that a child is in flow, or from a place of managing a schedule, adults might frequently, and often unnecessarily, interrupt a child's flow of learning with a request or to show them something: "Come here, I want to hold you now." "Look at that airplane!" Even when a child might appear to do nothing, in their inner world they might be working out a problem related to their social, spatial, emotional, artistic, logical, or other learning process. When an adult interrupts with a stern mandate or expectation for a quick transition, this sends a signal to the child that what was meaningful to them was not important enough to be acknowledged by their trusted leader. Whenever possible, let go of your own agenda and know that what children choose to do in the moment (provided it doesn't hurt them or anyone else) is exactly appropriate and part of their flow of learning. If that is not possible, remember to offer children the similar courtesies you appreciate when being interrupted or asked to change your plans. Something as simple as, "I can see you are really enjoying yourself with this project. Would you please find a good stopping place soon so we can get ready to go outside?"

"If I don't worry, I'm not a responsible person."

Most of us have been conditioned to worry as a sign of caring about another person or a situation. But the physiological effects of worry are detrimental to our health, directly influencing the nervous, muscular, hormonal, and digestive systems in a negative way. It produces tension that must be released in order not to cause sickness over time. Instead of worrying, we can firmly believe in our own or another's ability to succeed and master a situation. Encouragement such as "I believe in you; you can do it; I am here for you if you need me," is much more supportive than "I'm worried about you."

"I should work harder."

We've glorified hard work as the one virtue needed to succeed in life. We have historically held up people who sacrificed their well-being and kindness for their career. However, it is far more than a willingness to work hard that makes a person successful. You can see that in the current economy many people who have worked incredibly hard, many of whom have a college degree, are currently unemployed. In order to experience true success and fulfillment in work life, it must be in alignment with personal talents, interests, and passions. Life is full of unexpected events, challenges, and difficult periods of growth and change. Resilience and deep self-knowledge are fundamental to successfully use one's hard work and talents. Children discover and develop these vital skills in flow.

"I am too slow. I should be faster and more efficient."
The tight schedule of the average Western family pushes people to hurry constantly from one place to another. At school, children often do not get the time needed to finish a task, to deeply understand a concept, to talk with their friends, or to solve conflicts. After school, they may be whisked to soccer, violin, and tutoring lessons; they often do homework until late at night. Such a schedule does not allow them to enjoy the present moment and discover their personal pace in flow. Slow down your life with children. Whenever you can, create time for timelessness and free play.

"I am not beautiful the way I am."
Remarks by adults, even said in jest, such as "What the heck are you wearing?" or "Still loving the baked goods, I see!" instill an underlying conviction that someone is not beautiful as they are. This is reinforced by the unnatural beauty standard of fashion models, a manufactured idea of what is beautiful further distorted by the digital manipulation of all marketing images that is now the worldwide norm. Japanese tradition offers a concept called "Wabi Sabi," which describes the idea of imperfect beauty and expresses appreciation for the way things naturally are. The truth is that *beauty lies in the eye of the beholder*—we decide what is beautiful to us! Let's take a closer look at ourselves in the mirror and eagerly find beauty in our own "imperfections" and in those of our children.

"I will never understand this. I am just not smart enough."
Sadly, there are teachers who encourage these false sentiments in students by saying things like "Maybe understanding math just isn't in the cards for you." Very often we see children in traditional classrooms

being asked to complete tasks that are far above their capacity, within a grossly unrealistic time period, or via a prescribed method of learning that does not work for everyone's learning style. Pushing children to achieve ever more, creates incredible stress because they internalize the idea that they should be able to do what's expected, and that there is something "wrong" with them because they cannot. It is also frustrating for teachers who may blame themselves for not being good teachers.

It is well known that teachers at traditional schools often do not have the tools, hands-on materials, and time needed to teach in a way that children can understand. This is especially true for math. How many adults tell themselves they are not good at math and believe they will never understand? I used to be one of them. But when I did my Montessori teacher training, I realized I was completely capable of understanding basic and even advanced math using Montessori learning materials. Thus, it had been the teaching method that failed me, not my ability to understand. Instead of doubting a child's ability to learn, let's look into different ways of teaching at school, home, or other environments to give every child a chance to understand.

TRY THIS
Ways to show children your trust

By allowing children to learn in flow and play, to tinker and discover in their own ways, we give an empowering, positive message: *I trust you that you can figure this out by yourself.*

By not interfering with a child's activity, we give the message: *I respect your activity. It is important for me that you can play and work in whatever way feels right for you.*

By respectfully asking a child who is getting blamed for something what happened from their perspective, and then by helping them to make amends, we give the message: *I see something went wrong here. I trust you didn't know what the consequences of your behavior were, and I trust you will learn from this and do better next time.*

By empathizing and allowing each child in a conflict to state what happened from their perspective, and by helping children to find their own solutions to conflicts, instead of blaming, judging or punishing, we give the message: *Conflicts are part of growing up and they can be solved. I trust you also want to solve your conflicts and I will help you find your own solutions that work for all of you.*

By leaving a child's art or crafting work, written text, or any product *as is,* without making suggestions or improving it by adult standards, we give the message: *I saw that you gave your best, and I acknowledge that. Your work is just right the way it is. I trust that you will learn everything important in your own time.*

By giving the child as much time as needed to finish an activity, we give the message: *You are allowed to stay in the present moment and focus on your task. It does not matter how long it takes as long as you are enjoying it and learning in the process.*

Re-Parenting One-on-One

Susanne Stover, FLOW TO LEARN's Oregon-based parenting advisor shares how she was able to embrace self-care to be a more available, generous parent to her children.

One of the most daunting challenges of being a parent or primary caregiver is finding balance between caring for children and caring for oneself. Since we spend nearly all our time doing things for the benefit of other people, it's easy to fall out of the habit of self-care. Even when we do find a way to have some "me" time, there are no vacations from the lifelong commitment of being a primary caregiver. Today more than ever, parents hold themselves to high ideals, and this additional pressure can feel unrelenting—"Am I doing it right?" A parent's commitment to treating children with respect, no matter how they are feeling about life or their role as caregiver on any given day is an even taller order for those who were raised with traditional approaches that did not promote self-care.

Adding to the stress of parenting is our typically externalized sense of self-worth. Many adults were raised to measure success primarily through grades, accomplishments, skillsets, status symbols, medals, awards, and other metrics set by society. Questioning the idea that our self-worth is directly tied to what we do, what we produce, and how we perform doesn't mean we give up on accomplishing our goals. It simply means that those metrics don't define us. This was certainly true for me.

For the first few years as a parent, I was unable to accept the inevitable imperfection in my parenting, and so I became a stressed-out parent. Instead of having appreciation for all I was doing right, I could see only what I wasn't doing perfectly or sometimes even very well, and I was constantly judging myself harshly for it. I realized, no matter how I might try to encourage my children's positive self-talk, a child can easily sense what's really going on inside us, especially when it's habitual.

Six months after experiencing a serious complication giving birth to our daughter, when our son was two-and-a-half, I finally buckled under the pressures of working full-time, co-managing our farm, trying and failing to be the perfect parent and maintain a beautiful home, the challenges of marriage, and my dear mother-in-law's passing. My physical, emotional, and psychological faculties were reduced to shambles. Over the course of the following year, I spent a lot of time outside, in a flow state, trying to come to terms with and understand what had happened. I began to recognize that holding onto perfection so tightly was one of the reasons my body, mind, and spirit had to stop the overwhelm and toxic self-shame by shutting down.

I found that balance lies in a parenting paradox—to be always improving, yet always enough. Negative feelings toward ourselves sap our energy, our morale, and our motivation. The cumulative effects of stress on the body and mind are well-documented and can seriously impact our life if we don't take time to stop and sincerely say "I am enough." To the voice(s) in our heads that point out our failures, we can highlight everything we did today with love: the hugs we gave, the food we prepared, the clothing we washed or lovingly re-used because it was clean enough, the jobs we worked to provide for our family, the errands we ran, the events we attended, the toys we picked up, and the all-important investment in our own soundness of body, mind, and spirit. This kind of focus reduces overall stress, and in our case, it has created lasting positive effects on all our interactions. Practice looking around and making a note of what you did right as a parent today, saying aloud, "I am enough." If you feel a reaction, a rebuttal, or a denial after saying this phrase, try saying it again throughout the day. For a long time, I would hear a voice in my own head rebuffing such a claim. Eventually, the voice went quiet.

Now when I miss the mark as a mom, which still happens regularly because I am 100% human the last time I checked, I practice responding to the inner critics as my best self would respond to a child when they're unable reach a goal:

"You really wanted to spend more quality time with the kids today. I know you didn't want to yell. You felt overwhelmed. Look how well you showed up and apologized. See when you were fully present with them? It's okay that you weren't perfect. You did your best. Tomorrow is another chance."

Failure, when viewed properly and handled with love, is an essential part of success—only by living what doesn't work can we find exactly what does. Taking the time to look myself in the eye and affirm that I am enough, to treat myself with respect, and to emphatically forgive myself when I fall short of the intentions I set as a parent has become a fundamental building block of my life with children.

YOU CAN DO IT!
Trust children's willingness and capacity to learn

MOST OF US ARE CONDITIONED not to trust children. In fact, most of us are conditioned not to trust ourselves. As children we really need someone, at least one person, who really trusts us. This understanding adult firmly believes that we mean well, that we can reach our goals, and that we are worthy and complete as we are. Such a significant adult can strongly influence the self-perception of a child and enable them to keep finding and reconnecting to their safe inner core.

A child who consistently receives patient, loving feedback—even when they make mistakes—learns that they may not be perfect, but they are a good person. Continuously offering children our patience and the benefit of the doubt helps them develop the courage and the "spine" to do the right thing. It supports the core belief that they can always find goodness inside themselves, and that they can trust their own moral compass.

My mother always gave me the benefit of the doubt. I still hear her say, "I know you didn't mean to hurt this child, here, come, I will help you say I'm sorry and possibly make it up to them." When I broke something she said, "I know you didn't mean to break this. It's not a big deal, it could happen to anyone." And I remember as a child I was instantly confused when *something happened*—it was an interruption in my flow, when *I did something*. I remember that I genuinely never wanted to hurt a child or break something; I was just playing and experimenting. And when my mother gave me the benefit of the doubt, it calmed my nervous system immediately, it helped me believe that I am full of goodness, that it is okay to make a mistake, and that I can make amends to heal it. I was so relieved when she said whatever happened was a misunderstanding; that it happened by mistake. My mother never doubting my goodness helped me never to doubt my own goodness.

As a teacher, I have been that adult who believes in the goodness of many children. Often, I have received incredulous yet grateful looks from older children who aren't used to this kindness. I believe the benefit of the doubt changes something in a child: it reminds them of their own goodness and gives them permission to believe in it.

What is given to us in childhood considerably adds to how our inner world is established and the lens through which we see the world. If we experience love and trust in childhood, we are made more capable to create that for ourselves and for others and in adulthood. If we experience mistrust, neglect, and abuse, we are more likely to recreate these experiences as adults, because this is what feels familiar to us on a very deep level.

Learning to trust children is a process that takes time. We must outgrow not only our own childhood conditioning but also the weight of many generations of mistrust between adults and children. It helps when we learn to trust ourselves and our own capacity and willingness to learn. Just as it is safe to allow seeds to be seeds and trust they will grow into plants given nourishing conditions, it is safe to allow children to be children and trust they will grow into the persons they are meant to be.

I realized the significance of trust while working in RWB schools, where the bond of trust between adult and child is patiently cultivated. In response, children love learning and are naturally active, collaborative, and even eager to contribute with chores. This is how I learned that play is much more than a leisurely activity, and the drive for play is a child's inner compass for learning. I also came to understand that a lot of children's unruly behavior is a direct response to adults not trusting them. This is a fundamental truth explored in many of today's respectful parenting approaches (see Resources).

Although the mistrust between the generations has a long history, it can be healed. As the people with the power, it is the adults' responsibility to initiate this process. It's important to know that trusting children doesn't mean letting them do anything they want, or being scared of what they may come up with next. Instead, it means allowing children to choose their activities within the boundaries that feel safe, appropriate, and healthy to you and others who share the space. Of course, the better the environment is prepared, the easier it is to trust and relax. As our doubts diminish, the child's ability to learn in flow grows exponentially.

Trusting children is best learned through our experiences in real time, as we interact with children. It is okay to slowly ease into different ways of being with children and give increasing freedom over time, as we receive positive feedback from a child. Below are a few ways to soften our judgments and let go of fears as we deepen our trust.

TRY THIS
Encourage yourself and children

This week see yourself, your partner or co-workers, and the children in your life with compassion. Know that you, as much as the children around you, are a learner. You are all on your way! Put effort into replacing negative internal messages with positive ones. You might try the Emotional Freedom Technique (EFT). EFT is a simple, scientifically proven way to relieve anxiety, self-doubt, and inner criticism. The full method entails tapping at various strategic points on the body, making a great effort to feel and acknowledge any emotional challenge or physical pain, and then affirming that you love yourself anyway, no matter what. Here are a few templates inspired by EFT, which you might use to create your own encouraging phrases: "Even though a part of me doesn't fully believe it, I know I can do this. I am good enough. I am okay." Or, "Even though I made a mistake / I lost my patience / I (fill in the blank), I am okay. I forgive myself. I will do it better next time. I am doing the best I can."

This may feel silly or quite awkward at first, especially if you did not receive this kind of explicit encouragement as a child. It's okay to feel awkward. You are doing the best you can! Keep at it. You will slowly but surely become your own best friend and turn your mind into your ally. When you question any and all doubting and criticizing of yourself, you will become a safe person for yourself to be with and it will become easier to be a true ally for the children in your life.

Encourage yourself regularly, write inspiring messages, record yourself speaking them, or create posters, paintings, and artwork with them. This can also be done together with children. These messages can be hung on the wall or sent to each other in love letters. This will be healing for yourself and provide positive thought patterns for the children.

WEEK 44

BECOME A GENUINE NEEDS DETECTIVE
A different look at misbehavior

MOST OF US WERE RAISED in families and schools where "unruly" behavior was simply suppressed or punished. Only a few of us as children were surrounded by adults who sensed that our misbehavior was a request for help or for changed circumstances. Only very few of our young selves were asked *why* we weren't collaborating, and if we were asked, we might not have had the courage or the understanding to share our true feelings. *Vulnerable feelings are only revealed when children feel emotionally safe.*

In addition, many children, and often even teenagers and adults, don't have the verbal and social skills to express their needs effectively. Yet, — as Dr. Shefali, a clinical psychologist and leading parenting expert writes: "Our children are constantly telling us what's going on in their inner world through their behavior. But if we don't know how to decipher the clues, we can't get to the root of the behavior and therefore can't offer the guidance and support that's needed." When young children come across as unruly, they may simply need food, a nap, or a hug. "Misbehavior" is painful not only for the adults but also for the child—to behave in a way that a child knows is unwelcome requires them to be so uncomfortable in their own skin that they don't know what else to do but "act out" for the help and connection they need.

In fact, for long-term improvements in behavior, we must adjust external factors in the child's environment rather than asking a child to modify their behavior. In addition to co-regulating and modeling how to self-regulate, (explained in the next parenting insight), experiments with changes in a child's environment, diet, and daily rhythms may naturally improve behavior.

There are a thousand ways children might behave in unwelcome ways, and a thousand reasons why. *What is misbehavior for you?* If a child can't sit quietly at the table until everyone finishes their meal? If a child doesn't do their homework? If a child stole something? If a child addressed someone disrespectfully? If a child lies to you? If a child won't go to sleep? If a child won't finish the food on their plate? If a child hits another child? If a child runs away from you? Rest assured, none of these behaviors is done in spite, to upset you, or to enter into a power play with you. Events such as these could easily turn into a power play—and into upset for everyone— but only if no one bothers to find out *why* a child is behaving in this way.

In many instances, an empathic response changes the energy right away: "I see you are not feeling well, I think I understand, let's take a break." Instead of giving less loving attention or even punishing and isolating a child, provide understanding and companionship (as well as natural and logical consequences to keep everyone safe). Help a child heal and develop better behaviors. Sincerely ask which of the child's genuine needs aren't being addressed, and what you can do about it in the long run. What led to this behavior? Is there a misunderstanding? What is missing in this child's life now or on a broader scale? Flow companions are keen observers. We need to become *genuine needs detectives*!

As a loving parent or caregiver, our responsibility is to recognize possible reasons for misbehavior, address the needs we can see clearly, and give the children the benefit of the doubt for those needs we cannot yet know.

It is possible that, through making a few changes, you could significantly raise the quality of life for a child and witness dramatic reduction in instances of misbehavior. For instance, when children are generally fidgety, this may reveal a need for more movement: experiment with providing regular access to a playground, trampoline, bike-riding, or ball play (they may need more movement than you think!). When children get cranky, ask if they have had a glass of water today or ask if they would like to listen to a story so they can rest with you. When a child often cries over seemingly small incidents, they may need to release inner tension that stemmed from previous incidents. Patiently allow tears to flow and any other expression of emotion.

For more information about addressing children's genuine needs, refer to Week 20 as a guideline to experiment with smaller or bigger changes in a child's lifestyle. If you cannot change less-than-ideal circumstances, comfort your child, bond with your child, and try to do the best you can with what you have. Your willingness to truly see a child, non-judgmentally meet them where they are, and acknowledge whatever it is they are experiencing significantly reduces inner tension and misbehavior and while modeling empathy.

TRY THIS
Let the detective work begin!

This week, when a child misbehaves, respond with as much warmth and empathy as possible, and find out what is really going on. Of course, you can address any unsafe behavior right away, and for instance stop a child from hitting another or removing objects that might hurt the child or others. Then go a step further and reflect to yourself on why a child is acting out. Below are some basic guidelines that will help you determine what is going on underneath the apparent behavior.

LOOK FOR THE FOLLOWING CLUES
WHEN YOUNG CHILDREN ACT OUT REPEATEDLY

Ponder whether something in the environment can be changed.
Maybe the lights are too bright, the background noise is too loud, there is not enough time and space for movement and play, there is no quiet space, there are too many people around, siblings need to be in different spaces from one another, and so on.

Discover if the child feels comfortable in their body.
Maybe they ate too much sugar, are hungry, are allergic to something, or need to drink water. Maybe they are short-sighted, or they don't hear well. The child's shoes may be too small, they didn't get enough sleep, or they didn't get enough fresh air, and so on.

Observe how your child relates to adults.
Maybe they are scared of some adults? Maybe they don't trust some adults? Could you imagine why? Do they make eye contact? Do they come to you when they are upset? If you notice they are having trouble with any of these indicators of trust, try to talk with your child, and clarify possible misunderstandings.

From Dysregulation to Co-Regulation

Susanne, FLOW TO LEARN's parenting advisor, shares her research and insights about the buzzwords dysregulation, self-regulation, and co-regulation.

When my kids get overloaded, there are times they simply "lose it" and go into a full-blown meltdown. These are key opportunities for the adults in their lives to offer support, even as our schedules are inconvenienced by the time it takes. Severe outbursts of misbehavior are characterized as "dysregulation" in psychology. This term is now used widely in the field of child development to describe serious upset that can cause misbehavior, which is age-appropriate in all children until they learn how to "self-regulate." A dysregulated child (in the sense that they're unable to self-regulate their thoughts, emotions, and behavior) may not be able to express what they need, and it may take a few minutes or even a few days for them to feel clear enough, calm enough, and safe enough to share their feelings.

I regularly examine whether how I engage with my children might contribute to more frequent dysregulation, for example, by requiring that they stop what they're doing immediately without giving them time to accept and adjust to a transition, or insisting they explain their behavior before they themselves understand it. I consistently remind myself that these types of interactions are the opposite of connection in this context and will often further push my child away from their own self-knowledge and intuition, and even into a dysregulated state.

Whatever the reason for their upset, ideally, I can stay calm enough to accompany my child who has lost their self-control back to a balanced emotional state by practicing "co-regulation" with them. A co-regulation response might include soft touch, hugging, or rocking once permission is granted from the child, or simply staying present and offering non-judgmental freedom (a "safe container") for the child's emotional arc to complete. Once the child has calmed down naturally, relating to what they were experiencing is the next step to effective co-regulation. Some examples of relating could be, "You seemed really sad that we had to take a break for lunch. It can be so frustrating to have to stop a project we're enjoying before we're ready. That happens to me sometimes, too." Adults can develop a skilled intuition around when a child is ready to reflect on what happened and gently discuss ideas for self-regulation in the future.

One evening, I accidentally knocked over a marble track my son (five years old) had built in his room. That marble track was especially important to him, and he couldn't bear to leave it knocked over. He dissolved into tears, insisting that I put it back together immediately. I sincerely apologized for having knocked it over, saying that I completely understood that he wanted to rebuild it right away, but that it was bedtime, and we could do it together the next day. He responded to this limit by going further into a furiously dysregulated state. This time, I sat quietly on the floor, holding the boundary in a soft voice. I could have asked him to calm down and put him to bed, but something in me saw this as a golden opportunity. So, I let go of the bedtime goal, and recognized it was more important that I hold a quiet space and a firm boundary for as long as necessary, while allowing my son to feel the full arc of his emotions.

Eventually, he was able to respond in halting speech to my questions about how he was feeling. This was the beginning of the co-regulation, as he slowly began to calm down. He worked hard to express himself, and eventually came to me, still quite sad, but calmer. I held him for some time and related to how upset he was about the toppled marble track. His nervous system powered back down to a resting state. We laid in his bed together and had a close snuggle as he drifted off. The next day, we talked about what happened, and I let him know I was so proud of his efforts to share with me how he was feeling in the midst of such strong emotion. I asked questions about how he was able to calm down, and we reflected together on what happened. Practicing these skills during calm and happy moments make them more accessible to children and adults alike during times of upset. We use playful terms with the kids such as "vacuum cleaner breathing" for breathing deeply, "reverse blast off" for counting down to calm down, and the like. I use these tools as well, when I feel myself losing control of my emotions. The trust that's fortified when I acknowledge my own challenges with self-regulation can be a powerful bonding experience as I work together with my children to develop these important life skills.

RESPECT MUST BE MUTUAL
Kindly require and give respect

CHILDREN ARE BORN WITH a natural capacity for learning in flow, but they aren't born with social skills. Children don't need to learn *how* to learn but they do need guidance in socializing. They may naturally respect you as their significant caregiver, they may intuitively know about dignity, but they don't know yet how to express this respect with words and deeds. Socially respected behavior is learned behavior and some of it (for instance, table manners) varies by culture, faith or family. When we help children become aware of the unwritten rules of common courtesy, we give them valuable tools that help them navigate through life.

Many times, whenever necessary, kindly inform children that a person who shows respect to others through kindness is much more likely to be welcome anywhere they go. Social skills will help children make friends, mediate conflicts, adapt to various environments, and talk with teachers and other adults. Knowing about politeness helps them ask for what they need and graciously say *no* to unwanted offers. In Montessori terms, this area of learning for a child is called Grace and Courtesy.

When children feel emotionally safe, they *want* to learn what others perceive as respectful and how they would like to be treated. They want to learn from you how to be friends, how to be a part of a peer group, or how to be included in a table conversation. They are relieved to learn that it is okay to ask for what they need, and that there are certain ways of asking that work better than others. This knowledge helps children find their place in their own community and having good practice with one culture's common courtesy sets the stage for learning about other cultures.

In any relevant moment, give children concrete examples of respectful everyday interaction. Let them know: this is how you can ask for something; this is how you can let me know when you are unhappy with something; this is how you can respond if an adult asks how you are doing today. Modeling is the best teacher, so use kind words with your child and everyone else: *May I...? Can I...? Please..? Excuse me... Thank you. Would you be willing to...? Would you be so kind...?* All of these phrases are like keys to open doors and help establish friendly rapport between people.

Rather than the conventional way of requiring all requests to be accompanied by "please" and "thank you", try more open-ended and authentic ways to encourage polite interactions. For example, "Hmm, that doesn't feel good to me. Can you think of a different way to ask?" Children become quite skilled at asking for what they need with respect when reminded in this way, rather than having politeness imposed upon them by force, which of course, is not polite.

There are also many non-verbal ways of showing respect that need to be brought to a child's awareness: listening to someone without interruption; making eye contact (or sometimes being okay with not making eye contact); smiling, opening the door for someone; asking if a person would like to be hugged or touched; and whatever else feels important to you and your family. There are three main ways in which children learn courtesy over time: through direct (and polite) instruction, by imitating their role models, and by experiencing how it feels to be respected.

THREE MAIN WAYS IN WHICH CHILDREN
LEARN COURTESY OVER TIME

Through direct (and polite) instruction: Instead of scolding when a child seems to be (or is) disrespectful, we can make them aware of their behavior. How? Help them reflect on what happened and then give clear guidance on what could be done differently next time. For example, "When you ask me for help with angry words, it doesn't feel good to me. Here is how you can ask me in a gentler way: Can you help me, please?"

By imitating their role models: Children perceive how we treat ourselves and others, and they consciously and unconsciously internalize the same behaviors. We show respect to ourselves through self-care and positive self-talk when we make mistakes, and we show respect to others by relating to them with kindness and patience. For example, "Oh no! I left the car window down and the seat is soaked! Aw, that is so frustrating." Disappointment and then searching for a solution are authentic reactions for anyone to have. "Ugh! What I can do about this?! I'll go get a towel to keep my body dry. I wish I had remembered to roll the window back up! Well, it will dry. It's okay. Next time I'll remember!" This may not feel natural for those of us who have been conditioned to react negatively to our mistakes, but it is crucial to model positive self-talk for children in normal day-to-day life.

By experiencing how it feels to be respected: Certainly, the most effective and lasting way to teach children respect is to respect them deeply. Our respect for children and adults goes hand in hand with our own self-worth, and our unwavering belief that we all have the capacity to live respectfully, side-by-side, even if we don't agree on everything.

HERE ARE SOME WAYS YOU CAN SHOW RESPECT TO CHILDREN

☆ Avoid speaking about a child as if they weren't present—children can hear you. This all-too-common act makes them feel invisible and excluded and often leads to "acting out."

☆ Keep your promises, or don't make promises.

☆ Avoid asking children to make and keep promises. Most children are developmentally incapable of doing so and asking them to invariably sets them up for failure.

☆ Share information with children: For example, while traveling or running errands, share where you are at the moment, where you are going next, and what the child can expect once you arrive.

TRY THIS
"Stop, rewind, take two!"

It is completely okay to make sure your child gets a chance to learn the respectful behavior you deserve. We don't do children a favor by letting them be rude to us. This doesn't need to happen using authoritarian, threatening, or judgmental methods. Teaching polite behavior can be done in friendly, playful ways.

I have observed several adults who are great with children using the following phrase, when they feel a child behaved disrespectfully towards them: "Stop, rewind, take two!" This phrase inspired by filmmaking jargon was their loving, playful way of letting a child know that something didn't go very well and just like filming a movie, they offer the child another chance to repeat the same scene.

For instance, let's say a child swiftly grabs a marker from your hand without asking if you are done with it. Instead of scolding, "Don't do that!" we might say "Stop, rewind, take two! I would prefer you to ask me first, saying something like, 'May I have your marker, please?' Or 'Are you done with your marker and could I have it now, please?'" If this happens repeatedly, you can kindly say something like, "Ehm, excuse me. Do you remember what I'd *really* prefer you to do and say, if you need something that I am holding? Thank you for being so kind."

We must remind ourselves constantly that children are learning by example, and that none of their disrespectful behavior need be taken personally. Rather, they are truly asking for respectful examples and alternatives through every mistake they make, so they can learn "the rules of the game," or how to thrive in their lives as individuals and within their communities.

WHERE I END AND YOU BEGIN
Children need healthy boundaries

WE ALL COME FROM A STATE OF UNION with our mother in the womb, and we learn gradually through life experience what it means to be a separate individual. Over time we gain awareness of where "I" end and "you" begin, and we learn about our own and others' boundaries.

As we grow into adults, life shows us over and over what it means to be a distinct person and that we need to learn how to respect and set boundaries. Healthy boundaries enable a child to become a happy, creative individual who can also be a team player, co-creator, friend, and companion.

We teach healthy boundaries best by being aware of where "I" (the adult) end. This, for most of us, is an ongoing learning and healing process. Many of us grew up in families with blurry boundaries. Our parents often amplified our feelings with their reactions: They got upset when we were frustrated, scolded us when we complained, told us not to cry. Overall many of our parents had a hard time with our feelings. Of course, it's not easy to see a child cry or witness extreme upset and keep from becoming unbalanced as well! If we are scared of our own negative feelings, it's even harder to accept a child's "big" feelings.

Whenever we have enough inner resources to try to feel and maintain our own healthy boundaries, we know that *these are the child's feelings, not our own,* and *it's okay for them to go through this with our support.* Through this process of awareness, we do the child and ourselves a great service.

When we don't get triggered by their expressions, when we stay calm and allow them their feelings, we become a safe person for this child, and we keep ourselves safe. Instead of adding guilt, shame, and confusion to a child's feelings, we help them to simply feel the fullness of their emotions, and to let them go. Within healthy boundaries, when a child is upset, we slow down, we nod, we try to understand. We provide what a child needs most in the moment, whether that's a hug, a listening ear, or simply our affirming presence: *I see you and it's okay to feel what you feel. I am here if you need me.*

Dr. Shefali Tsabary, a leading parenting expert, writes extensively about the importance of parents having healthy boundaries and allowing children to have their own authentic feelings. For instance, when parents over-identify with their children and take it personally when, for example, their child gets excluded from a birthday party or refused a role in a school play, they add unnecessary suffering and conditioning to a child's life experience. Of course, it is really hard to see your child's disappointment or struggle. You may think that defending them and trying to fix things to take away their pain is best for them. However, instead of internalizing your child's negative feelings, or trying to solve their problems, it is much more healing when parents support children in coping with their disappointments. By showing your child that these are normal experiences and they can survive and again thrive, you help them know they are strong, help them build their resilience, and give them tools for future disappointments and struggles.

Healthy boundaries protect our individuality (and sanity) while allowing us to bond deeply with children. Children in turn learn to feel and exercise their own boundaries by witnessing our healthy boundaries. It is not necessary to have perfect boundaries in order to be a positive role model. For many adults, this is a skill in progress, and the effort is what counts. If you notice you are over-identifying, micro-managing, or otherwise intruding into a child's important development of autonomy and boundaries, you can correct your position as many times as needed. Modeling making amends for your own missteps is setting a good example for your children, as well, since no one on the planet is perfect.

TRY THIS

I am I—you are you

Notice the instances when your child was upset, and you were able to stay calm and comforting. Celebrate those moments and be proud of yourself; they are precious and healing for you and your child. Also notice the instances when you couldn't stay calm and try to find out why. Ask yourself: Might I have been particularly affected because I subconsciously remembered one of my own childhood experiences? Could it be that one of my own unresolved fears was triggered? If so, *that's okay.*

Your simple awareness changes the dynamic between you and your child. Your energy will naturally begin to correct itself because now you know that your reaction has nothing to do with your child. Whatever arose for you in interaction with a child can heal as you develop deeper understanding and self-love. Healing is often not a linear process; be patient with yourself as you learn how to allow children's experience to be their own.

THE FLOW COMPANION AS TEACHER
A glimpse of non-invasive teaching

EVEN THOUGH CHILDREN ARE CAPABLE of self-education and self-directed learning, there are many occasions when introductions or instructions are valuable. As a wise saying goes, "The teacher appears when the student is ready."

As a flow companion, be available to support children in the flow process and help them reach the next level in their activity. Develop the sensitivity to know when your input is suitable. You may prepare a complete introductory lesson or notice crucial moments when your child is open to learning. In any case, non-invasive teaching means to never teach skills or content against a child's will. Respect the integrity of a learner's boundaries, and honor a "no." This way, you are welcome as a mentor in their life.

Remember you are foremost a companion—only when necessary do you become a teacher. A child or learner chooses and accepts a teacher as a mentor because they feel inspired to learn from them and trust their guidance. Teaching at a time when a learner is not open to receiving creates tension and is in a way a breach of trust.

Not every situation needs to be transformed into a teaching moment; there's no need to volunteer information all the time. Allow children to come to you and ask you for more information. This will be much more powerful, and learners will more likely remember answers to their own questions.

When questions arise, if possible, help learners to find answers on their own, and feel free to share what you know about a subject when it is welcome.

Stay in tune with the child's flow process and remain at the learner's pace. As a flow companion, you speak exclusively for the benefit of the learner; there is no one else to please. If your student cannot follow your pace of teaching, you've missed the point. You must adapt absolutely to the learner's pace. For children that often means slowing down; sometimes this may mean providing additional information or learning challenges, or instructive steps that you haven't anticipated. The bottom line is this: for an empowering flow experience, we answer a learner's request for knowledge, and do not deliver a prepared speech or even a spontaneous lesson without acknowledging and completely adapting it to the receiver. Showing an activity or skill once may not be enough. Instead show it as often as necessary. Young children especially benefit from repeated demonstration of the same skill or activity.

Whenever possible, show an example of what you are explaining while you are talking about it. By narrating in simple terms simultaneously with your activity steps, you minimize misunderstandings. For instance, when you are introducing a microscope, have one at hand and point to each specific part as you describe it.

When introducing complex hands-on activities such as knitting, show each learning step, even simple ones, isolated from the next one; this is especially important for young children. Take the example in which you show how to cut out paper snowflakes. First share with a child how to hold scissors, invite them to practice freely until they feel confident with their tool, for example by doing simple paper cutting (each step should be allowed to take as much time as necessary). Then show how to cut along a line, then show how to fold a paper square in half, then in quarters, then show how to cut triangles into that folded paper square so they become snowflake patterns once unfolded. After each step you show you can wait for the child to imitate you, and practice as long as they'd like until they are comfortable with that activity. Remember that their intrinsic creative flow may take over for some time, possibly multiple days, as they experiment with their newfound skills. Be prepared at any time to let go of your attachment to the end-product of a paper snowflake. If you are making your own paper snowflake, consider completing it at the pace of the child.

Trust children to take the time they need, even if that means they create their own goals that appear to have little do with yours. When they are ready, they will very likely come back to the snowflake, but through a deepened learning that has become their own. This organic back-and-forth interaction builds trust as flow companions share ideas, introduce topics, and guide in a way that fully respects children's pace and autonomy to be in command of their learning.

In order to maximize the learning potential of a child's creative process, avoid directly interfering with their material. This way we don't take possible learning steps away from a child and we give them space to learn from their process. Show how you would do it with your own material. For instance, don't "help" with a child's picture by drawing the perfect flower on it, don't go with a red pen through a child's text, and don't solve a puzzle for a child. If a child wants me to draw a flower, I draw it on my own paper; if a child wants me to correct a text, I copy their paper and scribble my suggestions on the photocopy; if a child wants me to solve their puzzle, I may set a firm boundary of encouragement by saying, "Sorry, I'm doing something else right now," and give them time and space to solve the puzzle on their own or ask a peer. The puzzle may not be solved right at that moment, it might take weeks to solve and that is okay.

Tend to questions when they arise and set your child up to continue their flow process. Perhaps you remember an instance when you were following a talk and suddenly you didn't hear or understand a crucial point the speaker made. Very likely you continued thinking about that moment when you lost the thread and subsequent parts of the talk didn't really make sense to you anymore. This is why it's important that we address questions as they arise rather than at the end of a lesson. If a question is crucial to understanding instructions or content, it must be answered when it is relevant. In many cases, the answer will need to be worked with until a child feels fully confident to continue. You might encourage children to raise their hands when they have questions, versus simply interrupting, to encourage respectful habits in a learning environment.

Clearly, a child—just like a master—does not move hastily to the next step until fully skilled with the current one. Many adults have difficulty slowing down enough to learn challenging new skills, because we are conditioned to produce an end product quickly, instead of taking all the time we need to master each step. By providing children with an environment that supports their innate abilities to achieve mastery one step at a time, they lay the foundation for a lifetime of joyful learning anything they choose.

TRY THIS

Facilitate learning through asking questions

Asking friendly questions is a great way to inspire a learner and add additional dimensions to ongoing activities. If a child does not want to respond to your question, respect and support children in finding answers when their thirst for knowledge has been awakened. Remember that their answers do not necessarily have to coincide with your knowledge of what is correct. Very young children may respond in wildly creative ways. Sometimes, having fun with the process is much more important than getting the "right" answer. If we remember that the best learning happens when we're having fun, then silliness wins out over serious with children's learning processes. Trust that they will eventually find the truth of the matter. And they will have a great time getting there. Here are examples of questions that facilitate learning:

☆ What do you think about this?

☆ How would you do this?

☆ Where do you think this comes from?

☆ Who do you think made it?

☆ Do you also wonder how they made it?

☆ How long does it take to make it?

☆ What exactly is missing?

☆ Why didn't this work?

One day, at the Wild's child-based school, the Pesta school in Ecuador, Rebeca asked a group of learners who were playing with water, "Where do you think this water comes from?" This question lead to a sequence of grand learning steps, and a group of learners traced their water supply from the sink to the local watershed and beyond. Thirty-seven Pesta students between the ages of 12 and 18 ended up going on a self-organized bike ride (with the help of Rebeca and Mauricio Wild and other adults) to discover the primary source of their water supply. This legendary bike ride became famous through the Wilds' workshops in Europe. It lasted several months, and they traveled through Ecuador, Columbia, Venezuela and to Manaus, Brazil where they found the source of their area's household water. Of course, the teenagers loved this extraordinary adventure; they learned uncountable lessons from financing to teamwork. They experienced their own strength and limits in unforgettable ways. This is an impressive example of experiential learning.

GENEROSITY—THE GREAT HEALER

There is enough for you

IN 1970S, AMERICAN AUTHOR, INVENTOR, and futurist Buckminster Fuller was first to declare that humanity had reached a tipping point: While throughout human history, there had always been a shortage of food and other goods needed for survival, now there was *enough* for everybody in the world—enough food, enough shelter, enough love. However, he also predicted that it would take the human family many years to shift into this new way of thinking, since we have been used to struggling, hoarding, and fighting over supplies instead of sharing them. Furthermore, Fuller suggests that the assumption "there is not enough" *may actually be the cause and root for there not being enough*!

We can help our children shift into this new paradigm by nurturing the feeling that "there is enough for everyone" in our homes and schools. In fact, through modeling generosity, we empower children to become naturally generous, and who knows, perhaps even facilitate a quantum leap in human evolution.

Apart from modeling generosity, there is another significant way we can help children develop the feeling of "there is enough for me." Children need the security of trusting that their personal belongings are honored. Young children, especially, still feel in deep union with their environment. Sharing one of their personal things when they are not ready to do so is painful for them. Just imagine if someone were to force you to part with an item you felt you really needed and loved. When adults force children to share their things, of course they do it to try to teach children to be generous. However, this often backfires. When young children (and even many older children, who still have an age-typical, self-centered view of the world) are strongly encouraged or required to give something away they feel they really need, their egocentric point of view is reinforced. They feel misunderstood and are disappointed by the adult they trust and depend on. Additionally, the basic feeling of "there is not enough for me" is confirmed.

It is safe to allow a child's "childish" perspective within healthy boundaries, and let them know, "It is okay, I understand you, and I still love you." For instance, eight-year-old Luke doesn't want to share his stuffed animals when other children come over for a playdate. Instead of urging him to share, his parent can give in to his wish, assure him that he can share when he feels ready, or not share his special toys at all that day. In addition, his parent can provide different toys for the other children, or help mediate situations with constructive, supportive language: "You want to play with the rocket ship. Luke is still playing with it. He will let you know when he is ready for you to take a turn."

This way, by being able to keep or share on his own terms what he feels belongs to him, Luke has the experience of his wishes being respected and his trust in his parents deepens. Often, when children feel supported rather than forced to share, they are freed up to be generous of their own accord. Just like countless other aspects of a growing child, "help me do it myself!" certainly applies to sharing, as well.

When the feelings of "I am respected" and "I have enough" can be rooted in a child, and they grow up witnessing generosity, they will more likely share as they grow older. If children are forced to share against their will, they may hold on to their things more strongly over time, because a fear of scarcity has been reinforced in them. Whenever you can, allow children to safeguard things that belong to them, while letting them know that they can share when they feel ready. Assign specific places, such as drawers, corners, or a room to your child, where they can have a say over what happens with their things.

Often children love to have special places for treasures they found or that were gifted to them, such as shelves for special books and photos, boxes for precious toys, pouches for pebbles and crystals, and folders for their artwork (refer to Try This in Week 30). The child gets to decide what happens with the things kept there. If you need to change something there, consciously do it in agreement with the child. This is another way to affirm their primary feeling of "there is enough for me."

Sometimes children trust us with their wishes or desires for certain things or circumstances, but we may not be able to grant them. When this happens, we can still acknowledge that their wish is a genuine and valuable wish, and let the child know we would fulfill it, if we only could. Understanding and acknowledging is comforting and it creates trust. For example, your child might develop a strong attachment to a particular item at their school or a friend's house. Naturally, they would want you to allow them to take this item home with them to keep as their own. Even though this is not possible, it's important to acknowledge how valid the child's feelings are, and express empathy for how difficult the separation is. If they decide to take it home without permission, you can help them to return it in a matter-of-fact way, acknowledging how much they must love it, and taking it back to where they got it together (of course, making sure the child knows that they must not take anyone's things without permission).

The same basic principles can be applied to developing the feelings of "there is enough time," "there is enough food," "there is enough love for you." You clearly state and bring to awareness that "this is our day and we have enough time—we have all day!" To assure a child's nervous system that there is plenty of food, leave little plates of healthy snacks out such as celery and carrots, so they always have access to food. Place a water pitcher and glass nearby, so children don't forget to drink, they don't have to ask anyone for water, and they can simply serve themselves. Show children that there is enough love in the world by smiling often, by being available for hugs, and by being available to come see something a child wants to show you as often as you possibly can, while allowing for a gentle boundary when you need to focus on your own needs

The more genuine needs are met, including the need for a sense of ownership over personal belongings, the more a child's nervous system can relax and create the foundation for empathic understanding and behavior. Eventually, when the "joy of giving" is learned in gentle ways over time, children and adults experience a feeling of euphoria after acts of generosity. The research around this phenomenon confirms that giving, helping, and volunteering make us profoundly happy hence the name "helper's high."

TRY THIS

Experiment with healthy abundance

What are ways you can provide "healthy abundance" for your child? I call this experiment healthy abundance because there is also an unhealthy abundance: when children are flooded with toys, they get overwhelmed and it's hard for them to realize the true value of anything. Healthy abundance doesn't really require much stuff; it is more about the value you and your child assign to what you already have.

There are many ways parents and teachers can cultivate true generosity that stems from their inner motivation and provides a deep feeling of abundance that will allow for lifelong joy of giving. This week, using the following questions, find ways to provide healthy abundance for yourself and your child.

☆ Can you find places in your home where your child can truly have their own things and decide what happens there?

☆ Can you create days or at least an afternoon when you all relax, with truly enough time, and without a sense of needing to move on to the next activity?

☆ Can you make sure your child has access to fresh, light snacks whenever possible?

☆ Can you have days when you set your own worries aside and create an atmosphere of love and joy with your child?

WEEK 49

WE, THE HUMAN FAMILY
Celebrate diversity

WE, THE OLDER GENERATION, have the power to let children grow up with the notion that everyone is unique, interesting, and beautiful in their own way. When children experience complete respect for who they are and witness others receiving the same respect, this is what becomes *normal* for them. Our modeling is how they will treat others.

As young children we don't distinguish between people as we do as adults. In the first months after we're born, when we see someone, it is simply *mom* or *not mom* for us. As we grow up, we learn to label people according to our role models and environments. We adults have an enormous influence on how children will learn to distinguish between people.

Children are as comfortable with other people as we are. When children see you treat everyone with equal respect, including how you speak about them when they aren't around or when they make mistakes, that's what they will do. Be in contact with and let children be in contact with all kinds of different people. Let them see you be kind and respectful with everyone, and experience that each person is a complete individual, no matter what age, ethnicity, gender, social class, political stance, ability or disability. Let children grow up with the idea that we are one human family: we differ in many things, but we are equal in the dignity everyone deserves.

When children get curious, take time to explore together what differences and commonalities are between people. Here are some interesting things about the human family to teach children: *All people want to be happy. All people want to be treated with respect. All people have good days and bad days.* It is calming for the nervous system to know everyone belongs to one human family, and the child is part of it too. You can also explore how you and your child are different and what you have in common.

In addition to messages of inclusion and oneness, giving children the language to express differences is important. As they grow, children may have disagreements about many things with their peers or siblings, developing their identity, social skills, likes and dislikes along the way. Early on introduce the idea of "opinions" or "agreeing to disagree," for example, "One of you thinks oatmeal tastes best with blueberries, and the other thinks it tastes best with raisins. You don't agree on that, so you could agree to disagree and then everyone gets to have their opinion." Children are often quite pleased to find they can keep their opinions no matter what another says. Many times, once they allow one another this freedom, they find other ways to creatively compromise. Social skills that allow other people to have their opinion, without each person insisting they are "right," are essential for being able to participate in one's community, as differences of opinion are a fundamental part of the human experience.

Since we are immersed in a culture where equal dignity is not the norm, each significant adult needs to take responsibility for making a difference in their radius of influence. Children in the standardized school system need extra support in understanding that everyone deserves dignity, including them. They are compared with one another constantly, with their achievements and failures used as metrics by which many adults treat them differently. This and countless labels can create intense and painful experiences as they hear and internalize judgments: *this one is loud, this one is smart, this one is the class clown; this one is a troublemaker, this one is a prodigy, this one is an indigo child, this one has dyslexia.* Such labels restrict a learner and may become self-fulfilling prophecies. Children start thinking that their differences are weaknesses, that if they do not achieve in similar ways to others and something is *wrong* with them.

In the communities of RWB and child-centered education, and in books on education reform there are so many stories of adults revealing that their teachers gave *them* restrictive labels—*unable to focus, too much energy, cannot sing, cannot draw, terrible handwriting, scattered, will never be able to ... (fill in the blank).* It takes great effort to let go of these beliefs in adulthood, because throughout childhood and even as teenagers with adolescent attitudes, we are impressionable sponges who trust the adults in our lives. It's widely known that many people who made significant contributions to humanity struggled in school: Albert Einstein, Thomas Edison, Bill Gates, Walt Disney, Elton John, and Princess Diana, just to mention a few. Let's contribute to making diversity an asset instead of an obstacle, no matter the age or differences of the children in our care.

The emphasis on the benefits of diversity and on what the human family has in common doesn't mean we don't need to teach children discernment. But discernment must be based on things that actually matter, such as: *Is this person kind to you? Does this person feel safe?* This way children can grow up being comfortable with diversity, celebrating our differences, and learning from each other. The skill of discernment allows their nervous systems to assist them in recognizing true danger, and saves that reaction for when it's needed, rather than for when they are met simply with normal human differences.

When you feel a child is developmentally ready, also tell them little by little about the cruel history of humankind, the times when we didn't respect each other, and how we keep learning from our history. Let them know there is still much injustice in the world, and share how each of us can make it better by treating one another respectfully at every turn.

But most of all, let's show children the positive achievements of human culture. Show them the impressive works of classic and contemporary visual arts in painting, sculpting, photography, filmmaking, and architecture; the inspiring works of literature, poetry, and non-fiction; the uplifting, cathartic effects of the performing arts of music, dance, and theatre. Let them explore (in child-friendly ways) the philosophies, world religions, and spiritual traditions of the ages. Introduce them to the great masters in science, the altruistic doctors, inventors, political leaders, and visionaries that have moved human evolution forward. Take them to small farms, nurseries, animal shelters, artisan studios, and other inspiring people and places and let them see through all of these, that a meaningful, well-lived life is possible and achievable, and that there is much beauty and inspiration in the diversity of people.

TRY THIS
If a child gets bullied

If you suspect or know your child is discriminated against or bullied—no matter what the reason may be—don't take that lightly. In these cases, it is important to know that the children will *not* "figure it out," as some adults prefer to say. They need your strong help right away. If a child is exposed to abuse in person or cyberbullied, you should be the one who protects them. In addition, the bully needs emotional support and help in learning how to treat people respectfully. Here are some things you can do if a child gets bullied:

— Listen closely when a child opens up to you and let them tell you how they experienced the discrimination. Children often are not able to open up when asked directly about something that made them uncomfortable. Be patient and vigilant to when they are ready to share.

— Validate the child's experience and make sure they know what happened to them is *not right, not their fault*, and that no one deserves to be treated that way.

— Be sure not to become intensely angry in front of the child when they share with you. This may scare them or reignite their trauma. Let them learn from you how to handle being hurt without falling into the trap of extreme reactions. Stay calm, supportive, and clear.

— Let the child know that sometimes people don't know better because no one taught them how to treat people respectfully, but that does not make the behavior okay.

— Ask if there is something you can do to make the child feel better and use the tools for tension release provided in Week 11.

— If it feels safe to you, speak with the bully, including their parent, and help everyone involved find respectful ways of behaving with each other. Remember that children who bully are in painful places themselves.

— Make a complaint to the school or organization and let them know what happened to the child. Make sure they follow up on this incident and involve a counselor to speak with the bullying child and the bullied child.

— Invite presenters, encourage teachers, or speak at the child's school about human differences and how to respect, work through, and celebrate them.

Under California state law, in severe cases of bullying, including cyberbullying, the principle of a school will decide if the case can be solved with "restorative practices," (processes similar to mediation), or if further action is needed, such as filing a complaint with the district Office of Equity or its equivalent in your district. A school may refer an offending student (or teacher or any other school employee) to counseling and/or discipline them in a variety of ways, including suspension, expulsion, or dismissal from school.

PRETEND VIOLENCE AND WEAPON PLAY
A closer look

PRETEND VIOLENCE OR WEAPON PLAY often scares adults, but when initiated by the children, it is safe to allow within intentional structures and safe boundaries. When children spontaneously choose to play this way, flow companions can respect this as a part of children's internal world that must be expressed in a safe context. If we suppress these kinds of play, children may rebel, feel guilty and ashamed, or play these games hidden from our watchful eye.

There are three typical reasons behind pretend violence and weapon play. First, children naturally explore a great variety of archetypal roles, which include the warrior, the hunter, and the enemy. These archetypes are embedded in our collective consciousness and want to be experienced in a playful, safe context. Secondly and unfortunately, many children are exposed to violent scenes in movies and shows that they need to "play out" in order to process and integrate them (refer to Week 22). Thirdly, some children experience actual violence or witness it somehow in their lives. Violent scenes or real-life situations may create substantial inner tension, and children need safe channels through which to play this out. As a flow companion you can help them make peace with these experiences in a healthy way.

Pretend violence and weapon play can be healing when they are consciously accompanied by adults who make sure that these games remain safe and within healthy boundaries. What can be fully experienced, can be released. What we feel, we can heal. Here again the verse from the Tao Te Ching applies: "If you want to shrink something, you must first allow it to expand. If you want to get rid of something, you must first allow it to flourish."

When children would like to pretend-play violence or pretend fight with their swords and guns, flow companions need to stay close to them. Most of all, adults must define a specific place where this kind of play can occur and not allow it to take over other parts of the home or school, especially not interrupting children who are engaged in other activities.

Flow companions are invited to establish or co-create with the children rules that assure every person feels safe. For instance, let children know that whenever it feels too much for one of them, they can use a safe word like "stop," or they can come up with their own. Ensure everyone agrees that the safe word must immediately end the activity in progress. Whenever it's used, the children can check in with each other and see why someone doesn't feel safe. Flow companions make sure each child's wishes for safety are respected, and if a compromise cannot be reached, the adult might require that the game end.

HOW TO SAFELY ALLOW PRETEND VIOLENCE AND WEAPON PLAY

How to offer role play for several children:

When several children are involved in a role or pretend play that has some violent content, stay especially close. When a frightening figure such as an angry monster or cruel villain is part of the game, make sure each participating child knows about the safe word and that they can leave the game any time they wish. If you suspect a child may be uncomfortable or even scared, ask them if they still like playing this game, and assure them that they can suggest the game be changed or leave.

How to accompany swordplay or wrestling:

Help children take their time to thoroughly negotiate the rules of their games, before they play. They may decide on playing knights, pirates, or samurai warriors and create a complete storyline that they agree to play out. For example, "When I touch you with my sword, you will be my prisoner, and you have to come with me over there," or "While they are looking for the treasure, we'll escape the prison and hide in the forest."

Once physical pretend fighting is part of the game, it needs a prepared space, such as a circle laid out with a rope on the ground, or a designated area in the back of the yard. Children agree that as soon as they step out of the designated area, they don't play this game anymore. Create rules for or with the children that help everyone feel safe, such as "swords are not supposed to touch, only 'air-fighting' is allowed," or "swords may only be made of cardboard, not of wood." Such rules are possible but not always needed, and may arise out of the children's own agreements with one another if an adult poses open-ended questions, such as "How can we ensure that everyone feels safe?"

How to provide pretend play on the sand table:

One or two children can play out pretend violence on the sand table (as explained in Week 17) with small figurines, without disrupting anyone else. Figurines of soldiers, hunters, and dark or villainous characters may be added to the pretend play figurines, or taken out when not needed.

How to support children with arts and crafts:

Children may draw, paint, shape in clay, or otherwise express and explore these topics. Crafting swords, rifles, or battle ships often comes up when children are allowed to craft whatever they wish. Sometimes the activity of crafting such an item is enough for the child to process the internal imagery they may have developed around a action-packed scene they have heard or seen.

Pretend violence and weapon play aren't ideal or desirable with regard to cultivating flow; however, if they arise during spontaneous imaginative play, accompany it in a way that it may become healing for children. Talking about violence instead of merely suppressing it is a way to give it a place without having it unconsciously take over any area of a child's life. Make children aware that even though violence may be part of many areas of the world that surrounds us, we aim to create a world where violence isn't needed to find a solution or for people to get their needs met. Let children know that usually people use violence because they feel desperate and cannot think of any other solution to their problem or conflict. However, our human community is finding alternative ways to solve conflicts, such as taking a break to calm down, discussing a problem, deeply listening to one another, adjusting environments to genuine needs, and supporting each other in receiving all that is needed to survive and thrive.

TRY THIS
Three things to give to a child

Some gifts cannot be purchased; they are priceless. You can practice giving them to the children around you and to your inner child.

Modeling flow: Nothing is more magical and attractive to children as when you model an activity done with love. When children see that something can be done with love, it makes a deep impression, even though that may not be visible outwardly right away. It is a seed for the future. You may see them replicate it with a sibling, a friend, or even with you, very soon after they experience this love from you.

Giving comfort: Life is bound to be hard at times, and when it hurts most, we need comfort. The way we comfort children influences their ability to comfort themselves as adults. When a child is hurting, take your time to be with them. Bring them a glass of water or warm herbal tea and let them know that everything heals with time. Listen to them, and assure them that soon, everything will be okay again. When the worst is over, offer to do something wonderful, play a game, or a walk in nature.

Viewing things from a higher perspective: When a child trusts you with a sad story of what happened to them such as a challenge with a peer, bad grades, a disappointment, or a conflict with a teacher, do everything in your power to help them. Welcome the full experience of the feelings they are having, and invite them to write about or draw about their experience. Especially for older children, after a release of emotions, also offer the insight of a higher perspective, by asking questions (when they apply) such as: "Do you think this will still hurt next week, next month, or next year?" or "In some way, I believe, we were lucky, can you imagine how this could have been even worse?" or "What would you do if you were the parent and I was the child?"

DEBUNKING OUTDATED MYTHS
Next steps in childhood education

MANY YOUNG CHILDREN LOVE SCHOOL in the early years. They are excited to learn to read, to accomplish all the tasks big and small that are asked of them, and they want to get it right. They want to succeed so badly. Where does this initial enthusiasm go? Why do many children hate school after a few years? It is not because children are lazy or don't like to learn. In truth, standardized schooling hampers flow by over-activating the thinking mind while neglecting the body and emotions of a learner.

On the physical level, children are urged to sit more often and much longer than they would naturally sit, thus undermining their natural impulses for movement. This premature separation from their physical impulses creates tension and floods the mind with fear-based conditioning such as, "Something must be wrong with me. The teacher wants me to sit still, but I just can't." On an emotional level, young children continuously search for opportunities to bond with significant adults and to be lovingly witnessed and encouraged by them. And, most teachers also prefer to authentically bond with their students.

Let's give teachers the conditions they need to be able to become true mentors and flow companions for their students. We need to create different education models that are based on children's, teachers', and parents' needs. The New Learning Culture (NLC) school model (refer to the Afterword), which I designed using best practices in education, offers a school system that is in alignment with children's natural ways of learning while making sure academics aren't left behind. Read below how the NLC school model addresses some of the major challenges teachers face as they transition to more individualized education.

EARLY RIGOROUS ACADEMICS ARE NEEDED
TO SUCCEED. IS THAT TRUE?

Without a doubt, there might be times in someone's life when rigorous academic training is needed, for instance, to succeed on a test or to learn a complicated and precise skill. However, rigorous studying of academics doesn't need to take up a whole childhood. Most basic academic skills can be playfully taught at a child's pace. Montessori schools have long gone in this direction and, over the last 30 years, RWB schools have gone all-in with this experiment. From studies on progressive schools, unschooling, and homeschooling, we have seen that children can catch up in basic academics within a year or two, for example, when they feel ready to take the next steps needed for a high school or college admission.

Next steps in childhood education: Individualized learning goals allow children to learn at their own pace. Reduced or optional homework eliminates excessive stress in the family. Relieving teachers and students of the continuous pressures of standardized testing allows teachers to become mentors to the individual learner. Teachers can instead offer standardized tests when a child feels ready. The NLC school model provides a wide spectrum of child-friendly academic practices, which learners can access in a self-directed way or with the guidance of a teacher, yet always at their own pace and on their own terms. When a learner decides to take a standardized test, they receive all the help needed to prepare and succeed in the months before the test.

IF A CHILD CAN'T SIT STILL AND FOCUS,
THEY PROBABLY HAVE ADHD. IS THAT TRUE?

Undeniably, ADHD is a real challenge, and medication helps many people. However, it seems that an ADHD diagnosis has become a go-to solution when a child, even a very young child, is not functioning well in a traditional school setting. According to the Centers of Disease Control and Prevention, approximately 6.1 million children ages 2 to 17 had received an ADHD diagnosis in the US by 2016 (*NOTE:* Numbers vary in different statistics, depending on counting criteria). For many children—before trying to change the child's behavior through therapy or medication—it's worth experimenting with a different kind of education, perhaps in conjunction with other changes to their lives, such as nutrition and screen time. Even though many children might indeed be capable of sitting still from "school-age" on, they learn better when they can be active. Even when reading—if allowed—they will move their little bodies and find creative positions sitting and lying down. Many children cannot focus "on demand," yet they are perfectly capable of focusing on a self-chosen task. Let's strongly advocate that public education first offer alternatives to special needs learners, instead of or at least before turning to medication.

Next steps in childhood education: In the RWB schools and in other progressive schools, as well as in the NLC school model, learners may move and play indoors and outdoors as much as they need,—indeed, many children play all day. This educational approach only makes sense in thoroughly prepared, hands-on learning environments, as proposed in the NLC model. Prepared hands-on environments that feature a variety of flow activity stations naturally invite learning and discovery. Flow companions, mentors, and teachers skillfully support spontaneous play, flow, and self-chosen study as the most significant ways of learning, and help each child reach their next steps in their individual curriculum.

IF A CHILD LACKS SELF-INITIATIVE, THEY ARE LAZY, AND NEED MORE STIMULATION. IS THAT TRUE?

When a child isn't as active as other children, and when they show little interest and self-initiative, they are often seen as lazy and in need of encouragement. As their caregivers, we might get anxious they are missing out on essential learning opportunities. However, it's important to look more closely at what a child is experiencing before offering them an array of activities or insisting on their participation. A child's disinterest may stem from other reasons, and rarely is laziness (I personally have never known a lazy child). If a child comes home from school, they may need time to integrate the complex social interactions that are part of a school day. Children deeply feel the many spoken and unspoken invitations, rejections, expectations, and rankings, and they need downtime to find their place in all that (also read Week 26 "A Close Look at Boredom"). They may simply need to rest, daydream, and play quietly in order to restore their energy levels.

Next steps in childhood education: At RWB schools, as well as in the NLC school model, learners may rest, observe, and daydream as much as they need. I remember a six-year-old girl at our RWB school in Northern Italy who was completely inactive during her first weeks at the school. She would quietly sit apart from everyone and rarely speak or engage. She refused all the gentle invitations for play from peers and teachers. Her parents were getting worried, yet we, the teachers, kept trusting her natural process. We made special efforts to let her know her behavior is okay by frequently smiling at her and accepting her "No, thank yous" with grace. Finally, after a few weeks, she got up from her resting place, walked straight to the makerspace, and created a most exquisite card deck, featuring around 40 different hand-drawn snails, each doing something different: a water-drinking snail, a tree-climbing snail, a leaf-eating snail, a sleeping snail and so on. She was visibly satisfied, and she flourished in the flow learning environments from then on.

TRY THIS

Become aware of habits that sabotage flow

In order to cultivate flow in homes and classrooms we need to examine some of our habitual ways of being with children. Explaining, interfering, and nudging a child to do more than they want to do, while it may be well intended, often leads a child away from their own flow.

Explaining when a child isn't ready to listen: As a rule of thumb, explain something only if a child asks you a question. Especially when a child is busy doing something, don't volunteer your knowledge or "help." Let them be in their own process. Even when a child asks a question, especially a younger child who may not be cognitively ready for scientific explanations, sometimes it is appropriate to just ask the question back: "What do you see is happening with the water in the bucket right now?"

Interfering when a child is focused on an activity: In general, try not to interfere with a child's flow process unless it's absolutely necessary. Even if you see something that you would like to share, something beautiful, interesting, sweet or funny, consider holding back in order not to interrupt your child's natural flow. Maybe they will discover it on their own.

Nudging a child to do more than they want to do: During a flow process, don't nudge your child to do more than they personally want to do. Trust your child to set the perfect challenge for themselves. Even if you know they could do more, and that they are capable of higher achievements, there may be other reasons why your child is choosing to stay in their comfort zone for now. All inner aspects of the child need to be on board for an authentic, fulfilling flow experience.

YOUR RIPPLE EFFECT
Small changes for great impact

AS WE HAVE SEEN IN THIS BOOK, flow is not only doing something with gusto; it is so much more! Flow also has a significant *ripple effect*, "a spreading, pervasive, and usually unintentional effect or influence" (Miriam Webster Online Dictionary). When your child gets comfortable with their flow state, they are empowered to be who they are. Once you allow yourself to let go into an activity, be fully present with it, and abandon your worries of making mistakes—you are free! You experience a moment of vivid, colorful life that no one can take away from you. In this moment, you are the creator of your reality—you are the captain of your ship! You feel affirmed in your existence; everything feels just right. This feeling can be exhilarating or deeply peaceful, and it is contagious!

Just like a rock skipping on water and creating ripples with each skip, you affect others when you do things differently. Embracing flow brings you into greater alignment with your child's genuine needs and the truth of your own being. When you, for instance, prepare a water play station for your child, you are not "inventing" a game your child wouldn't play without that flow station; instead you are creating space for your child's natural, playful, learning drive: Young children (usually) love to play with water, and they will do so whenever they have a chance; if they can't find a water play station, they will play in the bathtub or with their water glass at the dinner table. Creating space for your child's natural way of being is giving a powerful message of positive feedback and your child will feel affirmed in their existence. They will feel loved and respected. This, in turn, gives them the self-confidence needed day by day, year by year, to create a healthy, strong identity: *I know I am worthy, and I know what I can do!*

Likely a remnant of our need to survive in early human history, the human brain is wired to have a negativity bias, which is the scientific notion that our memory gives more significance to negative experiences than to positive or neutral ones (further explained in WEEK 6). In order to consciously counterbalance this deeply ingrained thinking, I encourage you to look back at the process of reading this book and identify the positive ways in which you brought more flow into your life with children. Balance out any negativity bias that arises and highlight the benefits of inviting more flow into your lives. You can apply this practice to a wide array of contexts and focus on the good.

Think of your own and your child's progress not by comparing your selves to others but by comparing your selves to a year before. Here are some questions to ponder..

☆ What are the ways in which you created and noticed more flow?

☆ How did that affect your awareness and relationship with your inner child?

☆ In which ways did you notice or bring more flow experiences to your child?

☆ How has your home environment changed?

☆ For teachers: how did your classroom environments change?

☆ What are your favorite memories of this time?

☆ Are there positive effects (ripple effects) you observe in your partner, family, friends and their children, or at your workplace?

FLOW TO LEARN doesn't need to stop with the end of this book, the beginning of school, or with returning to daily life. Keep flow alive by continuing to create flow stations in your home. The spaces you create physically anchor what is first only in our thoughts, making it more accessible. For instance, if you have always wanted to play the guitar but have never learned it, start by creating a place where you would play it. Spend time seeing yourself playing the guitar, daring to imagine the melodies you might play, and how delighted with your music you and others would be. Look for guitars that are already in your life, maybe at a friend's house, and ask if you might try to play, or if they might even show you a few chords. As you become more strongly connected to this desire, wait for the right moment for a guitar to come to you or go out and purchase it. Encourage this visualizing in your children. Keep creating flow stations and adapt them to you and your child's current skills, needs, and interests. You might even stow away some prepared flow station "kits" for friends and family for when they come over. Flow is part of self-care, it is an expression of our natural being, and it is contagious. The more you practice it, the more you experience its value, and the more you inspire people to do that same for themselves and their children.

TRY THIS

Time for gratitude and celebration

Ah, the wonderful, glowing feeling of fulfillment after a flow experience! That sense of accomplishment and satisfaction! After children emerge from an adventure in timelessness and periods of intense concentration, you may see a look of gratitude in their face, and a smile that says, "Wow, that was fun!" Sometimes you might even receive some additional, unexpected affection from your child because they feel supported in their authentic self; they were able to naturally release tension during flow, and new wholesome pathways of learning and perceiving were created. Flow helps a child feel a little "bigger," and a little more of who they are meant to be.

Being in flow, even if it's just for a few hours, enveloped in that magical out-of-time feeling, is a gift we can give to ourselves. When we allow ourselves to be in flow or to be a catalyst for flow, we slowly realize that we as much as our children are smarter, braver, and more generous than we may ever know!

Making a conscious effort to notice those moments of fulfillment and embodied gratitude makes a huge difference in our quality of life and well-being. Create time for some moments of gratitude every day. At night when bringing your child to bed, is an excellent time to cherish the good parts of the day. Together, you can be grateful for small things and big things alike: *Thank you for smiling at me. Thank you for cleaning up. I'm grateful for the blooming tree. I'm grateful for our purring cat.*

It really doesn't matter for what or to whom we are grateful—it is the feeling of gratitude that matters because it is healing, empowering, and uplifting.

And gratitude leads straight to celebration. Make time to celebrate! Make time to party! Every small step toward a better quality of life for you and your child deserves your positive attention and celebration. A celebration can be as simple as a moment of reflection and a smile. Or it can be a tea party with your child, a dance party in your classroom, or a ritual like lighting a candle. At dinner, raise your glass and give a celebratory speech, express your gratitude, and then invite your child to give a speech. Give yourself and your child a thumbs up, a high five, or a pat on the back: *We are doing the best we can! We are making the best of it! We are on our way!*

List of reasons to be grateful:

☆ _____
☆ _____
☆ _____

List of reasons to celebrate:

☆ _____
☆ _____
☆ _____

List of dreams and flow projects for the future:

☆ _____
☆ _____
☆ _____

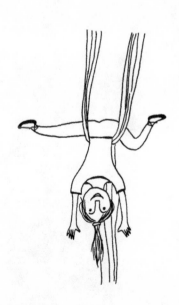

AFTERWORD

THANK YOU SO MUCH for your interest in FLOW TO LEARN. I hope you feel inspired and empowered on your journey into greater flow. Paradoxically, this optimistic book was born from a deep sadness. When I look around the globe, I see a thousand reasons to be depressed and frightened. Children all around the world are being abused, abandoned, and neglected. Standardized school, even though flawed, is often the best-case scenario; conditions are much worse for all too many children. In addition, the daily terrifying news of climate catastrophe with millions of species dying, and the never-ending stories of cruelty, poverty, and xenophobia cannot be ignored. In the face of this onslaught of so much violence, it's easy to slip into hopelessness.

Finding the Rebeca Wild based schools was a lifesaver for me. I was deeply inspired by their uplifting spirit. I became a teacher in this school model where children are allowed to be children. The time I spent with my young students changed and healed me. I realized what was at stake if I gave up on the world and, as time went on, I received ever more strength to become a protector and advocate for children. Finally, it has been the connection to my inner child that helped me rediscover flow states within myself, and she has kept a smile on my face.

My mother was very loving and provided me with a great variety of toys, puzzles, blocks, books, and arts and crafts materials, including a Montessori toy abacus, all of which she put in accessible drawers I could reach at any time. She was tuned into a universal wisdom and intelligence of the heart that carefully, consistently, gently tends to all living things. Even though she was not "perfect," she was perfect for me, and I am grateful to have experienced this in my childhood. We lived in a beautiful home with a garden in a 700-person village, and I went to public school in Catholic Northern Italy (a bilingual area, German and Italian, because it was part of Austria before WWI). After school and in the summers, I was able to play indoors and outdoors as much as I wanted, and I always felt safe because my mother was usually somewhere nearby. When I was a young adult, our neighbors humorously shared with me how often during the day they smiled to themselves when little Carmen called out loud "Mamma, Mammaaa!" from anywhere on the property, and they knew my mother would be there to care for me as fast as she could. Even though my mother had never heard of child-centered education, her intuition naturally provided a prepared environment for me where I could play and explore independently.

In contrast, it seems to me the detrimental parts of our culture have been created by minds disconnected from their inner child. It is this state of separation and its inherent pain that enables people to be so cruel. Flow is an effective way to reconnect our minds to the genuine needs and vulnerabilities of our inner child, and thus, our bodies, and of all life. Like many parents and educators, I believe that nurturing our inner child and the next generation with the utmost wisdom, love, and care is an act of powerful, healing activism. We might feel helpless witnessing the many problems of this world, but in our own environment, we can empower ourselves to create positive change.

THE REBECA-WILD BASED SCHOOLS

The Rebeca Wild based schools in Europe have been the underlying field of research for this book. "Rebeca Wild based schools/RWB schools" is an umbrella term that I am using in this book to identify all schools that incorporate Rebeca and Mauricio Wild's education approach. There are approximately 700 RWB schools across Europe and worldwide. These schools all differ slightly from each other, and you would know whether a school is an RWB school only by reading its mission statement (which usually also includes references to Maria Montessori) so they are not so easy to spot. It was Rebeca and Mauricio's request to course participants that their names not be used as part of any school's name because they feel each school is a unique entity that should have its own name and individualized approach. In addition, there is no official website about their work, and as a result, it is difficult to find information about them on the internet. I hope this book will contribute to keeping Rebeca and Mauricio's legacy alive.

In RWB schools, we support children to keep learning in a state of flow as they grow up. We achieve this by allowing them to choose their own activities in thoroughly prepared learning environments. Within the healthy boundaries of the school, children may play and learn at their own pace as their hearts desire. The myriad learning opportunities include time to explore the many hands-on materials such as Montessori math, language, and sensorial materials, pretend play and make-believe in elaborate doll play and block building areas, movement in their gym room and outdoors on the playground, tending to the gardens, crafting in the makerspaces, cooking and baking in the kitchen, working in the woodshop, resting on big pillows, snacking at the communal dining table, and communicating with each other and us, their teachers and flow companions, about anything that is important to them.

Inspired by Montessori education, Berlin-born Rebeca Wild (1939-2015), and her husband Mauricio Wild (1937-2020) created an experimental school, the Fundacion Educativa Pestalozzi (informally known as the Pesta), near Quito, Ecuador, in 1980. The Wilds initially founded this school as a kindergarten for their second son, hoping to avoid the disastrous experience their first son Leonardo endured until age 13. Needing an educational environment for both sons, the school grew to accommodate learners from preschool to high school. In this school, local children learned alongside children from ex-pat parents, which enriched both cultures.

In their yearly visits to Europe in the 1990s and 2000s, the Wilds held hundreds of workshops in which they shared their insights with thousands of parents and teachers. They sparked a grassroots movement of parent-and-teacher-founded schools across Europe and beyond. Many of their course participants traveled to Ecuador to visit their school The Pesta (the name derives from Johann Heinrich Pestalozzi, [1746-1827], a Swiss pedagogue and education reformer) to receive deeper insights into their methods. Here are some of the Wilds' core messages:

— The harmonious growth of a child is a natural and slow process. The task of the adult is to create appropriate conditions to meet the genuine, authentic needs of a growing child—not to try to speed it up. If, as adults, we are capable of not interfering with a child's natural growth, instead provide supportive love and healthy boundaries, we allow them to develop inner guidance and the ability to think for themselves.

— Based on Humberto Maturana's research (biologist and philosopher born in 1928) the Wilds realized that every living system—from a single cell to a large group of cells, such as a human being—creates and maintains itself from within; it shapes itself (adapts) in accordance with and reaction to outer circumstances; this process is called "autopoiesis." Love (supportive conditions) is the only driving factor for any living system to grow and learn.

— Hence, adults must create environments where children can move, learn, and interact in alignment with their inner realities and in loving, non-invasive, supportive relationships with their adult companions.

The Pesta in Ecuador doesn't exist anymore, but the over 700 Rebeca Wild based (RWB) schools today in the world, mostly in Europe, Spain, and South America, are alive, well, and growing in number. Some schools exist only for a few years, for the founding parents to raise their own children there; others grow larger and exist beyond the initial founders to serve other children in the community. Some schools offer only preschool and elementary school; others also offer middle and high school grades.

In the many European RWB schools, we witness that children's natural, self-motivated joy of learning continues throughout all their school years because it is nurtured and supported. These children have time to grow up at their own pace, and they experience individual, natural, balanced development of their body, heart, and mind.

THE NEW LEARNING CULTURE (NLC) SCHOOL MODEL
FOR NEIGHBORHOOD SCHOOLS

In order to help Rebeca and Mauricio Wild's basic ideas for neighborhood schools spread throughout the world, especially to English speakers, I created the New Learning Culture (NLC) school model. My model is not identical to the Wilds' model, yet upon Rebeca's request and green light, I used as much as I wanted from their model and added other elements I found necessary to make it a complete, teachable, adaptable template. The NLC model works for all levels, from preschool up through high school, and guarantees not only a custom, play-based education for each child, but also academic proficiency. It combines diverse elements with original ideas derived from my teaching experience to form a new school model in its own right. I included useful elements from Montessori education, the Reggio Emilia approach, Waldorf education, Forest Kindergarten, mindful education, the Freinet school movement, traditional schooling, and innovative teachers from around the world.

The NLC school model features a blueprint for a great variety of hands-on classrooms (such as an interactive math studio, a language lab, make-believe landscapes, a woodshop, a kitchen, gardens, playgrounds, and more), custom progress assessment in collaboration with the learner, a complete framework for providing "non-invasive teaching," and many strategies for "child-friendly academics" (terms I coined). It can be used as a whole, or its elements can be included in other school models (which has been happening in the US through my consulting work). Currently, I don't know of any RWB school in the US, and there is no New Learning Culture school yet. Let's hope this book and my upcoming books about the NLC model help these innovative, child-friendly schools spread.

There is so much more to be said, but we must stop here for now. Play and flow are crucial. They are vital. We become social beings through play. We become highly intelligent through play. And science confirms this. Thank you for caring for children and for the child in you by reading this book. I look forward to hearing about your and your child's experiences as you try the concepts and ideas in this book. Thank you for finding ways to flow through life together.

Carmen Gamper
March 2020

GLOSSARY

Archetype: The original model or a perfect example of something. (Cambridge dictionary)

Child-centered (or child-based) teacher: A teacher who gives priority to the needs, pace, and interests of a child.

Flow: A term coined by professor of psychology Mihaly Csikszentmihalyi describing a mental state in which a person is fully immersed in their activity experiencing a feeling of energized focus, enjoyment, and fulfillment.

Flow station: A place designed for people of all ages to pursue activities that lend themselves to flow.

Flow companion: An adult, teacher, parent, or anyone who inspires, creates places for, and supports flow activities for children.

Genuine Needs: Anything that is crucial to a child's mental, emotional, and physical health, happiness, and cognitive development.

Healthy boundaries: Knowing where *I* end and *you* begin and thus having awareness of personal and others' genuine needs and limits.

Inner child: Your inner child is the part of your personality that still reacts and feels like a child. (Cambridge Dictionary)

Masters of flow: A master is a person who is very skilled in a particular job or activity (Cambridge dictionary). Children are young masters of flow, because they effortlessly and frequently drop into flow during their spontaneous play.

Montessori: Dr. Maria Montessori (1870-1952) was a revolutionary Italian educator who recognized flow as the ideal state for learning. Her surname titles the child-centered education method she developed.

The NLC school model: The New Learning Culture (NLC) school model was developed by Carmen, the author of FLOW TO LEARN. It is a template created to support teachers in offering individualized, child-directed, hands-on learning, "non-invasive teaching," child-friendly academics, and custom progress assessment. Read more about it in the Afterword and in Carmen's upcoming books.

RWB schools: For the purpose of this book and in order to spread this knowledge, the author (Carmen) named schools that are based on Rebeca Wild and Mauricio Wild's approach, "Rebeca Wild based schools" or "RWB schools." Rebeca Wild (1939-2015) herself asked school founders not to use their name for schools (unlike Montessori) because they felt all schools are individual entities that should have their own unique name. The way to find out if schools are RWB is to check their mission statement. You could also do an internet search using "Rebeca Wild Freie Schule," which will take you to many Rebeca Wild based schools in the German-speaking areas of Europe. RWB schools (preschools, grade schools, high schools) offer learners a great variety of prepared learning environments for hands-on learning (flow stations) instead of traditional classrooms.

BIBLIOGRAPHY

Axline, Virginia. *Dibs in Search of Self.* Boston: Houghton Mifflin, 1964.

_____*Play Theory: The Inner Dynamics of Childhood.* Boston: Houghton Mifflin, 1947.

Bradshaw, John. *Home Coming: Reclaiming and Championing Your Inner Child.* Bantam Books: New York, 1992.

Breuning, Loretta Graziano. *Habits of a Happy Brain: Retrain Your Brain to Boost Your Serotonin, Dopamine, Oxytocin, and Endorphin Levels.* Adams Media, 2016.

Brown, Stuart. *Play: How it Shapes the Brain, Opens the Imagination, and Invigorates the Soul.* New York: Penguin, 2010.

Childre, Doc & Martin, Howard. *The Heartmath Solution: The Institute of Heartmath's Revolutionary Program for Engaging the Power of the Heart's Intelligence.* New York: Harper Collins Publishers, 1999.

Claxton, Guy. *Hare Brain, Tortoise Mind: How Intelligence Increases When You Think Less.* New York: Harper Perennial, 1999.

Csikszentmihalyi, Mihaly. *Flow: The Psychology of Optimal Experience.* New York: Harper Collins Publishing, 1990.

_____*Creativity: Flow and the Psychology of Discovery and Invention.* New York: Harper Perennial, 2013.

_____ *Finding Flow: The Psychology of Engagement with Everyday Life.* New York: Basic Books, 1998.

_____*The Evolving Self: A Psychology for the Third Millennium.* New York: Harper Perennial, 2018.

Donaldson, O. Fred. *Playing By Heart: The Vision and Practice of Belonging.* Deerfield Beach, FL: Health Communications, 1993.

Elkind, David. *Child Development and Education.* New York: Oxford Univ. Press, 1976.

_____ *The Power of Play: Learning What Comes Naturally.* Philadelphia: Da Capo Press, 2007.

Frost, Joe L., Wortham, Sue C., & Reifel, Stuart C. *Play and Child Development.* Englewood Cliffs, NJ: Prentice Hall, 2000.

Gandini, Lella, Edwards, Carolyn, Forman, George (Eds.) *The Hundred Languages Of Children: The Reggio Emilia Approach to Early Childhood Education*. Norwood, NJ: Ablex Publishing, 1994.

Gardner, Howard. *Intelligence Reframed: Multiple Intelligences for the 21st Century*. New York: Basic Books, 2000.

Gatto, John Taylor. *Dumbing us Down: The Hidden Curriculum Of Compulsory Schooling*. Gabriola Island, BC: New Society Publishers, 2002.

Gerber, Magda & Johnson, Allison. *Your Self-Confident Baby: How to Encourage Your Child's Natural Abilities from the Very Start*. New York: John Wiley & Sons, 1998.

Holt, John. *Learning All The Time*. New York: Da Capo Lifelong Books, 1990.

Knight, Sara. *Risk and Adventure in Early Years Outdoor Play: Learning from Forest Schools*. London: Sage Publications, 2011.

Kohn, Alfie. *Punished by Rewards: The Trouble with Gold Stars, Incentive Plans, A's, Praise, and Other Bribes*. Boston: Mariner Books, 1999.

Lansbury, Janet. *Elevating Child Care: A Guide to Respectful Parenting*. Malibu: JLML Press, 2014.

_____ *No Bad Kids: Toddler Discipline Without Shame*. Malibu: JLML Press, 2014.

Lawlor, Robert. *Voices of the First Day: Awakening in the Aboriginal Dreamtime*. Rochester, Vermont: Inner Traditions International, 1991.

Lent, Jeremy R. *The Patterning Instinct: A Cultural History of Humanity's Search for Meaning*. Amherst, New York: Prometheus Books, 2017.

Lipton, Bruce. *The Biology of Belief: Unleashing the Power of Consciousness, Matter and Miracles*. Authors Pub Corp, 2005.

Louv, Richard. *Last Child in the Woods: Saving Our Children from Nature Deficit Disorder*. Chapel Hill, NC: Algonquin Books of Chapel Hill, 2005.

Maturana Humberto. *The Tree of Knowledge: The Biological Roots of Human Understanding*. Boulder, Colorado: Shambala Publications, 1992.

Mellin, Laurel. *Wired for Joy: A Revolutionary Method for Creating Happiness from Within*. Carlsbad, Hayhouse, 2010.

Mitchell, Stephen. *Tao Te Ching*, New York: Harper Collins, 1988.

Montessori, Maria. *The Absorbent Mind*. New York: Dell, 1979.

_____ *The Child in the Family*. London: Pan, 1970.

_____ *The Discovery of the Child*. New York: Ballantine, 1986.

_____ *Dr. Montessori's Own Handbook*. New York: Schocken, 1988.

_____ *The Montessori Elementary Material*. New York: Schocken, 1973.

_____ *The Montessori Method*. New York: Schocken, 1988.

_____ *The Secret of Childhood*. New York: Ballantine, 1977.

_____ *Spontaneous Activity in Education*. New York: Schocken, 1965.

Nelson, Jane. *Positive Discipline: The Classic Guide to Helping Children Develop Self-Discipline, Responsibility, Cooperation, and Problem-Solving Skills*. New York: Random House, 1981.

Pearce, Joseph C. *Magical Child: Rediscovering Nature's Plan for Our Children*. London: Paladin, 1979.

_____ *Magical Child Matures*. New York: Bantam, 1983.

Pearsall, Paul. *The Hearts' Code: Tapping the Wisdom and Power of Our Heart Energy*. New York: Random House, 1998.

Piaget, Jean. *Play, Dreams, and Imitation in Early Childhood*. London: Routledge and Kegan Paul, 1972.

_____ *To Understand Is To Invent: The Future Of Education*. New York: Penguin Books, 2007.

Pink, Daniel. *Whole New Mind: Why Right-Brainers Will Rule the Future*. New York: Riverhead Books, 2006.

Plotkin, Bill. *Nature and the Human Soul: Cultivating Wholeness*. Novato, CA: New World Library, 2007.

Rathunde, Kevin. & Isabella, R. *Playing Music and Identity Development in Middle Adulthood: A Theoretical and Autoethnographic Account*. In R. Mantie & G.D. Smith (Eds.), *Oxford Handbook of Music Making and Leisure*. (pp. 131-149) Oxford: Oxford University Press. Published, 01/2017.

_____ *Experiential Wisdom And Lifelong Learning*. In J. Sinnott (Ed.), Positive Psychology and Adult Motivation (pp. 269-290). New York, Springer. Published, 2013.

_____ *Creating a Context for Flow: The Importance of Personal Insight and Experience*. NAMTA, 40(3), 15-27. Published, 07/01/2015.

Rechtschaffen, Daniel. *The Way of Mindful Education: Cultivating Well-Being in Teachers and Students*. New York: Norton, 2014.

_____ *The Mindful Education Workbook: Lessons for Teaching Mindfulness to Students*. New York: Norton, 2016.

Robinson, Ken. *The Element: How Finding Your Passion Changes Everything*. New York: Penguin, 2009.

_____ *Creative Schools: The Grassroots Revolution That's Transforming Education*. New York: Penguin, 2016.

_____ *Out of Our Minds: The Power of Being Creative*. Mankato: Capstone Publishers, 2017.

Sachs, Jonah. *Unsafe Thinking: How to Be Nimble and Bold When You Need It Most*. New York: Da Capo Lifelong Books, 2018.

Schrag, Peter & Diane Divoky. *The Myth of The Hyperactive Child*. New York: Dell, 1975.

Shapiro, Shauna & White, Chris. *Mindful Discipline: A Loving Approach To Setting Limits And Raising An Emotionally Intelligent Child*. Oakland, CA: New Harbinger Publications, 2014.

Singer Dorothy G., Singer Jerome L. *The House of Make-Believe: Children's Play and the Developing Imagination*. Cambridge: Harvard University Press, 1990.

Taylor, Jill Bolte. *My Stroke of Insight: A Brain Scientist's Personal Journey*. New York: Penguin Books, 2009.

Tsabary, Shefali. *The Conscious Parent: Transforming Ourselves, Empowering Our Children*. Vancouver: Namaste Publishing, 2010.

_____*Out of Control. Why Disciplining Your Child Doesn't Work and What Will*. Vancouver: Namaste Publishing, 2013.

_____*The Awakened Family: How To Raise Empowered, Resilient, and Conscious Children.* New York, Penguin Books, 2017.

Wild, Rebeca. *Raising Curious, Creative, Confident Kids: The Pestalozzi Experiment in Child-Based Education.* Boston: Shambala, 2000.

_____*Libertad y Límites. Amor y Respeto.* Barcelona: Herder, 2006.

_____*Educar Para Ser: Vivencias De Una Escuela Activa.* Barcelona: Herder, 2011.

_____*Aprender A Vivir Con Niños.* Barcelona: Herder, 2009.

Young, Jon, Haas, Ellen & McGown Evan. *Coyote's Guide to Connecting with Nature.* Santa Cruz, CA: OWLink Media, 2010.

RESOURCES

CONSCIOUS PARENTING EDUCATORS

— Janet Lansbury, https://www.janetlansbury.com
— Deborah Carlisle Solomon, https://deborahcarlislesolomon.com
— Dr. Shefali Tsebary, https://drshefali.com
— Dr. Chris White, www.essentialparenting.com
— Lawrence Cohen, PhD https://www.playfulparenting.com
— Hand in Hand Parenting, https://www.handinhandparenting.org
— Maggie Dent, https://www.maggiedent.com/

CONSULTANTS FOR PARENTS OF CHILDREN ON THE AUTISM SPECTRUM

Dr. Andrea Libutti, https://www.andrealibutti.com
Early Start Denver Model (ESDM), https://www.autismspeaks.org

CONSULTANTS FOR PARENTS OF CHILDREN WITH ADHD

Additude Magazine, https://www.additudemag.com
Dr.Daniel Amen, https://danielamenmd.com/

RWB SCHOOLS OPEN TO VISITORS IN EUROPE

Schpumpernudl, preschool, Telfs, Austria
www.schpumpernudl.org
Contact: Gabriela Bergmann: gmbergmann5@gmail.com

Lernwerkstatt im Wasserschloss, K through 8, near Vienna, Austria
www.lernwerkstatt.at
Contact: Theodor Feldner: office@matheomatik.at

Die Pfütze—La Pozzanghera, preschool through high school, Merano, Italy
www.pfuetzemeran.org
Contact: Claudia Zwischenbrugger: schule@pfuetzemeran.org

RESOURCES FOR HOMESCHOOLING

In California, there are several ways that parents educate their children at home: through an existing private school, through a public charter or independent study program, and in many instances by opening their own private home based school and filing the Private School Affidavit (PSA) with the California Department of Education (from the website of the California Department of Education https://www.cde.ca.gov/sp/ps/homeschool.asp).

Great resource: Homeschool Association of California https://www.hsc.org/

For other states and countries, please research your local resources and legalities.

RESOURCES FOR TEACHING

— Education Revolution (AERO), https://www.educationrevolution.org
  The American Montessori Society (AMS), https://amshq.org
— North American Montessori Teachers' Association (NAMTA)
  http://www.montessori-namta.org/
— North American Reggio Emilia Alliance (NAREA)
  https://www.reggioalliance.org/
— The Froebel Conference, http://froebelusa.org/
— Teaching and Learning from Preschoolers, Teacher Tom
  http://teachertomsblog.blogspot.com/
— Fairy Dust Teaching, Sally Haughey https://fairydustteaching.com
— The Curiosity Approach, Lyndsey Hellyn & Stephanie Bennett
  www.thecuriosityapproach.com
— Moving and Learning, Rae Pica www.raepica.com
— Mindful Digital Life, Claudia L'Amoreux www.claudialamoreaux.com
— Changing Schools from the Inside Out, Daniel Rechtschaffen
  www.danielrechtschaffen.com
— The Maker Movement, https://makerfaire.com/
— Children and Nature Network, Richard Louv www.childrenandnature.org

MENTAL HEALTH AND PERSONAL DEVELOPMENT

Dr. Daniel J. Siegel, https://www.drdansiegel.com

Dr. Daniel G. Amen https://www.amenclinics.com/

Emotional Freedom Technique (EFT), https://eftinternational.org/discover-eft-tapping/find-eft-practitioners/

TOYS AND LEARNING MATERIALS AVAILABLE ONLINE AND IN STORES

Orff instruments, building blocks, Montessori materials, Froebel materials, Waldorf dolls, felted animals and figurines, learning toys, games and puzzles, science materials, circus materials, crafting materials, art materials, household items, and gardening tools.

STORIES AND MUSIC: A FEW OF SUSANNE'S FAMILY FAVORITES

— Jenni Cargill Strong (all albums), https://storytree.com.au/
— Bill Harley (all albums), https://bill-harley.myshopify.com
— "Chickens and Other Stories for Young Children," Priscilla Howe
— "Nanushka, A Russian Children's Story," Ina Allen & Barbara Kemp
   https://store.cdbaby.com/cd/allenkemp
— "Listen to the Storyteller: A Trio of Musical Tales from Around the World,"
   featuring narrators Kate Winslet, Wynton Marsalis, Graham Greene.

MUSICIANS / ALBUMS

All albums: Andrew & Polly, Charlie Hope, Ella Jenkins, Kathy Fink & Marcy Marxer, Kira Willey, Lisa Loeb, Pete Seeger, Raffi, Tom Chapin.

"Dream Too Much" Amy Lee / "Meadowlark" Ann Zimmerman / "Everything is a Song!" Gayle Schmitt / "Kids" Keller Williams / "Who Let the Goat Come Off the Mountain?" Rick Jones / "Still the Same Me" Sweet Honey in the Rock.

More resources on https://FlowToLearn.com

INDEX

ACKNOWLEDGMENTS

HONOR AND GRATITUDE TO REBECA AND MAURICIO WILD.
Mauricio passed away in March 2020, when this book was first published. Rebeca passed away in 2015. They dedicated their lives to children and became trailblazers for the education of the future. Their unique presence, integrity, brilliance, and humility empowered thousands of parents and teachers to tread new pathways with children.
May FLOW TO LEARN help to keep their legacy alive!

I wrote this book in loving memory of my wonderful mother. Her patience, love, and dedication in raising me made me who I am. She passed away on August, 27, 2017.

I am deeply grateful for my family, and owe very special thanks to Johann Gamper, Cäcilia Haller, Patrizia Ratschiller, Hans Ratschiller, whose unwavering support throughout my whole life made this book possible.

Deepest gratitude to the FLOW TO LEARN team: Dana Anderson, editor and catalyst of this book; Susanne Stover, parenting advisor and developmental editor, who helped me keep the book grounded in the reality of parenting; Sybille Kramer, creator of the delightful illustrations of the young masters of flow; Louis Fox, advisor and filmmaker, who encouraged me to continue when I was about to give up; Michael Dubowe, Blue Growden, Asli Ors, and Robert Hickling, the book advisors; thanks to all the beta readers and special thanks to Iva Tashlick, Hamsa Patti Lutke, Alcina Horstman, Natasha Hadweh, Claudia L'Amoreaux, Joy Gallina, Nutmeg Baker, Susan Bradford, Sukaynah Aubrey; and last but not least, gratitude for my inspiring partner Ken Greenstein, who proofread the book and supported me in a thousand ways during the writing process. FLOW TO LEARN would not exist without your generosity, patience, and brilliant minds.

Gratitude and praise to all the Rebeca Wild based (RWB) schools who are pioneering the education of the future. Special thanks and kudos to All the teachers, learners, and parents at Die Pfütze Meran, Aktive Montessorischule mit Nicht-Direktiver Begleitung (Merano, Italy)—special thanks to Evi Spechtenhauser, Elke Valtingojer, Ingrid Kofler, Renate Kuen, and Claudia Zwischenbrugger. Schule Umaduma (Auer, Italy)—special thanks to the whole team; Kindergarten Schpumpernudl (Telfs, Austria)—special thanks to Gabriele Maria Bergmann, Walter Visenteiner, Margaret Fischer. Kinderhaus Miteinander (Wörgl, Austria)—special thanks to Gitti Dorfer, Astrid, Anita. Lindenschule (Innsbruck, Austria)—special thanks to Stefan Steve Heitzer, Lernwerkstatt Pottenbrunn (near Vienna, Austria)—special thanks to Christine Glaser-Ipsmiller; and all who are involved in RWB based schools around the world.

Gratitude to all my teachers, especially all children, and very special thanks to Maria Montessori, Rebeca Wild, Mauricio Wild, Klaus-Dieter Caul, Gabriela Maria Bergmann, Joseph Chilton Pearce, Mihaly Csikszentmihalyi, O. Fred Donaldson, Emmi Pikler, and many more.

Gratitude to all my consulting clients, including school staff, parents and homeschooling parents, all the New Learning Culture course participants, and my colleagues.

Sincerest gratitude to everyone who believed in my work, and special thanks to MS Cholleti, Waltraud Lun, Iva Tashlick, Valentine Gruber, Elisabeth Viertler, Dennis Marelli and the Marelli family, Robert Calef, Sabine Schwienbacher, Joe Ramagli, Doug Lerch, Daniel Rechtschaffen, June McCrory, Sundew Amber Mosher, Joelle St. James, Luisa Donati, Julie Schiffman, June Gorman, Chris White, Susan Bradford, Scott Bultman, Carsten Brandt, Anita Gruber, Carmen Bonora, Marion Fischer, Simone Rizzi, Michael Heel, Christiane Heel, Silvia Mujic, Moana Diamond, Navin Mahabir, Cristan Norman, Sasha Benedetti, Jerry Mintz, Starhawk, Kat Steele, Mali Apple, Carolena Kling, Arisa Victor, Bryce Ellory, Sabine Oberregelsbacher, David Traub, Sarah Shockley, Mar Oscategui, Lynn Scheurell, Vicki Abrams, Richard Miller, Britta Butler, Matthew Edwards, Wilana Anderson, Matthew Egan, Sandeep Goel, Heather Pederson.

ABOUT THE AUTHOR

CARMEN VIKTORIA GAMPER loves to spend time with children, and she has worked as an educator, advisor, coach, and speaker for child-centered education for over fifteen years. She became an expert on childhood flow states by supporting and witnessing hundreds of children learning on their own terms in carefully prepared, hands-on learning environments.

As founder of the New Learning Culture (NLC) program, she supports directors and staff of preschools and grade schools, parents and homeschooling families in safely offering child-directed, flow-rich learning environments. For FLOW TO LEARN, Carmen teamed up with Susanne Stover, mother of two marvelous young masters of flow, to create practical guidelines to bring the best of flow-friendly education into homes.

Carmen grew up in the Italian Alps, where she co-created a RWB grade school that thrives up to this day. She lived in Europe until she was 29 years old, and is now based in California.

ABOUT THE PARENTING ADVISOR

SUSANNE STOVER commonly can be found immersed in flow with her husband and two children somewhere on their small organic farm in Oregon. From gardening, exploring, or working with their farm animals outside to playing music, making art, or reading inside, she is grateful for the chance to rediscover the joy of life through the eyes of her kids.

Susanne has worked as an editor since 2010, has been involved in regenerative farming since 2007, and enjoys sharing farm life with their guests from all over the world. None of her life experiences could have prepared her for the realities of respectfully parenting two spirited children, but thankfully, she is an open-minded learner and they are patient and forgiving teachers.

SUSANNE, JOE, CEDAR, AURELIA

ABOUT THE ILLUSTRATOR

SYBILLE T. KRAMER is the creator of the delightful drawings of the *young masters of flow* in this book. She is an artist and teacher from Alto Adige/South Tyrol, Italy. She is married and she has two grown up sons, and two dogs. She discovered her love for hands-on learning materials when her children went to a Rebeca Wild based, Montessori elementary school, and after, when she homeschooled them through middle school.

Sybille turned her passion for hands-on learning into her profession and has since supported teachers and parents with the learning materials and classes she developed. She is one of driving forces of Homeschooling Italia, and also supports teachers in public schools.

Currently, Sybille is developing an online class for FLOW TO LEARN readers, featuring her delightful hands-on learning materials for preschool and grade school-aged children.

SYBILLE
TEZZELE KRAMER

CONTACT

For more articles and resources about the flow state in children, and to sign up for Carmen's newsletter go to: https://FlowToLearn.com

Visit Carmen's education website to find out more about her work in innovative education: https://NewLearningCulture.com

Reach out to Carmen for advice in child-centered, flow-friendly education for existing and emerging preschools and grade schools: Carmen@NewLearningCulture.com

MORE BOOKS BY CARMEN GAMPER

FLOW DISCOVERY JOURNAL:
Daily Questions to Spark Your Beginner's Mind
for Children Ages 5 to 105
by Carmen Gamper
Published August 2020

The FLOW DISCOVERY JOURNAL is a 60-day writing journal, activity, and coloring book for kids and grownups. Answering the journal's inspiring questions encourages the reader to discover their original thoughts, their unique flavor of intelligence, and experience the flow state of optimal learning away from screens.

The Flow Discovery Journal also invites grown-ups to play and remember the curiosity and fun they had as a child. Parent and kids, teachers and students, get to know each other better and build deeper connections while engaging with the fun explorations offered each day.
Available on Amazon.

CPSIA information can be obtained
at www.ICGtesting.com
Printed in the USA
BVHW031100230421
605721BV00006B/892